Testimonials

"In 1991, I was working at Villa Rosa, an adult psych facility. I worked the 'pool,' so I was usually on a different unit each day. One day I met Janiece. She had short hair, baseball cap, white t-shirt, old jeans, tennis shoes, and a look on her face that said, 'Leave me alone! Don't talk to me! I hate your guts!' I don't remember much more about Villa Rosa except that I worked on her unit a few times and we talked. A few weeks later, I ran into her at church, (San Antonio Christan Fellowship). She still had the ball cap, t-shirt, jeans and tennis shoes, but the '...I hate your guts!' look was gone. I think in its place was a look that said, 'Oh crap, it's that guy.' I was glad to see her, but didn't think much of it at the time. The next Sunday, I noticed the ball cap was gone! Each Sunday after, something else was different. Her physical appearance and her countenance were changing. Then, one Saturday, she walked into church…her hair was fixed, she was wearing a dress, her face was glowing, and Joseph was walking with her. The two of them were holding hands and had these 'cute little smiley faces.' (Their wedding) It was a very moving sight. Puts a smile on my face. I know this is quite long, but I needed to write it and relive it. My testimony is simple: When needed the most, and expect it the least, God shows how special we are."
Jim Autry

"Something we remember about Janiece is how God changed her whole countenance. Her facial features were changed to totally feminine in just a few short months. It was awesome to see God in action."
Jerry & Lu Tipton

"My heart went out to Janiece from the minute I first met her. She was broken, incredibly timid and ruled by fear. She had been through a lot, and didn't trust easily; yet she wanted to know her Lord so badly that she hung onto Him with all her might. She knew that Jesus was her only hope for love and happiness, and she stayed close to anyone in the church who showed her His love and who would be willing to help her heal and grow in her relationship with Him. I have had the privilege of watching her mature and transform into the woman of God she is today, and her story still touches my heart."
Deborah Nazemi-Lewis

"Janiece would always encourage me and be so happy to see me. She had a big smile on her face for everyone and her love for God was and is so obvious. She is a good role model of showing the love of Jesus to those around her."
Catherine Turner

"I have only known Janiece for a few years. In Christian fellowship groups it is sometime difficult to get to know people really well. Everyone, out of consideration for one another, tends to have a concept of church and the unspoken code of conduct. I am a rebel of sorts and have become less inhibited as I grow older. I can think of several times when I was a little bit outside the norm and could have been misunderstood by some, but not by Janiece. Janiece never misunderstands me, but to the contrary, she gets me. She is always positive and encouraging. She never fails to mention her love for me and remarkably, I believe it as truth. I think this truth she shares with everyone. What a powerful impartation of God's love."
Vicky Beauchamp

"As I read the manuscript of Janiece's story, I was in awe. I will be 65 this year and I have traveled to far places, known many people, experienced many things, but I was struck with the thought. 'I have never known anyone with so much to overcome.' This is a glorious testimony of the resurrection power of Christ Jesus to completely transform a precious life. Romans 12:2 and 2 Corinthians 3:18 in action!"
Donna Blevins Burttschell

"What a blessing and privilege to have Janiece in my life as a friend and sister in Christ. It has been an amazing journey over the years to witness the transformation of a woman in body, mind and spirit, through the mercy, grace and healing of Jesus Christ and the tenacity of a woman, who refused to stop short of all that God had for her. I am reminded of God's word in Romans 12:10-12 that describes Janiece's heart so well...'Be devoted to one another in brotherly love. Honor one another above yourselves. Never be lacking in zeal, but keep your spiritual fervor, serving the Lord.' I praise God and share in your excitement with the completion of this book, prayerful that God's powerful healing, mercy, and unconditional love be revealed to all who read it."
Christa Edwards

"I have known Janiece and Joseph since 1994. I had heard some of her testimony and attended their wedding. Until I read the book I didn't know the rest of the story. If you have had doubts about what God can or will do, this book will change your mind. In every area Janiece gives the glory, honor and victory to our Lord Jesus Christ for her healing, deliverance and restoration. This is a story of love; Janiece's love for God and God's love for His children."

Pat Navarro

"Janiece is a true wonder of the miraculous power & love of God the Father. He gave her life back after she had almost died and began a gradual process of restoration. She had to learn to see herself as a woman, a person of value, and one that had been completely forgiven of her past. The Church women began to work with her and the Lord blossomed her inner man into a beautiful rose, full of compassion and mercy for others, a zeal for God and a passion for a full and rich life. The work of Christ continues, her humility, patience with new believers and servant heart are the real treasures of life that Pastors and the people of God long to see develop and mature in His children. She is a true treasure of the faithfulness of our loving Father in Heaven and she will always have the respect and admiration of my family, the Church she serves and of her family."

Mike Paxton

"I first met Janiece in the 80's. I was a server at a Jim's Restaurant. She would come in at lunch time after her doctor appointment. At first all the servers were scared of her. She was a scared little girl who was badly hurt. They never gave her a chance. I remember asking her what happened to her arm. She told me. Many years later she walked back in my life a different person. She had found a better life for herself, a wonderful man, and a beautiful son. Her whole life changed for the better. She found God and he changed her life. You would not know it was the same person."

P.J. Ramos

SENTENCED TO DEATH, DESTINED FOR LIFE

Tell My People, I Love Them!

The Janiece Turner-Hartmann Story

by Joseph James

Photo at Left: Photo of Janiece shortly before their wedding, December 3, 1994. The gown was created by Alyce Alcock and what a gift of love it was in full brocaded material. Thank you, Alyce. Janiece and Joseph worked on the hat together as they added the flowers and long ribbons to the back.

SENTENCED TO DEATH, DESTINED FOR LIFE

Tell My People, I Love Them!

The Janiece Turner-Hartmann Story

written by
Joseph James

published by
VaryMedia

"Scripture marked NIV was taken from the HOLY BIBLE NEW INTERNATIONAL VERSION. © 1973, 1978, 1985 International Bible Society. Used by permission of Zondervan Bible Publishers"

ISBN: 978-0-9842422-4-5

Sentenced To Death, Destined For Life™
Destiny Path Of Life™
Joseph James and Janiece Elaine Hartmann
11844 Bandera Rd. #470
San Antonio, TX 78023, USA.

Visit us at:
SentencedToDeathDestinedForLife.com
DestinyPathOfLife.com

CONTENTS

ACKNOWLEDGMENTS

To my wife, Janiece, my precious princess, thank you for who you are and for your love and grace. I love you. What a journey you have had, including the miraculous intervention and continuous miracles. May you continue to blossom, more and more, all the days of your life. His rose, my rose, let the fragrance of His love continue to flow through you.

Daniel, you have had to endure some major hardships, but you've learned how to receive His love and grace to overcome. I am so proud of the young man you are becoming. Thank you for extending to us the time and grace we needed to finally complete this book. You have done without many things that others have enjoyed, but your time to enjoy is coming.

Desiree and Krystal, I know you didn't understand this journey much, nor the times we've been apart. I hope you remember the good times we've had together as much as we do. There are many more to come. You are so precious to us.

Virginia (Gin) Turner, so many thanks to you. I wish you could have been here for this day. You left us too soon, but I know you have been overseeing every page from heaven. Thank you for all the encouragement and perserverance to make sure that I would finish the project. You constantly remined me over the years to write Janiece's miraculous story. Many times, while I was writing, I could sense your presence looking on. I'm looking forward to the day I'll see you again.

Bob Turner, I am proud to be a part of your life and so grateful that you received me as I was and trusted me with your precious daughter. I can't begin to imagine the journey you and Gin have had to walk. Thank you for always being there.

Deborah Ursell, you never cease to amaze me. Your input and proofing of the book has helped to make it what it is. Larry, you and Deborah are so dear to our hearts. You have helped us so much in so may ways and in completing this book. Thank you for all of your support, help and encouragement over all of these years.

Dennis & Christine Goldsworthy-Davis, you guys gave up your homeland to forge a path in His Kingdom here in the hot Texas sun. You've been a voice crying out for years to let His Kingdom come. You've touched many lives already, but I believe you've only just begun. Thanks for your prayers and prophetic words that were life to us.

Oasis International Christian Center, City Church, San Antonio Christian Fellowship, different names, but a wonderful group of people you are. Some have come and some have gone, but most have helped in some way along the journey. Thank you all for being a part of our lives in one way or another. You know who you are and there isn't enough room to list everyone, although I wish I could. Your names are written on our hearts.

To the rest of our family, thank you for all you mean to us, to all you've helped us with. We take a part of you with us everywhere we go. When our lives touch, we can't help but carry some of each other with us. We must continually walk as His cloud moves, camp when we must, and always be ready to do it again.

Jackie Haag, how could we have ever gotten this far without your encouragement, your professional advice, and giving to us over and over through the years? Thank you for all you do in His Kingdom.

Leisa Barger, thank you for all of your professional marketing advice, help and direction. What a divine connection we have had.

To all of our proofreaders, Deborah Ursell, Pat Navarro, Donna Blevins Burttschell, and Daniel Hartmann, a special thank you for all of your precious time. It is a tremendous blessing, especially since I like to put commas everywhere.

Most of all, thank You my Lord, my Savior, and my King. I can't imagine a day without living in Your Kingdom here on this earth. I can't imagine living outside of Your presence and not hearing Your voice continually. I am so honored and so blessed to be living this life. It is truly more than I could have imagined or asked for. Lord, may Your glory be seen in our lives and through the pages of this book. As others have been honored and rightfully so, may You alone, receive the glory that is Yours.

Joseph James

FOREWORD

There is a saying in Yorkshire England, 'It is better felt than telt,' which means if you can experience something, it has a greater value than talking about it. This book is such an experience! The Janiece Turner-Hartmann story is about a true God given miracle! Written by her husband, Joseph, after years of walking with the miracle and living with the miracle, he decided to document it for all; so that others could believe that God is a miracle worker in the every day people, as He always has been and always will be.

I first met Janiece nearly 20 years ago, when she first came into our fellowship, one mid-week meeting. I have been privileged, with my wife, to watch the ongoing miracle ever since. She is modern proof of the ability of the Lord to heal, deliver and work His grace deep within a person's life. She is still the loudest person during a message, having never lost her joy and wonder at the amazing grace of her God. Her journey still continues, her hope still burns bright and her testimony continues to thrill.

This book, written in depth and with consistent detail, will at the least inspire you. It will bless you and will open your heart to all the possibilities of a life touched by a living God.

Who knows what miracles are awaiting all whose hearts are open to the potential of the God of Janiece. He is your God too!

Dennis Goldsworthy-Davis
Oasis International Christian Center
Great Grace International

DEDICATION

Bob & Gin Turner - 1952 - When They First Met

This book is dedicated to Virginia Sue Turner. I regret that she was never able to hold it in her hands. From the time Janiece and I were married, she kept telling me that I must write the story. Well, the story is now written and she holds a special place in our hearts. Bob found a note written to her by Jean, a dear friend, for her birthday in 1994. Jean also gave her a hinged, framed photo of "Footprints In The Sand." I have included this image along with the letter as it captures the essence of a woman who truly loved "her Jesus" and did everything in her power to let others know and feel His love through her life. We miss you Gin, but know you are watching from above.

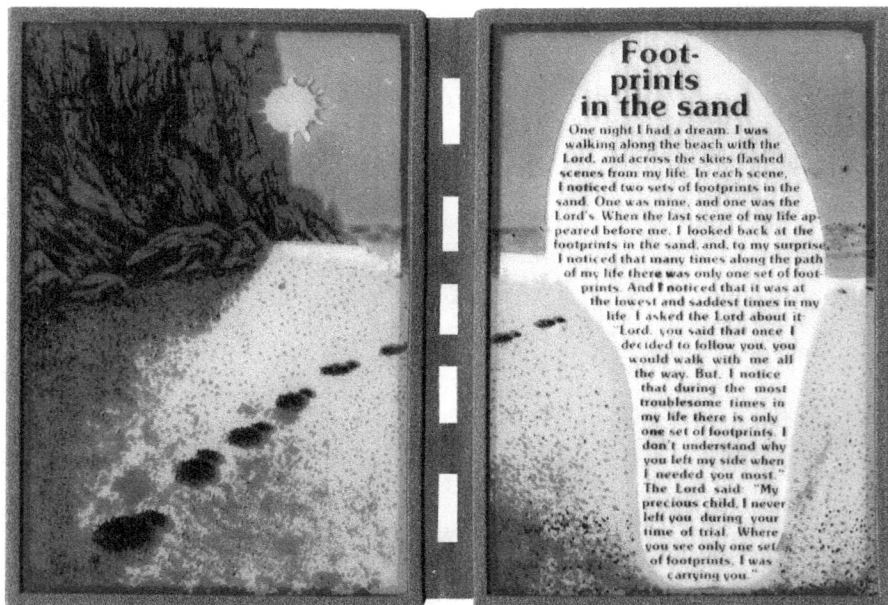

My Dearest Gin

Your surprise birthday party happened too quickly for me to find "just the right present" for you. I wanted something special to give to you from me...because you are so special.

Maybe this picture of one of my favorite places will always remind you of my love for you. There are elk tracks in the sand near the water's edge...you have made "tracks" or imprints upon my life the past sixteen years...dimly at first like in the dry sand but deeply etched now as we near the water.

The logs are rubbed smooth from years of living....our relationship is smooth and comfortable now because we've both been thru a ton of living but weathered the storms. We've shared the storms and they have drawn us closer.

The sparkles on the water remind me of the sparkle I saw in your eyes the very first time we walked in the office. The water laps softly at the logs and sand, soothingly, just as soft and soothing as your voice.

The wind's song from high on the mountains comes down the valley like a symphony played on icy rocky crags, keep green fir branches, golden aspen strings and dry reedy grasses in perfect harmony and I know God is the conductor. This peaceful melody washes all the hurt and care out of my body and fills me with joy. This happens again at times when I'm with you.

The strength seen in the rocky mountain tops is so like the strength I soak up from you when you talk with me abut Jesus and what his coming to the world means in our lives.

The ridges and peaks hold the valley so that it's beauty doesn't spill out and wash or blow away. Your hugs keep me that way inside and out.

So what I'm trying to say is thanks for being just the way you are and for caring about me.

INTRODUCTION

Please keep in mind, as you read this book, that it was written mainly from Janiece's perspective and how she reacted or responded to the circumstances and people around her. We have used other people's recollections and observations to enhance the story line and to provide a much fuller understanding of her journey.

Over a period of years and ministry, I have found that sometimes the truth isn't as important in someone's past, but rather, it is how they perceive that past in their own eyes. In this story I have laid a foundation, layer by layer, as it builds to a point of climax at the moment of the breakthrough. From that point on another foundation begins to be built as her life takes on a new meaning and a new journey.

Careful consideration was given to protect and cover those involved as much as possible, yet still revealing certain actions, reactions, and the necessary circumstances to achieve some sort of understanding of how she ended up at death's door, and what it took to reverse the process and bring healing. Janiece and I have exposed major parts of our lives in order to help our readers to understand the processes we can walk through in life, that there is hope, and that most of all, we can gain the victory.

We hope that as you read, you might be able to find something in our journey that might encourage you in yours. We hope you find your destiny and purpose in this life, and then live it to the full. Our greatest walk in life is not being a clone of someone else, but rather, walking the path prepared for us before the foundations of the earth, and at the end, receiving our victor's crown. Live life to its fullest with no regrets. Only One knows why we are here. It might just help us a bit in our journey if we find out what that reason is. Our gifts and talents are ours and no one else can walk the path we were destined to walk unless we refuse it. Live life on purpose, not by accident.

Joseph James

Janiece & Deborah (1967)
"Best Friends"

"Giggles, playing, sharing secrets, late night talks, exploring life's events, and being best friends come with sharing a bedroom while growing up."

"We came so very close to losing you."

"Praise God! Through His grace, here we are still doing the same thing."

"I love you, my precious sister."

Deborah Turner-Ursell

Image at Right: Joseph created this image to enhance the poem he had written for Janiece on April 28, 1994. These will be available in print soon. Please check our website link at the back of this book for updated information.

My Rose

There was once a rosebush all beaten and rent,
    If one were to see it, they'd consider its life spent;
But along came a man one day, He reached down from above,
    He carried it home with Him and showered it with love.

He placed it in some fertile soil, in His shelter all secure,
    He gently clipped the broken parts and allowed them to cure;
The plant had seen much trauma, but His love would bring it through,
    And then the time to transplant it, in the center of His garden view.

The little plant was honored, it didn't know what to think,
    And the many fears that held it back, even they began to sink;
The little plant, in the Master's plan, was proud to be a part,
    To bring Him glory and honor was the cry of its heart.

The growing, it seemed slow at first, as the new shoots appeared,
    The new life so tender, yet its protection secure;
Finally, a bud appeared, came the time to unfold,
    The little plant was all afraid and anything but bold.

To succumb to its fearfulness would cause the flow'r to fall,
   To expose itself again to pain brought back the tears and all;
Then it felt the Master's hand and heard His gentle song,
   He urged it just to bloom again and to know He was along.

As the petals started opening, a hush just filled the place,
   To those staring in amazement at the plant that was defaced;
The one that seemed 'could never be,' was now the Master's choice,
   His glory, He has shown us in the power of His voice.

So, open up you plants of His and let your fragrance air,
   Let the beauty that's been hidden be seen everywhere;
God is not a mean old man, nor one that He should lie,
   But now, He's here among us and on Him we can rely.

The Master, He sees everything, nothing's hidden from His view,
   As He died upon the cross, He was looking right at you;
He's felt the sting of pain and death, He knows what you're going through,
   So why not let Him heal your wounds and make you good as new.

Joseph James 04.28.94

SENTENCED TO DEATH, DESTINED FOR LIFE

Tell My People, I Love Them!

Chapter 1

A Path Of Twists & Turns

Love Breaks Through

This story begins on a rainy day in July of 1991, on the Northwest side of San Antonio, Texas. The 'Sentence Of Death' had been issued and there was an eerie feeling of the certainty of its judgment in the atmosphere. A young woman, in her early thirties, is seen standing on the front porch of a home for the terminally ill. She is smoking a cigarette and listening to her headphones. Normally, she would be sitting out in the front yard with her smoke; however, today the rain has forced her to stay on the porch. Her gaunt, anorexic figure displays her state of mind. She was depressed all of the time. Her constant cry is, "God! Will you please take me home? Just take me home!" She cried out over and over in her mind as she listened to a song by Metallica called "Sanitarium," trying desperately to drown out all of the voices inside of her head.

Janiece Elaine Turner had been through years of extreme pain and misery. She was tired, extremely exhausted, and she just wanted it to be all over, finished. The voices inside of her head would not leave her alone. Unbeknownst to her,

---

Photo at Left: Photo of Janiece when she was a little girl, December 31, 1961

she was getting her wish. Soon it would be all over, but it would not be the way she had expected.

After almost eight years of pain, surgeries, mental institutions, treatments, drugs, and medications, the doctors finally came to a new conclusion, aided by a new technology called the MRI (Magnetic Resonance Imaging). They told her family that the myelin sheathing around the nerves in her brain were dying and this was causing her brain cells to die. At the time, they called it Demyelinating Syndrome. They told her family there was no hope for her and asked them if there was a place that she could stay comfortably until she died, because the mental hospitals could not help her anymore and also, they were so expensive. Taking into account the doctor's advice, they decided to place her into her oldest sister's caregiving home for the terminally ill. The family was told not to tell her she was dying, for fear that this time she would be successful in taking her life, after all the numerous attempts she had made in the past.

There was something very special about this dreary, rainy day, however. This day was different. It was not like all the other days before. This day was special, because it was the fulfillment of a promise from a long time ago. This was the day that death would be sentenced and life would begin to blossom.

As she continued to listen to the music and continued to smoke her cigarette, the front door opened and her sister walked out. Janiece pulled the headphones down to her neck so that she could hear. Her sister only spoke a few words this time out of frustration and then went back inside. It was the same words she had heard from others over the years. "Do you want to stay sick forever?"

Aware, for the first time in many years, she suddenly exclaimed, "No! No! I don't want to be sick forever!" As she was turning around to face her sister, she reached down to put the cigarette out, but by this time, her sister had already gone back inside.

Janiece opened the door and looked for her sister. She walked up to her. "No!" she exclaimed. "I DON'T want to be sick forever! Now what…"

31 YEARS EARLIER…

Family Life

Janiece was born into a middle class family. Her early years spanned the entire 1960's decade. Her dad, Bob Turner was a lithographer, printer. Her mother, Virginia, or Gin as she liked to be called, was a homemaker while the children were young. They had three girls and a boy, Starr, Deborah, Janiece and Bobby. Starr, the eldest, is five years older than Janiece. Deborah is twenty months older than Janiece and Bobby is nine years younger than she.

When Janiece was around the age of nine in Colorado Springs, Colorado, Gin launched out in her own Avon business. Later, after they returned to San Anotonio, she went to business college and entered the corporate world as an administrator for a local CPA company. Sometimes, Bob worked extra jobs, including weekends, to provide for his family during the tight times financially, to buy property, to take care of emergency financial needs, and to take vacations. The family went on many vacation outings together and explored some of the old ghost towns of Colorado and some of the canyons in Texas, Arizona and Utah. They bought property in different places for investment and fun. The properties also allowed the family to camp out together and have a place to just get away and rest. While the family had a lot of fun together over the years, as the children grew into adulthood, there were some instances that came in to challenge this love.

Bob is an explorer at heart and loved to find places for the family to see. While they were living in Colorado Springs, Colorado, his fellow workers would ask him every week, "Where did you go this time, Bob?" They would spend most weekends checking out the various ghost towns nearby, single lane mountain trails that took four-wheel drive and other places of interest. His fellow workers were hungry to hear about his adventures because they were natives who had not even ventured out to the places around them. This is where Janiece gets some of her pioneering and exploration spirit, we think.

Current Events

Janiece was born at the Nix hospital in San Antonio, Texas on April 11, 1960. This was the year John F. Kennedy was elected as the 35th president of the United States of America, with the first presidential debates being held on TV. It was the beginning of the famous, "Swinging Sixties." The birth control pill was released to the public this year and the first working laser was demonstrated.

During the decade of the Sixties: John F. Kennedy, Lyndon B. Johnson and Richard M. Nixon became U.S. presidents. The Cuban missile crisis developed which involved the U.S. and Russia. The space race started and the U.S. sent men to the moon. The Vietnam war spanned the decade, while

Martin Luther King Jr's. "I Have A Dream" speech was given. John F. Kennedy, Malcolm X, Martin Luther King Jr. and Robert F. Kennedy were assassinated. The Peace Corps. was established. Category 5 Hurricane Camille, with 190 mph winds hit the Gulf Coast. Touch-tone phones were introduced. The first computer programming language BASIC was created. The first ATM (Automated Teller Machine) was opened in Barclays Bank, London. Feminism in the United States and around the world gained momentum in the early 1960s. In 1968, "Women's Liberation" became a household term. The Manson Murders took place in 1969. The Woodstock Festival, in upstate New York, took place in 1969. Psychedelic drugs, especially LSD, were widely used medicinally, spiritually and recreationally throughout the late 1960s. There was a music explosion from Elvis, The Beatles, The Four Seasons, The Supremes, Grateful Dead, Bob Dylan, The Rolling Stones, Simon & Garfunkle, The Beach Boys, Jefferson Airplane, Pink Floyd, Bee Gees, Jimi Hindrix, The Who and many more. The highest grossing film of the decade was "The Sound Of Music." The hippie movement began. The bikini and the mini-skirt were introduced into the fashion industry. Billy Graham and C. S. Lewis were among the spiritual leaders. Marlon Brando, Charlton Heston and Julie Andrews were in full swing in the movies.

Cultural Expectations

The cultural expectations of the 60's, were tumultuous. With the peace movement, the women's liberation movement, and the anti-God movement with the Bible and prayer being removed from public schools in 1962, the moral foundations of conservative parenting and schooling were breaking up and parents were being caught in a cataclysmic storm of epic proportions.

Janiece's parents were caught in this period of changes. They were determined to raise their children with moral values and proper manners. Bob had been forced to go to church and was determined to have his children grow up with the choice to choose when they were old enough to decide on their own. They believed in corporal punishment as did the public schools during this time period. They were very protective of their children and used every means available to ensure their children were safe, loved, and had the best advantage to enter adulthood.

Asthma Attacks

Janiece developed chronic bronchial asthma when she was eight weeks old. Her parents had to take her to the doctor on a regular basis in the beginning, because she was having such vicious attacks that she could hardly breathe. The doctors would give her a shot of adrenaline which would help some. Dr. Sweeney was Janiece's physician and he taught her mother how to administer the allergy shots at home to help strengthen her immune system. However, there were still times when the attacks were so severe that she had to be brought to the hospital. One day, the doctor told them that they needed to have air conditioning in their home, because the dry air would help her tremendously. At that time, there wasn't anyone in their whole neighborhood in South San Antonio that had air conditioning. This was in early 1960, so they looked around the city and bought a Friedrich air conditioner, which cost over $600 at the time. Air conditioners were so expensive, because they were new to the market. It made all the difference in the world for her, but she seemed to be allergic to everything. Her mother had to continually dust the house, including the baseboards and walls. This is the same air conditioner they later took to Colorado when they moved from San Antonio. They stored it in the basement while there, because they found they didn't need it there and brought it back with them when they moved back to San Antonio. In Colorado, they didn't need it because it was a different climate.

Janiece recalled, "I had asthma since I was a baby, an infant. It was called chronic bronchial asthma. A lot of times I would have to be rushed to the hospital to get a shot of adrenaline and later on it was a shot of epinephrine. They didn't have medications like Primatine Mist out on the market yet when I was little. Those came out later when I was in my teens. Until then it was always having to rush to the hospitals or clinics, but most of the time it was to the hospitals."

Dog Attack

When Janiece was three years old, Gin, Bob and the girls were next door visiting with their neighbors. At one point during their visit, Janiece was outside with the neighbor's dog, a Chow. She had her arm around its neck, like in a hug. She was feeding it her Graham cracker cookie and when she took it back, the dog snapped at her and bit her. Its teeth caught her right under her nose, ripped through her flesh, down through her upper lip and it also punctured the inside roof of her mouth. They immediately got into the Rambler, with Janiece in the front seat with them. She had her head on her mother's lap. They went to the emergency room at Santa Rosa Hospital in downtown San Antonio. She was required to take the complete series of rabies shots, because the bite was so close to her brain, so they began to administer them immediately. Even though they tested the dog as quickly as they could, she had already completed all of the painful shots before the results came back.

Her parents decided right away to get a plastic surgeon to repair her lip. Miraculously, one was there at the hospital and was very renown. Bob states, "The Lord took care of that, because it could have easily been a hair lip, really exaggerated." The tear was right through her top lip. The dog's teeth penetrated so deep, that they turned one of her permanent teeth around and when she got braces, years later,

Photo Above: Photo of sisters, Starr, Janiece with bandaid on her upper lip from the dog bite, and Deborah (from left to right)

they had to use a spring to slowly turn it back.

The lip atrophied after the bite. It was the orthodontist, years later, who encouraged her to continually massage it, by stroking it downward with the side of her index finger to stimulate growth, to get it to return to normal. Now, you can't even tell where it happened.

Baptism Of Water

Janiece recalls, "When I was growing up, my parents were Baptists. I do remember Mother loved Jesus. She even told me that she went to a different church once when she was younger, and it went over like a lead balloon with Janiece's grandmother because they spoke in tongues there." Janiece said that her mother told her, "They had the Holy Ghost. They had joy in the Lord."

Janiece continues, "However, when I was little they didn't go to church. Our next door neighbor was Baptist. He seemed like he knew the Lord somewhat and was involved in the church. We would go with our next door neighbor, Mary Ruth, to Vacation Bible School in the summers. They had studies where you had homework. One time, there was a contest for memorizing the books of the Bible and we only had to memorize the Old Testament. Well, I memorized it forward and backward and I won a Bible. I was so excited. I wanted Jesus so bad during this time of my life."

"Sometime during one of these weeks I told my mother, 'I want to go up, Mother, and be water baptized.'"

"She said, 'Honey you need to understand.'"

"I replied, 'All I know is I've got to go up there.'"

"She said, 'Honey you have to understand what it is all about and why.'"

"But I would say, 'I have to go up there, I have to go up there. I was like driven from a little kid. Please, please, please! It's like I am going to die without this. Please, I got to have this. I got to have Jesus.'"

"As it turns out, Mother finally said OK. On my way up there it was like I could hardly hold my emotions together. So much love! I got baptized finally and every time I messed up I thought I needed a new baptism. You know, it's like cleaning up again, dunk me again and wash all that stuff off."

"I don't know why I stopped going. Didn't get to go much, though. Life happens you know. Other kids happen around you and stuff happens. I drifted away!"

The Devil Is Real

"I always felt different, tom-boyish and different from Starr and Deborah. I wanted to play rough and they didn't. I just wanted to have some extreme fun. I liked tree climbing and hiking. They did too for a while, but then boys came into the picture," said Janiece as she thought about some of the gender struggles she was having at such an early age.

Colorado Springs, Colorado

The family moved to Colorado Springs, Colorado in April 1969 and stayed until December 1970. Bob took a printing job there to get away from the big city. Later on, they moved back for two reasons, one being that his stepfather suffered a stroke and his father-in-law suffered a heart attack. They wanted to be near to help their families. The other reason is answered later on in this chapter.

Janiece recalled, "It was here that I first started working out with lifting weights. It was really neat when we moved to Colorado Springs. I was nine at the time, in 1969."

"Back then our street, North Circle Drive, ended at a T intersection at North Union Boulevard. Now, it doesn't. It continues on as Fillmore Street. They have since expanded that road into a loop that goes around the city. There was a church at the end of our street. It was Bellevue Baptist, but is now called Heart Of The Springs. We went there for a little while. Deborah started going to that church with her friend. Later, I went along with her and also Starr. At the corner was a cherry tree. I remember that, the cherries! Wow! I was so glad it hung over the fence. They didn't like us picking the cherries, but kids will be kids."

"The bluffs were across the street from our house. We would go out there and play catch. We had our baseball gloves and baseball too. We picnicked a lot too."

"I really did like it there in Colorado, but I didn't like finding out that there was a devil, that he actually had a presence and that he was mean. I didn't like finding that part out. He was scary!"

"My parents used to like to watch 'Project Terror' and 'Twilight Zone.' Starr was going through some stuff during this time, you know, the teenage years finding out who you are and then realizing that there are boys. They are not just boys anymore. Now, they're cute. Wow! We are five years difference in age, so that made a big difference between us."

"I remember Starr talking to someone in her room once. I told her, 'Shhhh! If I can hear you, Mother and Dad can hear you. You better tell those boys to leave before you get in trouble.' I figured they were talking through the window.

I mean, we did stuff. We were kids. We didn't always get to have company."

"She said, 'Well, there's nobody here. There are no boys here.'"

"I said, 'Right! Sure! I hear you. If I can hear you, Mother and Dad will be able to hear down the hall. Just telling you!'"

"And she replied, 'They're spirits.'"

"'Oh, sure they are!' I replied."

"She said with a warning tone in her voice, 'They don't like to be mocked either.'"

"I replied in unbelief, 'Okay! Sure! Whatever!' I found out differently later on."

"Then, some time later, when I came home from school something happened. I have always thought that this couldn't have possibly happened because it was too weird, too unnatural, that it couldn't have happened, but the experience was real and very vivid in my mind to this day."

"One day after school, I came home. Starr was usually home before us. She went to the high school and I went to Audubon elementary."

"No one was at home this time, though. I looked into Starr's room and I saw her shoes slide under the bed. Well, right away I was breath-taken. I was just gripped with fear. I could barely breathe, it was so scary. Then, they popped right back out. Oh God, it was like my chest was hurting. It was an ultra-paralyzing fear. I ran out of the house and it seemed like I didn't even open the screen door, rather I just pushed through it and I kept going. I kept trying to avoid her window, while I was going next door to my best friend's house to see if he was home. I mean, her window was right there and there was my best friend's house. I kept trying to keep out of the view of the window. I was so terrified! No one was home and I thought, 'that's not right either. There is always somebody there, gosh, either, Tom, or Donna, or Steven.'"

"I was looking for someone to be home somewhere, but no one seemed to be home. I walked up towards the school and a short while later, I thought I'd better get home or I'm going to be in trouble. So I got back home and it was like nothing had happened to the screen door. Everything was fine. I told Starr what had happened and she said, 'I told you they don't like to be mocked.'"

"I said, 'Okay, so I'm not messing with you anymore.' From then on, I was afraid of her and them. At that point in my life, I was more aware of them, even more so than my love for Jesus. From then on, every scary show was even more scary than before, because now there was a life to it. It was real. It wasn't just a show anymore. I was a real scaredy-cat. I was afraid of the dark, everything."

"There was an earlier time, before we moved to Colorado Springs, that I was crying out in the middle of the night, 'Mother! Mother! Mother! Mother!' She came to the door and I said, 'Watch out! They'll get you!'"

"She asked, 'What?'"

"I exclaimed, 'They're everywhere! They're like giant animals, like giant turtles, frogs and stuff! Don't come in, but help me!' I didn't know what to do. I was so scared."

"She said, 'Aw, honey, there isn't anything here.'"

"'They're all around!' I exclaimed. 'They're all around!'"

"She said, 'Honey, you're sleeping.'"

"I said, 'How can I be sleeping if we're talking? They are all around!' She came in and she comforted me. Oh, gosh,

I remember so much of the time, I just wanted to make a device that I could telescope out to turn the light switch on from across the room. You know, so that I wouldn't have to actually get up. I knew that when I turned the light on they weren't going to be there. Turn off the lights and I could see them again. It was only in the dark that I could see them and I hated the dark. I was so afraid of the dark. I didn't like being awake before anyone else and I didn't like being home before they got home. I never felt safe inside, anywhere alone, anymore. I felt safer outside. I didn't feel safe inside, ever."

Just One Of The Boys

Janiece changed the subject at this point, "Along the way though, I just enjoyed being a kid. I liked to climb things and play football. 'The guys' on the street were just the guys on the street. They were my buddies. I was their quarterback. They would come knocking on the door and ask my mother, 'Can Janiece come out and play?'"

"Sometimes, I would have asthma attacks and I couldn't go out and play. Mother would have to tell them 'no,' to which they once replied, 'Well, she's got to! She's our quarterback!' It was then she understood how they felt about me."

"Starr and Deborah had their friends that were their age and they were girls. There weren't any girls my age close by, but that was fine with me. I was having a good time. I wanted someone to be rough with and just play. To me, we were just playing, climbing trees and jumping off of the house. Jumping off of the house would just unnerve Mother. She would get so mad at me. It made her really mad, but now that I am a mom, I found out that it scares you when it's your child."

Drugs, Rock & Roll

Janiece continued on, "Starr went to some parties that our parents didn't know about and she was exposed to drugs and Rock and Roll. Rock and Roll was big in the 1960's. This was from 1969 through the end of 1970, while we were still living in Colorado. The thing I remember the most, when I think about the drug scene, was seeing Starr sitting on her bed once. We had a basement, which was like another house downstairs, except without the kitchen and living room. There were two rooms downstairs and a bathroom, a den where the pool table was located, a workshop, and a laundry room. Starr was just sitting on her bed and was moving her finger in a figure eight in front of her."

"I asked, 'What are you doing?'"

"She said, 'Trails!'"

"I said, 'Trails? What?'"

"And Starr said, 'Yeah! This looks soooo cool.'"

"I said, 'I don't see anything.' She said something about LSD or something, that she had taken it and it makes you see things."

"It's like, 'Okay! Sure!' It was really weird."

"Later on, we would all sneak outside and smoke or something. This is how she would get herself from getting in trouble. She would get us to take a drag on the cigarette. This way she could smoke in front of us and she didn't have to always hide it from us when Mother and Dad were gone. You know, 'draw the other kids in and they are just as guilty.' So, I wasn't going to say anything, because my goose would be cooked too. I found out later that it was at night when you could see the trails of the cigarette butt. You could see it and I finally got it. That's what that was all about."

"I caught her smoking something else one time. I asked, 'What's that? It smells different, real different.' She handed it to me. I took some of it, coughed, and said, 'That stuff hits you hard at first. It's harsh.' That's all I remember about this in Colorado. Rock and Roll was neat. I liked it. Mother and Dad could not take that music. They did not want that stuff in the house."

Bob recalled, "The boys that Starr wanted to be with were the long haired hippies. I told them that nobody is coming in here looking like that. I told Starr, Deborah and Janiece, 'Do not ever come around with a boy with long hair, earrings or anything on him like that. I am not going to have hippies around here.'"

"One time Starr came into the house and asked Gin for the scissors. About fifteen minutes later she had a boy come in. She had cut his hair off. He wanted to date her so bad that he let her cut his hair."

"There was an abundance of drugs available there, even in junior school. In high school, the girls could wear halter tops and short shorts. I was determined that this was not the place to bring up three girls. Starr had gotten really wild during this time, smoking, sneaking out and staying out. It was a really bad influence."

"I found another job back in San Antonio, we moved back and it was just great. If anyone here just had pot, they were considered really bad. It wasn't that way there. In Colorado, even in junior school, you could get any type of drug you wanted. There were hippies all over the place. Their parks were full of them. I kept the kids away from this."

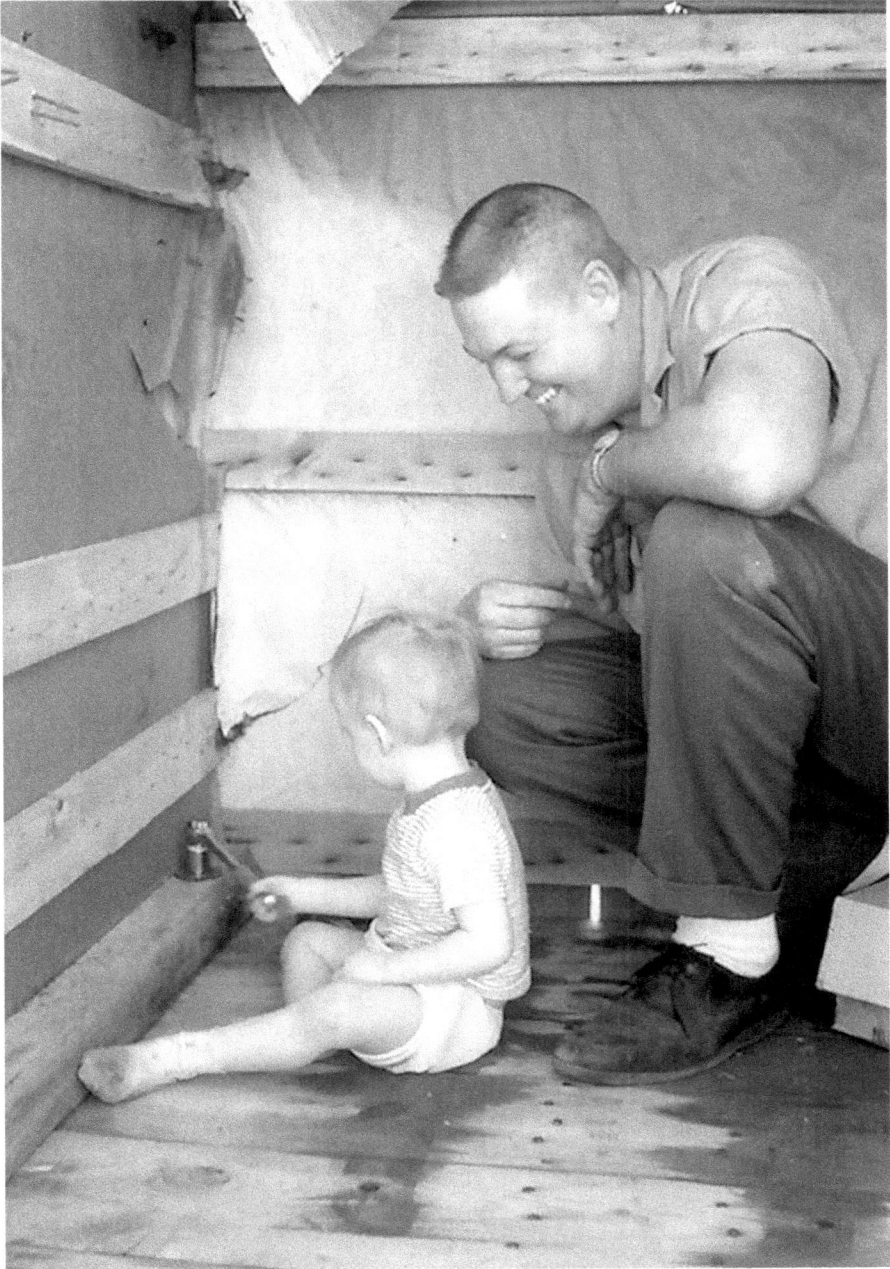

Photo Above: Janiece and Bob in what is going to be the girl's playhouse. She is learning how to use a ratchet at a young age.

Chapter 2

Times Of Unrest

Overview Of Love Snapshot

Since the very nature of this story builds a layered foundation to establish Janiece's overall perspective, it tends to get very one-sided and conclusions can possibly be drawn by the reader that could become exaggerated and false where it concerns her actual family life. In all of her outbursts and thoughts throughout the rest of this story, one can tend to get the wrong impression of family life. Therefore, I am including a small section here, of the fun times and love that permeated her life and helped to build a good foundation in her life.

Reflecting On The Good Times

Janiece remembered a time when she was little, "I remember playing 'Red Light - Green Light,' 'Mother, May I?', and 'Simon Says' with my sisters. We used to play 'Cowboys and Indians' and even dressed up to look the part."

"Dad would bring home 55 gallon drums and we would

Photo at Left: Photo of sisters, Janiece and Deborah playing 'Cowboys and Indians' at their home on the south side of San Antonio. The dog that bit her was from the yard next door in this photo. Janiece is lying on the grass.

race on them on the ground like the log roll races in the water. The whole family had Chinaberry fights in the back yard."

Janiece recalled climbing the Chinaberry tree, picking and dropping the berries to her dad, when they were team mates. They also had an above ground pool where they spent many hours of fun, playing and splashing around.

Her dad would bring home the used rubber blankets from the printing presses and they would line them up on the ground like a make-shift 'Slip-N-Slide.' He also taught each of them how to swim. He taught Janiece how to high dive, play basketball, pass the football, and shoot her BB gun at targets. He also took her dove hunting.

Janiece and her sisters would go exploring together on the properties Bob and Gin had bought. They took lots of vacations together during the summers, where they added to their exploration experience. When they built a cabin on one of their properties, he taught them how to construct it with various carpentry tools. He showed Janiece how to use a double-sided axe to cut down a bunch of trees. He didn't tell her how many to remove and while he was doing something else, she cleared out too many trees, almost removing all of the privacy the trees had given. She was having fun and didn't want to stop.

Running Away

However, during her early teenage years, the stress of school and life was starting to drown out the good times. Things became hard and difficult for her. There were many things she didn't understand, including the changes in her physical body as well as her mental state of mind. The identity crisis that was beginning and increasingly messing with her mind, began to overshadow so many things. The pressure was building and she couldn't keep it in any longer.

Janiece had a paper route during this time and one Friday she was out collecting the money on her bicycle, when she met up with a friend. Even though it wasn't dusk yet, nor time for her to be home, her mother and dad were already driving around in the truck looking for her. The rule for her was that she needed to be home by dusk because of the asthma attacks that could sometimes be brought on by the night air. Just prior to them driving up, a friend had invited her to a party. They saw Janiece talking to her friend and assumed she was playing around, instead of collecting money for her paper route. Her dad sent her friend away and told her they would meet her back at the house. She ended up getting a spanking. After the spanking, Janiece talked to her mother. She said, "I don't understand. It wasn't even dusk yet. I didn't do anything wrong. Here's the money. See, I collected the money."

Her mother told her, "I don't want to hear it. I can't do anything about it."

That night Janiece packed her bag, took the money and left.

One night, during the time she was gone, she stayed at her friend Carolyn's house and slept on the sofa. She was awakened in the morning by the police. Carolyn's mother had called the police while she was still asleep. She had been gone from home over a week and a half and everyone was concerned for her safety. She had a bag of marijuana on her person at the time and asked the police if she could go to the restroom first. At first they weren't going to let her, but then they did. She flushed the bag down the toilet. Then they took her to juvenile detention.

Until her parents could get there, she had to attend school during regular school hours at the center. They called her out of class to talk to the social worker. Her name was Gloria. Gloria wanted to know what happened and why she left. Gloria said she was going to call her parents in next and they would all talk together. Janiece was so scared. In her mind, she thought she was 'dead meat.' She thought she was going to get another spanking and that was the main reason she had left in the first place.

The social worker told the three of them that Janiece had the choice, to either go back home with them or go to a girl's home until she was eighteen. Janiece asked the social worker what was the legal age that she could move out of her parent's house and was told it was seventeen.

Janiece asked Gloria if it was okay if she thought about it over the lunch hour, since it was time for lunch. The two of them had lunch together and met up with her parents again after lunch.

Janiece had only one request for her dad, which was going to decide where she would choose to go. Her request was: "Dad, if you promise to never spank me again, I'll come home." It was then she saw tears in his eyes. Through all of the hardships and struggles, especially in her teenage years, the love she knew from her father had faded in her mind. The thing that was most prominent now was the fear and anger she felt towards him. When she saw the tears, it touched her heart so deep inside and gave her hope again that things could change. This glimpse, however, wasn't enough to break totally through all of the pain and torment she felt inside, but it was there. He promised her that he wouldn't spank her again. She went back home with them and he kept his word.

R.O.T.C.

Janiece chose to take R.O.T.C during her ninth grade in school, as a freshman, because it was the better of the choices. The other two choices were Physical Education or Pep Squad. The asthma kept her from doing so many physical things that she wanted to do. It was a handicap and it really hurt.

In R.O.T.C., she felt embarrassed most of the time, because of the dress uniform she had to wear. It consisted of a blouse, skirt, vest, knee-high socks, tie, hat, and nurse's shoes. Pants weren't part of the girl's uniform and she felt practically naked in the dress. She thought the guys uniforms looked cool. This embarrassment became like a continual crushing blow to her spirit being dressed up in something that didn't seem right to her. It was foreign and awkward. She did like working with the rifles though. That was fun to her.

First Girl In Printshop In High School

Getting into print shop class in high school was a 'boys only' thing and became a challenge. Her dad, being an experienced printer, went to talk to the printshop teacher to get his approval before the principal would allow her into the class. Bob had more experience in printing than the teacher did. The teacher gave his approval, so she took Printshop I & II in her sophomore and junior years.

Janiece was so adamant about being in printing that she even chose the class over going to Driver's Ed and getting

Photo Above: Her print shop teacher, EJ Bradley wrote this in her year book: "Janiece: I will always remember the girl who wanted to be a printer more than anyone I ever knew." Janiece is in the center of the bottom row. The two girls sitting next to her, on the right, were in the secretarial part of the class and were not printers.

her driver's license, because the classes were held at the same time. Later, she had to get a hardship driver's license when she was 17 so that she could get a job for the ICT (Industrial Co-operation Training) program at the school the next year. Her class hours were from 11:30 - 3:30 in the afternoon for the ICT class.

She had tried to get a job with Speedy Printing Company, but wasn't able to get it because she didn't have a driver's license at the time. This was the main reason used on the application for getting a hardship driver's license dated May 2, 1977.

Mechanic's Helper - High School

Janiece had been interested in mechanics and one day she went looking around for a job that she would enjoy. She drove down to Commercial Avenue where she saw a little shop off the beaten path called "Big Johnny's Garage." She heard Spanish music playing as she got out of the car. She went in and asked for the owner, and he was the guy she was talking to. He was about an inch shorter than she, had beautiful bluish green eyes, and had a stocky build. She had asked him to see the owner specifically, because she wanted to get a job there. He spoke in broken English. He was from Guatamala and this was his shop. He didn't have any workers to help him. She told him that it looked like he could use some help around there. She said she was only looking for part time work. He looked at her like 'You must be kidding! Hiring a girl!' She told him that he could try her out for free to see if she was worth it. He said, "Well, I can't pay you much." She replied, "Pay is not the issue here. I just need enough for gas for my car and some play money. How's $45 a week?" She ended up working there for quite a while. She was dropping transmissions using a floor jack. Then he would dismantle them and she would wash the parts with gasoline. He would then repair them and she would re-install them back in the vehicles.

Her dad had already taught her how do some things, like tune-ups, rotating tires, replacing thermostats and this gave her the desire to learn more. At Big Johnny's, she also learned how to change out starters, solenoids, brake master cylinders, oil changes, and how to remove just the flywheel or torque converter without removing the whole transmission. If she wasn't careful though, she would end up wearing the transmission fluid all over her clothes. Also, if she didn't line up the gasket correctly or tighten it too tight, the gasket would tear and leak, and she would have to do it all over again. They didn't have drain plugs on the transmission pans, so it was hard to stay clean. There was a special dismantling process to removing transmissions and if she didn't do it right, it could be very dangerous. I know, I have also done mechanic work.

Moved Out, On Her Own

Shortly after Janiece turned 17, she moved away from home. She couldn't wait to get away from the house because of all of the stress of having to be perfect in school. She couldn't do the school work because of her comprehension problem and was on restriction a lot. It was too much stress and she was buckling under it.

She met Carol Neimeier when she went to work for Tri-Way Printers & Mailers. She found out that she had an apartment, so she asked her if she could be her roommate. Carol agreed and that was what they did. Janiece moved out and called her mother who was at work. Her mother thought it was a cheap shot that she called her but wasn't going to call her dad. The reason she called her mother was because she was afraid to call her dad.

She had a 1965, light blue Ford Galaxy 500 at the time and she just moved all of her stuff over to Carol's apartment. She transferred from McCollum High School to Edison High School because she now lived in a different part of town. Her mother signed an affidavit making Carol her guardian.

Bob recalls, "She lived over to the north of downtown

with Carol and she was only 17. We were told we couldn't do anything about it, because she was of legal age. She was living over there and doing that for a little while. It wasn't too long, however, when we talked to her that she decided she would like to come back home and go to school. It was a lot better living at home. It was a lot harder out on her own than she had thought. She came back only with the condition that she finished school and she did."

Janiece even went to night school at Fox Tech High School to complete the two extra classes she needed, Government and English III, so that she could graduate with her class at McCollum. She graduated with her class in 1978.

Photos Above: Top: Bob, Steve, Deborah, Gin and Janiece working together and building their cabin on one of their properties; Bottom: Janiece with the double-sided axe, Bobby, and Gin; Next Page - Top: The family on a camp out in the mountains; Middle Left: Deborah & Janiece watching television on the floor with their dad, Bob; Middle Right: Janiece receiving her high school diploma from McCollum High School in 1978 in San Antonio, Texas, that she worked so hard to accomplish; Bottom: Janiece, Deborah, Starr and Bob playing catch together next to the bluffs across the street from their home in Colorado Springs during their stay from 1969 - 1970

Photos Above: Top: Gin talking to Janiece; Bottom: Janiece and her nephew Jimmy; She was in the electrical trade during this time.

Chapter 3

A Man's World

Choosing Her Path

Janiece had just graduated from high school in 1978 and her dad wanted her to either get a job or go in the service. First, she went for some testing for the Army. When they found out she was asthmatic, they said they couldn't let her into the service. No one with asthma could be accepted. She had completed one year of ROTC in school, so she could have come in at a higher grade or classification. They suggested she try the Air Force. Of course, they were being sarcastic about it.

She took the advice anyway and went to the Air Force and completed the testing. They asked what field of training she was interested in and she told them she had been in printshop class and had worked in a mechanic's shop. She told them she was good with her hands. They told her they would give her a list of careers after the testing so that she could make a choice.

She especially remembers doing the testing that had to do with the cogs, wheels, crankshafts and camshafts. It was all about how each one makes another one turn and she had to answer questions about them. It just made sense to her. That was her biggest area of strength. She wasn't really good in math, but she could visualize how everything would work in a series of gears. It made sense to her and was easy. They told her, that because of this, she would be good in aircraft mechanics.

Even though she had gone to the Air Force to enlist, she was really not wanting to get into the service because that meant taking more orders. As it was, she was having a hard enough time living at her parent's house, plus taking orders from an ROTC sergeant at school, and she wasn't too keen on getting her backside chewed on all of the time in the military.

She really didn't care for working in the job force as a printer, but it would be better than being in the service. Her dad asked her if she had any luck and she told him that she was waiting on a response from the results of the testing.

In the meantime, her dad knew a master electrician that worked at Bexar Electric Company. He frequently came to his shop to see what kind of repair or wiring they needed on the printing equipment. The guy would then send one of his crews to do the work. His name was Mike Fryar. Her dad told her he would go ahead and set something up with him.

Janiece wasn't for sure, but went for it anyway. Her dad set up the appointment and she went in for the interview. Mike wasn't available when she arrived, even though the appointment had been set up with him. She decided to wait out in the waiting room until he got back. She felt she had a better chance waiting for Mike, since her dad knew him, rather than talk to anyone else. There was also the fact that no other women were in the field at the time. Carol, the administrative assistant, told her that she could talk to Bob Weik instead if she liked. She didn't know that Bob was the owner. She was determined to wait and talk to Mike. He was her way in, or so she thought. Time kept passing by and finally the admin rose up and asked her again. She told her that Bob Weik was still available if she wanted to talk to him. Janiece remarked, "If I have to, I'll meet with him." She followed her into his office. She had been thinking that he was someone under Mike and didn't have as much authority and she wanted the best shot at the job.

She walked into his office and saw this really big, beautiful desk. The man behind the desk stood up and introduced himself. He was real polite. He said that this was an unusual field to enter for a woman. She replied, "But you don't know me. I've done printing. I took two years of printing in school. I was a mechanic's helper for quite a while and loved that. I smelled like gas all the time, but you know, I am not afraid to get dirty, or sweaty, or cut, or hurt. I'm a good worker. I learn fast. You can try me out and hey, if you don't like me, you're not going to hurt my feelings if you fire me."

He must have been impressed, because he later gave her a chance and told her when to show up for work at the residential shop on the north side. They also gave her a list of all the tools she was going to have to purchase. Before too long, they were ordering a uniform for her. She loved it from the very beginning. She became the first woman electrician in San Antonio, Texas in June of 1978.

First Woman Electrician

What is really interesting about the whole scenario, is the timing. The day that Janiece found out she was accepted into the Air Force, she was also offered the job with Bexar Electric Company. She went from having nothing to having a choice between two jobs on the same day. That was a no-brainer for her. She didn't really want to get beat up on in the service, so Bexar Electric sounded good to her.

Bob Weik, the founder and owner of Bexar Electric, started out in his garage with his own crew and before too long he had two locations in San Antonio. Janiece started out working for them in the residential shop, just north of the San Antonio Airport.

It wasn't long and one of the supervisors asked her if she knew about AIECA. She hadn't, so he explained to her that it was an Association for Independent Electrical Contractors of America. It was an apprenticeship program and he thought she should think about it. She asked him what the difference was between being a helper and apprentice. He told her she'll get a pay raise, to which she replied, "I'm already on!" He said to wait a minute because she would also have to go to school. She's thinking, 'I just got out of school. I don't want to go to school again.' He continued on with his coaxing, "The other thing about this is that you don't stay at that lower level. You keep going up and you can get your journeyman's license faster. You can still get your license without the school, but this way you learn about residential and commercial, and you won't get stuck in residential work." She thought about it for a while and then accepted. She was not only the first girl in the electrical trade, but also in the school to be an apprentice. She would attend the school twice a week for four years, after work.

There was only one person in Bexar Electric that she didn't like during the four years she worked there. She loved everything about the job. This person though, was a leadman and must have felt a competition thing. She loved that she was good at the job and fast. She learned what her journeyman needed and handed them tools and supplies even before they asked for them. She always had the truck loaded and stocked. She wanted to do the best job possible to bring honor to the company.

They tried to play a couple of pranks on her, but her dad had pre-warned her about this. One day, they told her to go and get a bucket of air. That one didn't go anywhere at all. She couldn't believe they asked for something so far out there.

Her dad had told her a story of what happened to him once at Alamo Iron Works. They asked him to go get something for them. He knew it was a prank, so he went to the theatre and watched a movie instead. When he got back, after the show was over, they asked him if he had found it. He just told them that he hadn't and kept on working. They didn't know any different.

Janiece was a good helper and hard worker so most of the journeymen wanted her around and even to be on their crew. There was a rotation with the helpers where each helper would be rotated to work with different journeymen or leadmen over a period of time. A leadman is not yet a journeyman. They haven't tested for the license yet, but have logged a lot of time, experience and training. Helpers were rotated to different crews by the supervisor. The supervisor also lines up the crews for the jobs needing to be done.

Green As Grass

Janiece remembers a funny story when she first started in the electrical trade. She was wiring for her first air conditioning unit outside. It was on a Bexar Electric job site.

She was still as 'green as grass.' She had these really nice and new Klein side cutters. It wasn't the normal 110 volts she had been working with, but this set of wires had two hot legs and it was 220 volts. She wanted to cut the wires to where they would fit well in the box. They told her she would have to use kerneys (metal wire clamps) to join the wires because they are larger than the other wires she had been using. The wire nuts were not big enough to use on these wires. Then she would have to wrap it to seal the connection with rubber and electrical tape. Her thoughts were that if she cut them the same length it would work better. She got a good bite on them with the cutters and she heard a big "boom." The cutters flew out of her hand and she couldn't hear for a little while. The electricity had notched out a hole in her cutters the size of the wires. They were brand new cutters that were now useless. They never told her not to cut both wires at the same time, but even so, the wires should not have been hot. The power should have been off. She thought someone was messing with her and turned on the breaker. The guys knew what had happened by the sound they heard and were all laughing. She could hear them. They knew she had tried to cut both wires at the same time. She kept the cutters for a long time as a reminder of what not to do. This was one of those lessons learned by experience.

Just One Of The Guys

When she first went to work for Bexar Electric Company, she thought that many of the guys didn't think she would make it. However, after a while, they accepted her more and more and it became a lot of fun. They drove to the job sites, sitting three across in the front seat and sweating at times, especially in the sweltering heat and high humidity of San Antonio in the hot summer sun. The residential shop of the company used the older trucks for their work. They received the hand-me-downs from the commercial shop when they were given new trucks. She said it like this, "We got what runs down hill."

The shop she worked at got the ancient trucks. They looked like some of them were from the 60's. In the heat, they sweated all over each other. It didn't matter much to them, they were just working. They found out right away that she was just fine with it and it was good to have her around.

When she switched over to the commercial shop, it was like night and day difference. She had to think differently. Everything was newer and nicer. The guys were more well-mannered and even protective of her. The commercial shop was larger and so were the wires. She went from running romex wire for residential housing, to single wires that were up to 1.5 inches in diameter, as well as having to measure, cut and bend pipe and then pull the wire through the pipes.

One of the toughest tools she had to work with in the residential shop was the auger bit. Sometimes it would catch on a nail as she drilled through the top wood plates and would twist her body around because of the high torque of the half inch drill. At the commercial shop, however, they worked with metal studs and had hand-held punchers to knock holes through for the EMT (Electrical Metallic Tubing) pipe. The punchers looked similar to a huge paper hole punch that had two handles and was about eighteen inches long. One of the hardest tools for her to use was the rotor hammer.

Janiece recalled, "One job we did, was on the Ingram

Park Cinema. On the outside wall we had to drill through the concrete. The walls had rebar, round steel bars, running through them and we didn't know where each bar was because we couldn't see them. So if we were drilling and the bit caught on the rebar, the drill could easily smack us in the face. If a person was on an extension ladder and sometimes we were up as high as fifteen feet in the air, it could get really scary."

Sometimes, they used jack hammers to break up the concrete in order to lay in pipe and floor plugs. She liked the 60 pound jack hammer because it was fun, but the 90 pound was really tough. She didn't weigh too much more than it. She weighed about 132 pounds at the time. When it broke through the concrete into the dirt below, it usually went straight down to the end of the bit, pulling her down with it. Then she would have to pull it out by herself, yanking, tugging and moving it side to side, if necessary, to get it out.

They also used scaffolds and hydraulic lifts for the heights rather than using ladders all of the time. The lifts were electric and could be driven around. Sometimes, she would have fun and mess around with her journeyman, Adrian. One time, when they were working high up on the lift putting a box up or something else, she was over at the controls and bumped it, up, down, up, down. He looked over at her and she was like, 'What?' She had her arms next to her side as if she didn't do anything. They had fun on the job even though they worked really hard and did good work. In the commercial shop, there was a lot of pride in the work they did. They felt good that they did a good job. "In Bexar Electric Company, in general, they weren't lazy workers," she said. She found this out from working at some of the other shops in town and it was like, "Whatever you know. If it's not perfect, no biggie." Her foundation, however, was that you do it right or don't do it at all. That is what she was raised with at home so when she went to Bexar Electric it was the same kind of concept. You do it right or get out of the job. Just leave! Their work reflected back on Bexar Electric Company.

Injured & Blackballed

Janiece completed all of the school requirements and received all of her certificates for each class. She was just shy 116 hours to get what she needed from the on-the-job hours needed before she could take her journeyman's test, when she was injured on the job. She was so close and yet so far away, really far away.

She injured her back, when she was working for the commercial shop of Bexar Electric on a job for the Gunther Hotel in downtown San Antonio. They were pulling wire into the electrical panels floor by floor. She hadn't noticed that she had even strained her back at all because she had just kept busy. At the end of the day, they loaded the trucks and left after they had finished. They went to a bar after work, which was the normal thing they did on Fridays to shoot pool. She bent over to break, but when she tried to stand up she couldn't. It was so painful that she could hardly move at all. They helped her sit down and later helped her to walk out and get into her vehicle. She was out of work for a long time. The doctors did all kinds of testing. She was even starting to lose feeling in her feet and her back was constantly spasming. She also went to a chiropractor for a while to manage the pain somewhat. They even tried a Myelogram, but couldn't find anything. MRI's were not even available at the time. When she got well enough to return to work, no one wanted to hire her. Bexar Electric told her they were laying people off and they laid her off too. Later, she found out that it wasn't so.

She went from shop to shop all over San Antonio trying to find work. One day she talked to her fourth year teacher, Tom Sandoval, who was also the chairman of the AIECA, and asked him if he would hire her on with his company, Allied Electric. He told her that he didn't usually do that, but he would try her out for a while. She told him she couldn't find any work, because no one was wanting to hire her because of her back injury. He told her that the word was out that she had been blackballed.

Tom had her operate a service truck to run service calls because he didn't really have any crews. He did a lot of service calls in air conditioning, as well as electrical. She didn't know anything about air conditioning, so she did some of the service calls concerning electrical. He tried to encourage her that she would be able to handle it. She told him she wasn't used to leading anything, especially a service call. Everything she had done up to this point was new construction. She didn't know how to go into something old and get it to work, much less how to troubleshoot it. She was scared as "all get-out," to be sent out on a job and have such a responsibility. Sometimes she would get to the job and someone wanted to talk to her. She didn't know what to say. She would freeze up and couldn't think. She was conscientious about overlooking or spending too long on a job, because she didn't know how to troubleshoot and her time was costly. This was constantly on her mind.

She told Tom one day, "Are you kidding, sending me out

alone? This isn't good for you. It's not right for them."

He told her, "Don't worry about it I have faith in you."

She thought, "Well, that's one of us."

She was so nervous. To even drive the van she felt nervous. She had driven the large bucket trucks before and felt more comfortable doing that than she did doing this. Just driving the van and knowing she was alone on a service call caused her to think she was a wreck, a basket-case to hear her say it. There weren't any cell phones then, either, so if she had a question, she had to find a landline. She was a wreck most of the time. She doesn't remember much of this time at all other than being a wreck most of the time.

Sold All Of Her Tools

She was also trying to get into the Kingdom of God during this time period while working in the electrical trade. She remembers selling her tools at one point because of what she was told to do, and felt like she had cut her arms off just by selling them to a pawn shop. She had spent a fortune on those tools, but through a false prophetess was coerced into selling them. She had multiple sizes of hole saws, knock-out tools, and channel locks in addition to other highly specialized tools for the trade. The prophetess told her she needed to dress like a girl and stop that kind of work. "It was a man's job. That's just not girl stuff." She said it wasn't feminine and that it was not a girl's place. She was actually told to quit and not to do that kind of work. By trying to be obedient to what they said was the Lord's will, she did what she was told. It got worse though, and some time later, she broke free from this group.

Later on though, she bought some more tools and went

back into the trade. She doesn't remember exactly how everything played out, but she had been blackballed and then coerced through deception, to give it all up. It could have been the reason she didn't go on to take the journeyman's test for her license. She was so close to having the hours she needed for the next step in this field. She had a lot of fun doing the work and it seemed to bring a sense of satisfaction to her life, and some sort of stability.

(Appendix A: Timetable of Janiece's Electrical work record)

Tell My People I Love Them!

Photo Above: Gin, Diamond, Janiece, and Brianna at Janiece's house warming party at her new house

Chapter 4

Glimpses Of Glory

Drums & Electric Guitars

Janiece was in her twenties, when Starr, her oldest sister, tried her best to get Janiece to go to church with her. Occasionally, she would try to go, but would sometimes have an asthma attack at the front door or something like that, that kept her from going inside. It was really extreme, like something was trying to keep her out. Janiece said it was like, "We're not letting her go in there." It had nothing to do with the people. It was a spiritual thing.

At one point, her sister was telling her about this one church. She was staying at her mother and dad's at the time. She had stopped by and had a poster of the meeting with her.

Janiece recalled, "First off, she asked if I'd take her to the store. I was a captive audience of hers when I got in the car. She knew she couldn't talk me into going to church again, but she pulled out a poster and it was a Morris Cerullo concert or something like that. I exclaimed, when I saw what was on the poster, 'At a church?'"

"Starr replied, 'Yes! These churches have drums and electric guitars.'"

"I said in disbelief, 'No way! They don't have electric

guitars and drums! Churches don't have that stuff!'"

"Starr continued on without missing a beat, 'Oh, yeah! They do!'"

"I had taken the bait, hook, line and sinker, 'Oh! Well! Maybe I will come then.' It was a crusade. There were drums and guitars. That is what really got me. I thought to myself, 'I got to see this!' It was really funny that something like this would pull someone in, someone unsaved."

Miraculous Healing

Well, Janiece wore glasses at this time because she had astigmatism in each eye. This crusade was a healing crusade. During the service, they asked that anyone who needed healing to come down to the front. Janiece was thinking, 'Oh, here comes the test!' She was going to put this healing thing to the test, to see if God was real. She wanted to know if God was real. "I gotta know. I want to know if He is real." She thought, 'Healing? I got something that needs fixing, my eyes.' She didn't even consider the fact that she needed healing for the asthma, too. She put her glasses on her seat and went up to the front.

As the minister stepped up in front of her and began to lift his arm up towards her to reach out to her and touch her, her legs lost their strength and she fell down to the floor. He didn't even get to touch her. The Lord stepped in Himself, sovereignly. She didn't know anything about falling out, or being slain in the Spirit at that point. When she had regained consciousness, she realized that everyone who had been around her was gone. She had been out for a while and when she came to, there were funny sounding words coming out of her mouth. She said, "It was the weirdest thing and there was

72

no coaching going on either. It was scary weird." She was so scared. She thought, 'What is happening to my mouth?' The few people, who were still around her, were almost dancing with joy about what they were witnessing. They had already heard the story of Starr's little sister. They had been praying for her over a period of time. They had already been excited when they found out she was coming to the crusade.

Janiece was wondering how long she had been out, so she looked up towards the clock that was all the way in the back of the building. "Oh, my gosh, it's almost ten o'clock. We've been here that long?" Then it dawned on her, "I can see the clock! He healed my eyes! My eyes are healed!" Of course, she said this after she could talk in an intelligible language, English. She didn't even get hurt when she fell down. She had fallen so fast, that no one was ready to catch her. It was totally a Sovereign thing. Now, she felt so light and free, versus the heaviness and burden she had earlier, almost high. She was so wowed. All she wanted to do was stay close to her sister and not get near anybody else she knew including her friends anymore. She wanted to learn what she could about Jesus. Starr and her next door neighbor, Elizabeth, used to go to church together at the time. Janiece started going to church with them.

She had gone to church when she was younger. As a teenager, she went with her sister, Deborah and now she was back again, at least for a while.

Fixing Up The Honda

Janiece had a Honda CVCC that she drove. She wanted to fix it up some, so she started looking around for parts. One day, on her way to work she saw a Honda just like hers a few doors down from where she worked. It was the same color, but was not working because the engine was gone. She stopped by and talked to the owner. She made a deal with him to buy the car, so that she could get all the parts off of it that she needed, but she would have to remove it from his property. She talked to her boss, John, about using his forklift to pick it up and bring it over to the shop. He ended up getting it for her because of the insurance liability issues he would face if he let her use the forklift. Once he moved it to the shop, she was able to get it to her home. She removed the parts she needed and then put them on her car.

A Detour

Some time had passed, after the healing of her eyes, and another voice came close to her. It was a wolf in sheep's clothing that came around to detour her from the path she was on with the Lord.

There were a few people who started hanging out together at the church she was attending. This one young lady introduced herself to this young group and they introduced her to Janiece. The group was telling Janiece that this lady was a prophetess. She hears from God.

Janiece was amazed, "Wow! Really! What is that about? What's that stuff?" She wanted to know more.

Once, when they were meeting, this prophetess told Janiece that she had a spirit of anger that needed to be cast out. She needed deliverance.

Janiece was open to anything, "Whatever I need! Ok!"

Janiece was put in the middle on her knees with everyone else around her. The lady kept commanding, over and over, "All right! Spirit of anger come out, in Jesus' name! Come out!"

Janiece was waiting for something to happen. She was actually looking for something to happen, wondering what it was going to be like when it happened. Will she know it? She was in agreement and wanting it out.

The lady kept on speaking, "Spirit of anger come out!" After a period of time had passed, the lady was really getting all riled up. Janiece started to get scared and wondered if she was alright. She was getting louder and louder. Before too long the lady said, "I said come out!" and she slapped Janiece in the face.

Janiece was like, "Do that again and something is going to come out! I'm going to come back at you! I know you are supposed to turn the other cheek and I will for a little while, but you keep that up and we are going to go around and around."

She slapped her again and Janiece felt like she just needed to get out of there. 'This isn't safe anymore. This is bad. This isn't Jesus.' Janiece got up, and ran out.

At some point later on, she went over to see Pastor Fender at the church and told him what had happened. He called all of this young group together and told them that this lady was a false prophetess. Some people are like this. They come in to try and get others to follow them. He instructed them to not have anything further to do with them. The wolf had accomplished its mission. This incident tore the group apart and they didn't hang out together after that.

Out On A Street Corner

One time, when Janiece was involved with a group, they forced her to wear a dress and made her stand on a street corner to solicit money for them. She gave away everything she had for their cause. She sold all her electrical tools, in addition to everything else, and gave the money to them.

Janiece recalled, "When they took me over to the pawn shop and I sold all of my tools, I felt like I had just sold my hands. I had three big tool boxes. The tools were worth $1000 alone. I felt like I cut my hands off. They said it was the thing that held me back. All I had left was my Honda."

They made her sell her tools, because they didn't think she should be doing that kind of work. Janiece kept trying repeatedly over the years to get in the fold, the church, but something kept coming around to detour her. This was the time she quit her electrical job and tried to be what she thought the Lord wanted her to be. She was like a lost sheep and the wolves were taking advantage of her. Each of these incidents were building layers of hurt in her heart, and with each one, she was building defensive walls around her heart.

The Shirt Off Her Back

Janiece and Deborah shared a story with each other.

Deborah told Janiece, "I remember the time everything in your apartment got stripped because you gave your apartment keys to a girl you met in Villa Rosa. You were so generous."

Janiece replied, "I would take groceries to people and just give them stuff. It's a good thing I was still under the guardianship back then."

I added my two cents to the conversation, "Well, a lot of that still hasn't changed."

Deborah chided, "Hey, you want the shirt off my back, no problem!"

Janiece joined in the fun, "Yeah, and especially back then,

because I didn't think it was a big deal to run around without a shirt, did I?"

Janiece continued, "I gave Bobby the Hyundai. I gave Valerie the Honda or tried. Dad said, 'You are not giving it away. At least get $50 for it.' I gave it to her anyway. Dad went with me to help me change the title, because I didn't know how to do that."

Thinking fondly about how her dad always loved to go with her to the car dealerships, Janiece said, "I always asked dad to help me pick out a car. He loved going with me and talking to the sales people. He got the biggest kick out of that because he knew them and how they worked and they weren't going to mess with his kid."

Turning The Tables

Years later, in late 1993 or early 1994, she turned the tables on her dad, when she bought her new 1994 Ford Taurus wagon. She kind of took his place and he was more on their side. She learned well.

Janiece said, "The car dealership kept trying to change the pricing on me when we went to buy the car. After a while of listening to their stuff, I said, 'You know, I don't want to listen to this junk. You guys can just keep all of your cars.' I couldn't believe that came out of my mouth. And Daddy was like, 'Yeah, let's just go.' I felt real good that my daddy's got me covered. They said, 'Oh, no, no, no, no! We'll work with you.' I said, 'Don't tell me that. He's told me how you guys are. I'm too tired. I don't want to go through all of this.' I learned it from him." Her dad was the one who was more patient this time around.

Photos Above: Top: Janiece helping her dad with building a rock garden; Bottom: Photo of a press in a printing shop in Colorado Springs, Colorado

Chapter 5

Daddy's Little Girl

Changing Course

After she had been healed from the back injury, she searched and searched and kept trying to find a job. She had sold her tools during the church, cult thing that didn't work, so she didn't have any tools to work with during this time. It just so happened, that her parents were moving and needed someone to do work on their new house. They had bought the second floor of an old Army barracks, that the Alzafar Shriners had bought from the Army and had used for a time. They were going to move it to their property, renovate it, and make it into their home. It was a 30 x 80 foot structure and was in two sections. It needed to be gutted and she was really excited about doing some demolition work. She asked if she could do it and had a blast tearing it apart. Her dad had to slow her down, so that some of the walls could remain in the structure. It was only a shell by the time she got through with it. Her younger brother, Bobby, did some of the work also.

After the demolition work was complete, her dad asked her if she wanted to do the electrical work too. She was kind of scared about that because she wasn't licensed. They ended up finding a master electrician that would allow her to work under his license. Her dad had the blueprints and she told him that anything goes. If he wanted to add any extra switches, plugs or anything, she would be able to do it. He could customize the electrical in any way he wanted it to be, including any outside electrical and exterior lighting.

Janiece was going to do the work for free, but her dad insisted that they pay her what she was getting paid at her prior job. Back then it was $6.15 per hour and that was a lot of money to her. This income went a long way for her because she was single.

She went and bought some more tools to replace the ones she had sold so she could do the work. Later on, she would be able to help people in their homes, by doing small electrical repairs. She did all of the wiring for the house and the exterior fixtures.

Following In Daddy's Steps

Janiece was the first woman printer on an offset press in San Antonio. Bob Turner said, "I don't know of any other woman, even to this day, that was in offset printing."

Janiece had taken Printshop I & II during her years in high school, and after she finished the work on their house, her dad checked into getting her a job with the company, where he was working as an offset printer, Performance Business Forms & Graphics. She wasn't able to start out as her dad's helper, even though she really wanted that, because he already had a helper. He told her that she could start out in the bindery. Since she had the back injury not long before, she was still very protective of her back.

In Printshop class she had learned how to do masking and stripping, so she already had the necessary skills to work in the plate department, too. She was able to work in the bindery, the shop, and stock. She learned how to operate the butane forklift. She had fun with it and thought it was 'Way cool!' She was very attentive because her focus was to never cost anybody anything extra for any job she ever did.

She began working in the bindery, cutting paper, folding, saddle stitching, padding, boxing, and shrink wrapping. She helped some with masking and stripping, and plate making. She kept bugging her dad to let her help him on the press. She really wanted to be his helper to fulfill her dream of being daddy's helper. Finally, after a while, he acquired more work and his helper was needed to help with the other smaller presses. The press she started helping him with, was an old press. It was an old two color press that had two sets of rollers. She started out learning how to wash up the press at the end of each day. Her dad would leave around three in the afternoon and she would stay until around four, to clean up and get everything ready for the next day. Then one day, August 12, 1983, as she was doing the routine cleaning, something unthinkable happened. Her thumb got caught between the rollers of the press and it started pulling her into it, inch by inch.

Sex Change Consultation

During a span of roughly ten years, Janiece had a relationship with another young lady. She knew it was wrong and every now and then would break it off. She struggled with a male/female identity crisis from some time around the age of thirteen. She pleaded with the Lord to either change her body or change her mind. After years of anguish in her soul and struggling with this embarrassing issue, she had lost all hope of a miracle and made an appointment with her doctor, in order to counsel with him about the procedures to undergo a sex change operation. He had already informed her that it would require psychiatric counsel before any doctor would even consider doing the surgery, but he wanted to talk to her first about it and be sure that's what she really wanted.

This was the only way she believed she would ever have peace. She felt like, 'I'm just not right.' She felt like she always thought like a guy, but it wasn't like she felt she was gay. The gay thing was a total turn off to her. It was wrong in her mind and embarrassing. That was a wrong lifestyle in those days. She felt robbed that she was neither female nor male. She knew right from wrong and to her homosexuality, lesbianism, and gay was wrong, although she did go to the gay bars where at least there she was accepted. She wanted a sex change. Her mind and her body didn't match and it wasn't fair. She had been crying out to the Lord since being aware that her gender was wrong as she was going through puberty. "Please! God! Change my mind or change my body! Something's got to give!" She would cry out over and over again to no avail.

Finally, after so many years, she had enough and felt like the sex change was her last resort and her only way out. The main thing that really bothered her about it was that the results of the surgery were going to be so grotesque looking to her in her mind. This would not be normal either to her. There is only so much that can be changed medically using the existing body parts and then adding additional enhancement by using male hormones. She really wouldn't be able to have a real and fulfilling life anyway. It would be impossible, but she thought that maybe it would bring her some comfort. At least it would bring her closer to looking the part, as far as outward appearances were concerned.

It is important to note here that every time Janiece tried to get closer the Lord, she cut off her relationship with her girlfriend. She would see it as wrong and would just walk away from the relationship.

The day she was scheduled to see her doctor for counsel to begin the sex-change process a very traumatic detour would begin. It was the same day her thumb got caught in the rollers of the printing press.

The Gender Issue

Deborah began, "I really think of it as gross. There is really no other way to explain it. As far as it concerns our personal life, it would be as if someone you really love has a blemish on their nose. It's not attractive, but that's not who they are. It doesn't affect your love for them."

Janiece shared a discussion she had with her mother about the subject years earlier. "Mother told me, 'I don't condone it, but I don't condemn it either.'"

Deborah stated, "I didn't agree with it. I didn't like it, but it didn't affect how I felt about you or my love for you, or the way I thought of you. I adored Diana, *(not her actual name)*. I thought she was such a grounding force in your life. When nobody else could get through to you, she could and she had common sense. She really, really cared. She cared about your well-being. Other than that, your relationship, it was something like, don't think about. Don't think about it in that way because it tended to get in the way of a comfort level for me. A sex change, it's like I don't get it, but I'm not living in your shoes. Just like the mental illness, I don't get it, but I'm not living in your shoes. In general, I tend to live my life that way anyway. My personal feeling is, I don't support the gay and lesbian lifestyle in any way, shape or form. It didn't get in the way of how I felt though."

Deborah continued, "I kept wondering. How far back does this go? Was it part of all this mental thing? Is this really who you are? Going back! Okay! I can remember incidents like you crying and asking me, 'Please, show me how to walk like a girl!' It was when you were a young teenager, probably before a dance. 'Show me how to be a girl!' Well, how do you show somebody how to breathe? Okay, let's work on it, let's walk. That lasted about ten minutes. I didn't have any idea what was going on back then. It was more of the tomboy thing. Clearly, you were a tomboy. We all knew you were a tomboy. You were very comfortable in that. I had no problems with that. I don't know that anybody else did either. And then, when you got asked to a dance and then asked me to please help you walk like a girl, it's like okay, that didn't seem unreasonable. I mean, no different from how to put mascara on."

Deborah thoughtfully continued, "As I reflect back, when you were talking about a gender change and all that, it was like, is this a part of the mental illness? When did this start? Then you go back and start looking back."

The Relationship

Janiece piped in, "Diana and I were together for about ten years. We started seeing each other when I first started working for Bexar Electric. I went to the electrical trade school until 1982, so we got together as a couple not long after I started, maybe '79 or '80.

Deborah said, "She was coming to the family things by then. Like you, this was new to her."

Janiece added, "It was new to mother, too. It was new to me. To everybody, it was new. It was embarrassing, kind of, and it was scary, real scary. She would stay the night while I was still living at Mother and Dad's house. She stayed the night a lot. She was at the gatherings. She was over there all the time and on weekends."

Traumatized

August 12, 1983

(Please note that this section is very graphic in nature due to the type of injury and the description of it. Please skip to the next section, "Miracles At The Hospital," if you would rather skip it.)

On this day, when destiny seemed to be heading a predetermined way, the unthinkable happens and completely changes the course.

Bob recalled, "We were at the end of the day and Janiece was going to wash up the press, which she had done day after day. I was already leaving our department to go into the bindery and then out the back door to where my car was parked. As I started out, the guy on the cutter said he was having trouble with it. Well, it had to be programmed, so I said, 'Okay, I'll give you a hand.' So I put down everything that I had, my lunch box and all that, and went over and was programming the machine for him. Then, all of a sudden, I heard the loudest scream. I wasn't even sure that it was a scream. It was like a squealing brake, like a hundred times more. I ran to where I heard the sound and Janiece had her arm into the rollers in the lower unit, with the cylinder on the upper unit turning around and around, chopping her arm. I was the only one who could've gotten her out of the press, and this is why I say it was a miracle. Anyone can stop the press, but you have to know how to disengage the second unit to get her out. It was a miracle that I was still there, instead of being on my way home."

Bob continued, "I had to get her out of there and then John Schlinder, my boss, and I took her to Northeast Baptist Hospital. That was just a miracle, but that roller was just chopping her arm so badly, every time it went around. Later, Gin came back with me and stayed with me, while I washed up the press. It wasn't just the ink from the rollers that I had to clean out on that cylinder that kept chopping her, but her flesh was on there too and it was also in the rollers. If I had not been there, I don't know what would have happened to her. She would have probably bled to death right there. No one else knew how to open up that section of the press. When I pressed the lever to let it loose and then turned the wheel, it flew open and hit her in the knees."

Janiece yelled, "Dad! My knees! My knees!"

Bob replied, "No, honey! It's your arm." He was thinking about her arm, but her knees were being pinched as he was separating the rollers.

Bob continued, "It went back so fast and hit her so hard. It was a miracle, because only God would have kept me there. Simple little decisions made the difference. If I would have told the guy on the cutter to just work with it, that he could get it, I would have been gone. Instead, I decided to stay and give him a hand. I was very familiar with that cutter and knew how to operate it. It was a new computerized cutter that had to be programmed. The guy was fairly new on it, so I wanted to give him a hand. I ordinarily go straight on out through the back door and straight home, which was approximately 30 minutes away and there weren't any cell phones then. I was still in the building, but there was a wall in between us and just a doorway. I heard her over the press making its noise, and over us talking. I could have heard her probably a half a block away. I remember it was hellacious."

Janiece kept trying to hit the stop button with her left hand as she was being pulled in, but she couldn't reach it, because it was recessed and just out of her reach. It wasn't like the safety shut-off buttons on equipment today that are mushroom shaped and easily accessible to push.

Bob added, "Another factor, was that on the newer units they had a shield around the rollers, so that you can't get caught in the rollers. This was a very old model and didn't have a safety feature on the bottom unit. There should have been a recall on this unit for safety upgrades because this wasn't the first time an accident had happened on this model press in this same part of the press. There had been another accident on this particular press before. After the accident, I had an electrician come out and install a trip wire across the unit to prevent another injury like this. I was able to take a photo and show the Meihly, (manufacturer of the printing press) representative, that this is what they should have had on the unit for safety."

Miracles At The Hospital

Deborah & Janiece recalled the incident together.

Deborah recalled, "Mother called me. I was at work and went straight over to the hospital. I didn't get to see you, because they already had you back in surgery. That first day, there was very little interaction. Mother had just told us what had happened, when Dr. Michael Earle, the orthopedic surgeon, came out. I remember a myriad of things from then. I met his brother Mark and the reason I remember his name is because he said, 'Mark, Mark, the hair lip dog.' Dr. Lebaron Dennis was the plastic surgeon and he also was at the hospital at the time she was brought in."

Janiece said, "Both of these doctors were leaders in their field and just happened to be at the hospital at the same time, when I came in. I got the best from the start."

Deborah continued with the hospital scene, "I know that when we were at the hospital there was a lot of crying from Mother and Daddy. You know, we're worried and they got you in the room and we didn't know the extent. Daddy just kept saying that he couldn't believe that when he pulled you out, your arm came back out. He was just like, 'Her arm came back out.' He was just totally amazed your arm came back out. I know they were dreading going back to the shop and cleaning up."

Janiece interjected, "Dad wouldn't let anyone else do it, though. Mother told me later. The shop wanted to call the Peace Corps, because they were familiar in doing those kind of cleanups. They are so sweet. They just come in, take care of stuff and leave. It was so gross and all that for anyone else to do. It was his kid."

Deborah said, "They came in and said that you had just shattered your arm and that is when they explained you had degloved it. They talked about you losing the skin. They said it was a body injury because it went above the shoulder. You had lost the skin from there and had broken bones. They were already talking about a new technique of skin graft. I mean, that night they said, 'There is a new technique for skin grafts,' to where they mesh it and that it was a new technique. They said, 'Basically we take the skin and we put it in a mesh roller that spreads it out.' He compared it to a yard having sprigs of grass, so it would grow in between. He said, that's what they'll be able to do. They don't have to take as much skin to do it. He said they were confident they could save the arm, but they weren't sure about the function. From there, it was day after day, finding out what your needs were."

The Injury - Medical Description

The following is a medical description of the injury to Janiece in Dr. LeBaron Dennis' notes dated October 10, 1983. Please note that this description is of a graphic nature and is in medical terminology.

Dr. LeBaron Dennis' notes dated October 10, 1983.

The patient is a 23 year old Caucasian female, who was severely injured in an accident at work. Her right arm was caught in the rollers of a printing press, carrying her arm into the machinery up to the shoulder. The rollers degloved most of the skin and subcutaneous tissue from her arm. The skin of the hand and the wrist survived. The skin of the forearm, elbow region, and entire upper arm was peeled off of the underlying muscles and bones by the roller action. The joints at the elbow and the wrist were also crushed. The skin from the degloved flaps, was saved and applied as free skin grafts. Other skin grafts were necessary to finish the process of recovering her arm with skin. Once the arm was covered with skin the orthopedic injuries became prominent, and she is being prepared for wrist joint reconstruction. Following that, she will have elbow joint reconstruction and release of a serious soft tissue flexion contracture, which locks her elbow at 90 degrees of flexion.

When she became conscious after surgery, she was so angry. She didn't want anyone around who even spoke the name 'God' in her room. She even went so far as to have the nurses put a sign on her door in the hospital, 'If you're going to talk God, don't even come through the door.' She didn't want to see a chaplain or anyone along those lines. No one was invited from the churches. Her sister Starr couldn't come in either. She was mad that He let it happen. She knew, 'He didn't make it happen because that was not His thing, but He could have kept it from happening.'

Surgery After Surgery

Her first surgery was administered on August 12, 1983 with the last surgery ending on October 1, 1986, over three years later. Additional surgeries had been scheduled and started, to add an additional abdominal flap from her side to the arm, but was abandoned, mostly because of her mental condition as well as financial restraints. Her last visit with Dr. Dennis, to continue with the second abdominal flap, was on January 17, 1989. A surgical procedure had already been administered, by cuts to her side and then reclosed, to begin the process that was eventually abandoned. The reason for the 27 month delay was because of all of the mental challenges she was having during that time period. Dr. Dennis refused to continue with this last surgical proceedure, until she was stable enough emotionally to continue.

(See Appendix B for actual photos of the press & illustrations)

Photo Above: Photo of a press in a printing shop in Colorado Springs, Colorado. The press in the foreground shows some of the visible rollers in the press.

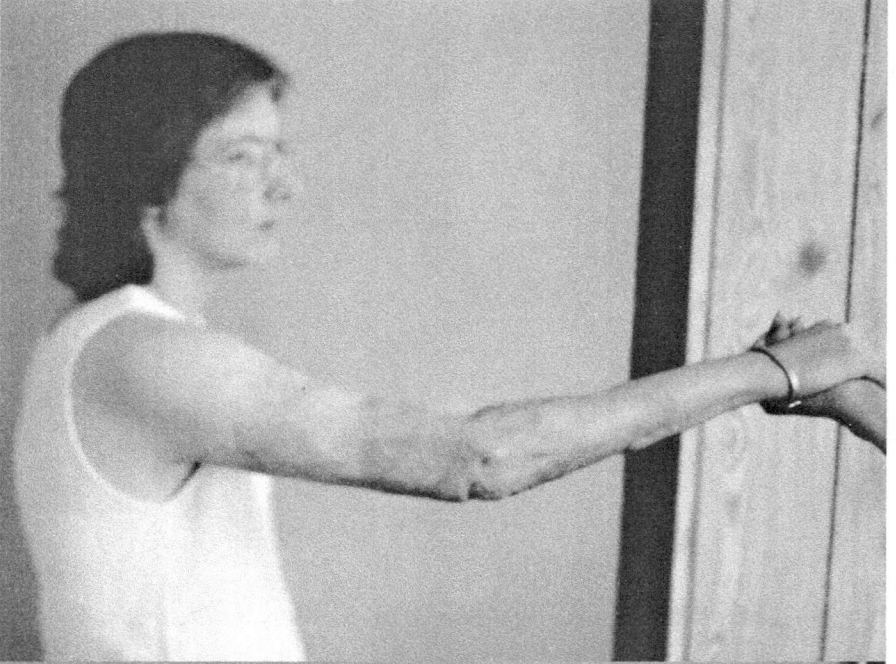

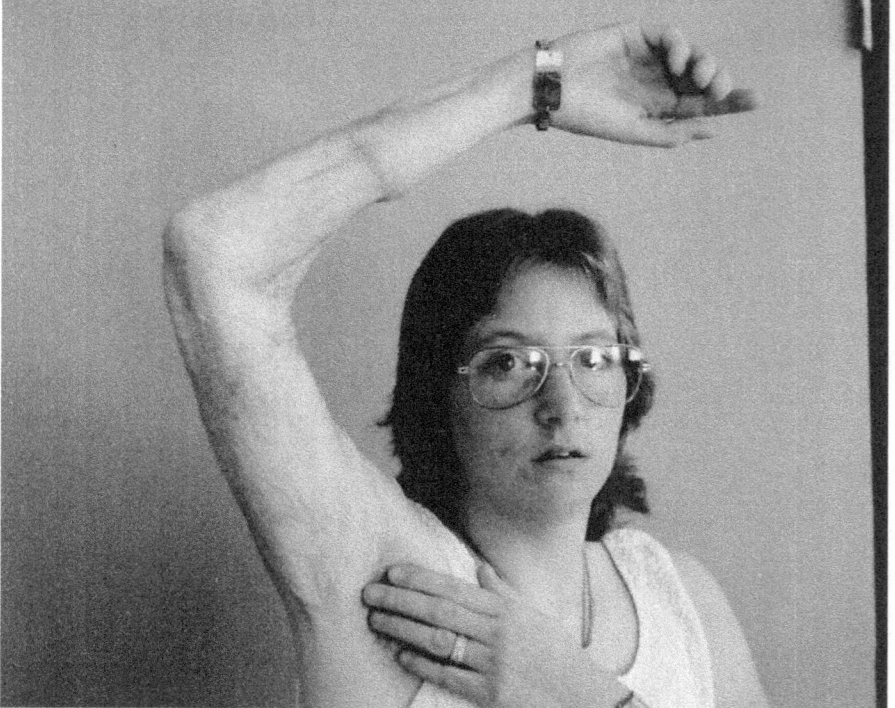

Chapter 6

It's Mine!

You Can't Have It

Janiece recalled, "When I first came out of surgery, right after the accident, they told me they didn't know if I would be able to keep my arm because the ink was ground into the bones. Unless they could get it all off of the bones, they would have to cut the arm off because of the risk of infection. They showed me this tool that almost looked like a spoon, but it had a blade on one side and they would have to use it to scrape the bones."

I told them, "Oh you're going to get it all off because I am right handed and I'm a tradesman. I got to have my arm so you are going to get it all off. You are going to do just fine. You are going to clean it up good."

They said. "Even if we do, you won't be able to use it."

I said, "Yes, I will! I'm a tradesman! I got to have it! Yes, I will! I need to! This is my life! I am right handed and that is

---

Photos at Left: These photos show the surgical and reconstructive miracles that took place. These photos were taken before the abdominal flap from her side was cut and then permenently attached to the under arm and elbow section to provide extra padding for her arm and elbow.

just the way it is."

They said, "No, you'll probably have to use your left hand to move your arm around."

I said, "No, I'm not buying that."

Making A Sailor Blush

There was a funny part in the midst all of this trauma and grief. Her mother and dad thought there was a funny reaction on the part of the surgeon when he came out of surgery. He said, "Wow! Your daughter has a really colorful mouth."

Her mother used to say that she could make a sailor blush. A couple of weeks later, her mother was even scared to be near her, for fear that she was going to be struck by lightning, because of all the anger she was mouthing at the Lord.

Janiece had hung out with the guys all the time. It was not just the electricians, but she was also around the plumbers, a/c techs, the roofers and the carpenters. It was all men and just her. She was the only woman on every job site where she worked. There were no exceptions. That is where she picked up everything. They wouldn't say it in front of other women, but they did in front of her.

She remembers, that because she had been hospitalized for so long in the beginning, that even her legs felt like rubber bands when it was time to get up and move around. The first hospitalization was just a few days shy of being a full six weeks. They had told her during that time, not to do anything without asking for a nurse because if she fell, or bumped her arm she could lose it. That put enough fear in her in the beginning to keep her obedient.

Cut It Off

Janiece told of the unwrapping incident, "My arm was wrapped for a long time and I couldn't see any of it. It looked really big because of all of the wrapping around it. When it was time to debride it, however, they unwrapped all of it. It was so tiny and grotesque. There were quarter inch staples all over it that were holding on the new skin. Debriding was getting all of the old, dead, scabby skin off. First, they wheeled me down to a big whirlpool. I got in and it was pretty hot water. They poured a Betadine solution into it. They had all of these gallon jugs. They also made sure Mother and Dad were there the first time. I didn't know why, but they did. It was going to be the first time I was going to see my arm since the accident. The bandages around my arm made it look like I might have had a normal size arm in there somewhere."

She continued on, "Now, I was pretty muscular and was proud of my build. I worked at it really hard. I didn't know what I was going to see. They started unwrapping all of this gauze off of it and everything that was stuck to it. My arm was in the water so that there would be no sticking and it would just come off real easy. As soon as they unwrapped it and lifted it up, I was horrified. I couldn't believe THAT was mine. I said, 'No, cut it off! Cut it off! You got to cut it off!'"

She finished the story emotionally, "They said the reason why they had my parents there, was because if I was to bang my arm, I might lose it. It was so traumatized already. They knew that this was the reaction I would have and that is why my mother and dad would have to be there. They were so strong for me, comfort and strength, you know. I kept saying, 'No, cut it off! Cut it off! That's not mine! I don't want that thing, that ugly thing! I'd rather not have one than to have that, because it was so grotesque and it was so tiny.' It had the staples all over it, the raw and bloody look. They were actually afraid I would throw my body around and bang it. I was kind of thrashing about, trying to get out of the tub. I don't even know what I was thinking, but that was my first reaction."

In this injury, there were three traumas that transpired; the injury itself, seeing the arm the first time after the bandages were removed, then all of the excrutiating pain from the multiple surgeries, reconstructive and cosmetic, to follow.

Growing New Skin

Deborah shared, "They were growing skin, too."

Janiece remembered the pain, "Yeah, by separating it. They were able to save some of the skin from my arm. Some of the fatty tissue survived, and they were able to stretch the surviving skin over the muscles. The skin grafts from my legs were so thin, you could see the pore holes through it. The doctor said, 'I want to show you what we are actually doing. There is this thing, almost like a push lawnmower, except for it is smaller. It's a press and it has like spikes. It makes a mesh out of the skin. It is not whole and solid.' I went, 'Wow! Cool!' He met me on the cool level. They took this skin and placed it, so that it was able to grow, so to speak. It is similar to placing sprigs of grass on a lawn and it fills the gaps itself."

The Contraptions

Janiece and Deborah discussed this time together.

Deborah began, "I remember you coming over and spending time with us after one of your surgeries. You stayed with us, Larry and me. I remember you were trying to take a bath. You had this contraption on your arm, (an airplane splint), and you had all of the bandages. You were supposed to change the dressing, but the bandages wouldn't come off and it was lifting the skin. I remember we worked on it and worked on it and we couldn't get it. We had a neighbor, who was a nurse and she came over and helped. It was really just trying to get the bandages off to change them. Again, just these images of you just sitting there in the tub, trying to soak them off and not being able to."

Janiece said, "The skin was stapled on with ¼" staples. I even remember the gadget he used to get them out."

Deborah added, "I know you had that gadget to where your arm wouldn't move. You had screws all in between. It looked like some odd metal thing. I thought, 'How uncomfortable can that thing be?'"

This was a device with four screws. Two of the screws were screwed into two of her hand bones and the other two were screwed into each of the bones in her forearm. They were joined by two plastic tubes filled with a concrete-like substance to keep the wrist stabilized, being that it was crushed. This was in place while they were completing the initial skin grafts and some other surgeries.

Janiece elaborated, "I couldn't feel anything for a while. Still, I don't have a sensation in every place and there is one place I touch and I feel it some where else. I didn't feel all of the muscles. I felt the bones, as far as bone pain and the muscles as far as pressure. I felt the pain the most where they peeled the skin off from my legs for the skin grafts, when they took off the plastic covering and air got to it."

Deborah said, "Once we were talking and I said something about your surgery, something about not knowing when it was. You were saying something about it or I didn't know how many surgeries you had. You said, 'Well the least you could do is remember how many, for all I've been through. You don't have to remember each one and all of the details, but at least remember how many I've gone through.' It was like so many you had gone through, because there were tons of them, 28 to 33."

Physical Therapy

Janiece recalled, "The doctors kept telling me that I'd never use it, but I kept asking, 'What can I do to make it work?' I was going to occupational therapy and they would massage my arm. I used to love this part of the day. I'd go in and they would put hot packs on my arm. I would lay there about 15 - 20 minutes and it would relax the muscles. They were trying to stimulate the muscles. Nothing was working. I would try my hardest to get things to move. I couldn't think hard enough to get my fingers to move. It wasn't happening, but they would come in and put the Nivea lotion on it. It is kind of greasy-like, and they would massage it. Over time it got to where I could feel it. That was cool. There are places that I still can't feel and our son, Daniel, is so cute about that. He'll touch it in certain areas and ask me, 'Mother, can you feel that?' 'What? What?' I reply. He is so cute. He is always checking to see if I have feeling, I think, because He knows that we are holding out for God's promise of total restoration and healing to be coming about."

A lot of the skin grafts were already complete, by the time they sent her to therapy and it was time for her muscles to be re-stimulated, to see if there was hope for them to work. The doctors didn't have much hope that the muscles would work again. The muscles had received so much damage and trauma. They thought she was going to have to move her arm around, by using her other arm for the rest of her life, because of the trauma to the muscles. She would go to therapy a few times a week and the therapists would put the hot packs under and on top of her arm. It heated up the arm and got the blood circulating through it. It felt really good to her. The pressure on her arm felt odd to her because the packs were heavy. In some places it actually hurt. They would leave them on the arm for about twenty minutes. Then they would take them off and apply some warm Nivea lotion to her arm and would rub it. They would massage her arm muscles. It would stimulate activity in the muscles and also soften, stretch and moisten the new skin because it would tend to dry out. Her muscles would cramp in position and the massage would help. They would also help in straightening out the arm so that it could become flexible again.

She would try so hard with her mind just to make a finger move. She did this everyday, all day long, just trying to get something to work. They told her not to worry about it, that if it was going to happen it would. They kept reassuring her, that it would take time, because the muscles hadn't been used in such a long time. They said, "We just have to keep stimulating them. The muscles were traumatized and then not used for so long."

Work! Arm Work!

Deborah said, "The most amazing thing to see, was for the amount of damage that you had, to have your muscles work again."

Janiece interjected, "Remember, they always said I would have to use my other hand to move it around."

Deborah said, "Well, they said you were not going to have fine motor skills. You would probably be able to have gross motor skills, but you would not be able to have strength and you were not going to be able to do the fine things. That all turned out not so. You worked at it."

Janiece said, "The different apparatuses attached to me felt like a cramp all day long. I just wanted it to work quickly so that I could get back to work. I work with my hands. I am right handed."

Janiece remembered, "I eventually had some apparatuses that I could put on and remove that would help bend my arm back out. It got stuck shut. When that one skin graft grew shut inside of my elbow because most of the skin grafts were done at the same time, they had to recut it, get another strip, attach it and then keep my arm straight out. Then my muscles would spasm and get all tight. I remember sleeping at night and I would have to keep my arm up in the air. In the morning, it would hurt so much to bring it down. It was breath-taking just to get it back to normal because the muscles had been so traumatized from all of the past. They weren't responding to every nerve and everything yet."

Humbled

Janiece said excitedly, "When I went to occupational

therapy and first saw the weight machines that used cables I was excited. There was a chair next to it and it had weights on it with handles. I asked, 'When can I do that?' They looked at me like, 'It's like you can't even move it right now by yourself. You have to use the other hand.' I asked them over and over again almost every time I went to therapy, 'When can I do that?' They finally said, 'Okay, fine! Go have a seat. Let's settle this thing.' I couldn't even! My fingers wouldn't even work."

She tried to will it to work, but it wouldn't. It would not obey her thoughts to make it move. Her therapists were kind of just rolling their eyes. Everybody did this at first, so they were used to it. They said it was mainly the guys that did it, though.

She came back over to them all humble and asked what it was going to take to get it to work. She was real depressed that it wasn't working.

She asked them, "How come the connection is not there? It's here," (she pointed to her mind), "its automatic." They told her she just has to keep working it. 'Don't give up, just keep working at it and keep pressing it.' She just wanted to get the fingers to work and they said that things will work on the shoulder first. So, they kept moving the arm around from the shoulder, massaging the muscles as they went. They would also try to get her to do dexterity exercises with her thumb and fingers.

Dexterity Again

The web between the index finger and the thumb had all but disappeared. Because of the surgeries on the thumb, it had grown together and she didn't have the normal separation between the index finger and the thumb. The doctor told her, "You'd be surprised, but like your lip, you can open it up again. Just always massage it when you are sitting around with nothing to do. Just work it and massage it to help redevelop the web." The doctors had completed three separate surgeries on the thumb alone to repair all the damage. That was the first part to go into the printing press. She massaged the web until it finally opened up to its normal width. It was the same process she had to use with her upper lip, after the dog bite when she was three.

Bit by bit, she was able to get her thumb to move and then gradually to start touching her fingers, one by one. It took a while to get the fingers to move separately from one another. It was so hard for her to get her fingers to work with her brain. She would be so tired after therapy just trying to get her mind to get the different parts of her arm and hand to work. The arm can't move without the shoulder, then add the elbow, wrist, fingers and thumb all at the same time. It was very difficult for her to do the side lifts with her arm, like in the jumping jack motion. She would get so tired, just trying to lift her arm up off of the table in front of her. She was so grateful that the therapists were so patient with her. She learned a love and respect for everyone in that trade, including the nurses and the whole field, because of the patience they extended towards her. They had endurance.

She could hardly wait until she could try to start grabbing the small cones with her hand and fingers. Because the cones were larger at the base, she could put her fingers over them and go down until it stopped and then try to hold them without them falling out. She found she wasn't able to lift even the lightweight cardboard cones at this time. She couldn't hold them. She had to reach forward, moving her shoulder and elbow, because they placed it just out of her reach. She went from, "I can't do it! I can't do it! I can't do it!" to "I will do this! I will do this! I will do this!" She thinks she must have sounded schizophrenic to them because she went on and on. It was so tiring to her.

Rolling A What?

Deborah & Janiece share again.

Janiece said, "I had both surgeons for quite a while. Dr. Dennis would have to wait on Dr. Earle for some things and vice versa because some surgeries were skin related and some were bone. At one point, they had to make a choice of whether to cut the outside forearm bone at the wrist, the head of the Ulna, or to fuse the wrist. If you fuse the wrist you had strength. If you cut the bone you had mobility. I chose mobility. I figured I could work the rest, but at least it would be able to be mobile. They were always waiting on each other."

Deborah said, "I remember, after one of your later surgeries, you called me and you were so excited. You were like, guess what, I just rolled a joint. I do have my motor skills. I thought, 'Oh, Janiece!'"

Janiece said, "I used to drive my stick with my left hand." (her Honda with 4 speed manual transmission) "That's when I really started driving with my knee a lot. I had to shift with my left hand."

Deborah started, "Why you had a standard with an arm injury is just…"

Janiece interrupted, "I already had it before the accident."

Sliding Down

All of these surgeries were going on during the time she was heading on a downhill slide emotionally and mentally. She was seeing a psychiatrist, Dr. Elizabeth Mitchell, during this time period. The initial diagnosis started out with clinical depression, just depressed from an accident. They didn't have the term 'Post Traumatic Stress Disorder' coined yet. It kind of made her wonder if they had developed some of those names, as they were continually trying to describe her emotional downhill slide.

She wanted to do so much during the period of all of the physical therapy, but she couldn't. She would practice with some things at home, just trying to speed up the process. They created special splints at the center to help using plastic that they could heat and mold to her arm. They had molded various positions, according to what she needed to work on at the time and also to stretch the muscles and bones back or at least close to their original flexibility. The stretching was constant and somewhat painful all day long. She couldn't wait to take them off to catch her breath. She was also on pain medication, Vicodin, Darvocet, etc. They had created a special sock for her arm, so that she could put the Nivea lotion on it overnight and cover it with the sock. If she slept with her arm down it would hurt when she awoke because the muscles would cramp and then she couldn't move it out of that position for a while. Or, if she slept with her arm up, she couldn't bring it back down quickly. It was stuck in that position for a while. That was excruciating pain. They had one mold for the forearm and wrist and then just one for the hand. They would use hooks on these, as well, with the use of rubber bands to help stretch each limb in whatever position, to help with flexibility. This was used especially for the wrist, to help it to twist, as well as move in different positions.

She had between twenty-eight to thirty surgeries, all of the physical therapy and then all of the mental distress and hospitalizations that lasted over a seven year duration. She also had a drug abuse problem during this time.

Elbow Padding

Dr. Dennis sent a letter to Dr. Mitchell on January 23, 1985, advising her of the upcoming surgeries to remove two flaps from her side and attach them to the underside of her arm for padding. He wanted Dr. Mitchell to monitor her mental condition throughout the process. If she got to where she was no longer able to handle the stress, they would either slow down or stop until she could improve. Following is a copy of that letter:

Dear Dr. Mitchell!

I saw Janiece Turner on 15 January 1985. She complained of two problems. The first problem was the presence of the unstable scar/graft over her right elbow with healed ulcerations and abrasions due to ordinary movements, such as resting her elbow on a table. This unstable ulceration cycle is to be expected inasmuch as she has lost the soft tissue padding that is normally present over the point of the elbow. It will inevitably worsen.

The second problem was a tight scar contracture band running anteriorly down her right arm and crossing the antecubital space. This contracture starts high on her upper arm and results from the injury and skin grafts that were applied. Her band has been stretched, (by physical therapy), but I do not expect any further improvement.

The solution to each consists of putting skin and sucutaneous tissue over the two areas. In Janiece's case, this means transferring pedicle flaps from her trunk to her arm. The reconstruction of the elbow problem would involve a flap from her flank that would wind up covering all of the point of her elbow and would be the size of a hand's span. The problem on the front of her upper arm and elbow could be reconstructed with a flap from the side of her chest. These body flaps would leave large mars on her trunk with skin grafts applied to the donor beds of the flaps. The flap off the chest would not compromise her breast. There should be a good prognosis of the success of these flap transfers. She still would have a residual mid-upper arm level.

I am talking about two operations. Each would involve her being in St. Luke's Lutheran Hospital with general anesthesia and care on an open ward. The time interval between procedures would be three months. I am considering preliminary procedures to help develop these flaps to increase the chances of their success. These preliminary procedures are called "delays." The "delays" can be done on an out-patient basis under local or general anesthesia. The timing between the "delay" procedures would be approximately 10 days. Once the delays (usually 3) have been completed, the flaps could be rotated. I need to give this some thought as to these and other technicalities.

The timing of the reconstruction will depend on your assessment of Janiece's ability to work within the structure of the reconstruction schedule. She presents a positive attitude for getting on with the reconstruction.

She was told several times that this reconstruction was

not going to restore her arm and that her arm still will be scarred. Her expectations must be realistic and not full of magical thinking.

Sincerely,

LeBaron W. Dennis, M.D.

Janiece remembered, "There were a lot of surgeries because of the two flaps they were cutting out of my side to place under my arm for padding. My elbow didn't have any padding. It was just skin over the bone. It had a piece of wire sticking through and I kept bumping my elbow and snagging it on things. A balloon was placed under the flap and would be gradually filled with a solution until it had been prepared for removal to the arm. There were multiple outpatient appointments to accomplish this. It was draining on my emotions because I was already having a hard time. They had already removed and attached the first flap to my arm when Dr. Dennis said, 'I am not doing any more until you are more well. You are not stable. I am just not going to do it.' They had already made incisions and were beginning to work on the second flap by now. It was like he was talking to a child, who was always having tantrums. I didn't take it that way at the time, but as I look back, that is how you would treat a child whom you knew very well and you would recognize when they were having a tantrum. Thus you pull back on whatever it is and they finally get right."

Deborah said, "You knew you wanted it over with and yet you knew you still had 'x' number of surgeries to go."

Janiece kept telling them, "Let's just do the next one. Let's just make it better. Make it better."

Deborah said, "Well, the balloon surgery on your side

seemed to take forever."

Janiece interjected, "It took so many injections to blow it up with all that saline. That was the flap they were removing from my side to attach on the bottom side of my arm and elbow for padding."

She continued on with the process, "First he had to kill and separate the nerves. Then he had to cut it and then sew it back up. That was one surgery. Then the nerves were separated. Later, he had to go back in there and reopen it after it had grown shut. Then he put the balloon in. Then I had to wait for it to heal up before he could start injecting it because he didn't want to tear it all back open. All that time and I was pretty much a 'basket case' during this. This was the last bunch of surgeries he did. He did it to cover the elbow, because there was a wire there that used to stick out and it would snag my clothes. Plus, I didn't have any cushion or protection for my elbow. Later, He told me, 'I'm sorry I didn't get it all the way around there, I know you wanted it for the padding, but we made it look good.' To this day, I still protect it, because it is still a little exposed. He told me, 'Yeah, we can finish it all the way around,' but it turned out the finances weren't there to complete it or the insurance or we settled or something. However, they did start cutting my side for the second flap, it was just never finished. I was fine with it, though."

Photos at Right: Top Left: Photo showing the incisions that were healing with the inserted balloon that was being inflated to separate the fatty tissue from the muscle to attach to her under her forearm and elbow; Top Right: Janiece wearing a wet suit to protect her arm from the cold water in the pool, sometimes the shower water was also too much for her, either too hot or too cold; Bottom: Janiece in the hospital during the time they attached the flap from her side to the bottom of her arm and elbow while it was still attached partly to her side. This was to make sure the graft would transfer from her side to her arm, and that it would grow on to the arm.

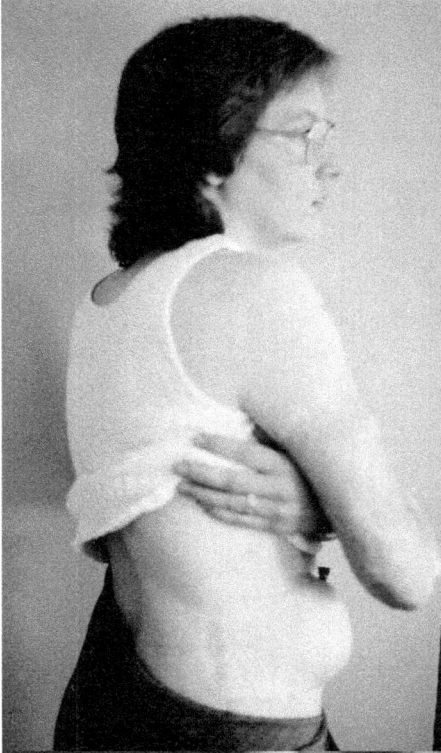

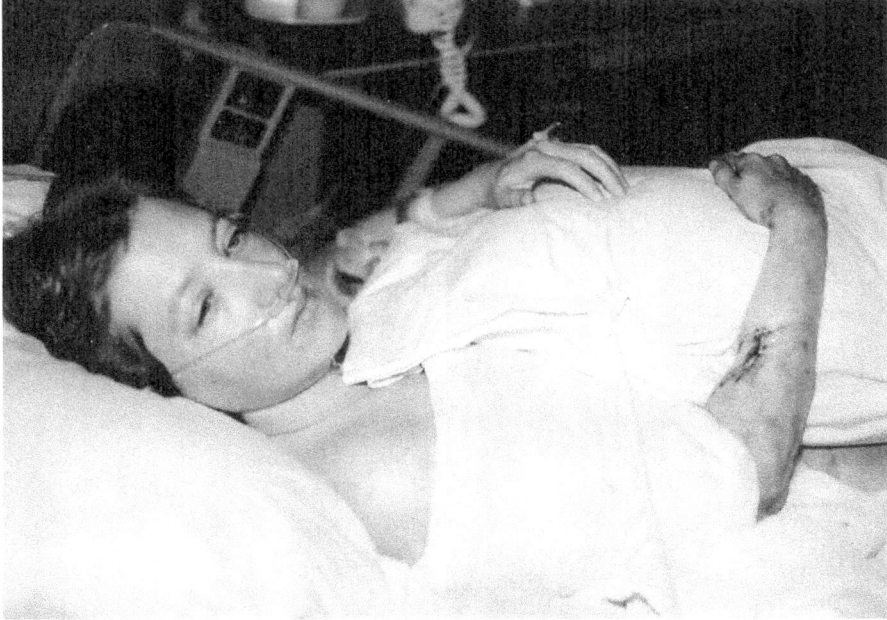

Chapter 7

Sentenced To Death

Depression Sets In

Janiece was in the North East Baptist hospital from August 12, 1983 to September 17, 1983 when she was discharged from the time of the accident. By that time, she had undergone eight surgeries. In the short three weeks that followed, her mental condition would rapidly deteriorate. Her doctor had become increasingly concerned about her. She was becoming very angry, even to the point of severely injuring herself and possibly taking her own life.

On October 10, 1983, Dr. Dennis recommended that Janiece see a psychiatrist before undergoing any more surgery. She had a choice between a female and a male psychiatrist and she chose Dr. Elizabeth Mitchell.

Following is the text that was included in the above document from Dr. Dennis to Dr. Mitchell. Please keep in mind that the description of the injury is of a graphic nature and is described in medical terms.

Photos at Left: Top Left: Janiece wearing her 'Fists Of Steel' t-shirt on September 17, 1990; Top Right: Janiece at a friend's house in Fayetteville, NC; Bottom Left: Janiece at a family gathering at Christmas 1989; Middle Right: Janiece holding her niece, Brianna; Bottom Right: Janiece with her smoke and her dog, Alteria

October 10 th, 1983
RE: JANIECE TURNER

The patient is a 23 year old Caucasian female, who was severely injured in an accident at work. Her right arm was caught in the rollers of a printing press, carrying her arm into the machinery up to the shoulder. The rollers degloved most of the skin and subcutaneous tissue from her arm. The skin of the hand and the wrist survived. The skin of the forearm, elbow region, and entire upper arm was peeled off of the underlying muscles and bones by the roller action. The joints at the elbow and the wrist were also crushed. The skin from the degloved flaps was saved and applied as free skin grafts. Other skin grafts were necessary to finish the process of recovering her arm with skin. Once the arm was covered with skin, the orthopedic injuries became prominent, and she is being prepared for wrist joint reconstruction. Following that she will have elbow joint reconstruction and release of a serious soft tissue flexion contracture, which locks her elbow at 90 degrees of flexion.

Emotionally, Miss Turner became very disturbed and is going through mixed emotions, which incorporate extremely strong feelings of anger, anxiety, denial, frustration, and bewilderment. She was receiving medications, while at the North East Baptist hospital to help her sleep. She had a very low pain threshold and was receiving stronger medications, such as Mepergan, until the time of her discharge. She had been hospitalized almost six weeks. She requested a psychiatric consultation while in the hospital, when she recognized being in a distraught state. The pychiatrist who saw her felt that he could not find fault with her feeling and never saw her again. Since discharge from the hospital, her emotional distress progressively worsened.

She has been unable to cope with the serious residual disfigurement of her dominant arm. Her thoughts have ranged from self destruction, to amputation of the arm and fitting with a prosthesis, to wishing for magical solutions; and with the associated discomfort, finds that she is unable to get away from her acquired deformity. A profound anxiety crisis appears to have erupted.

To handle this situation, a consultation is sought under semi-emergency conditions with Dr. Elizabeth Mitchell for evaluation, treatment, and further disposition.

LeBaron W. Dennis, M.D.

Psychiatry

Janiece shared, "I had quite a few operations already, when my plastic surgeon said that they had already done everything that needed to be done, ie. reconstructive surgeries. He was not going to do any more cosmetic surgeries, until I saw a psychiatrist. He said, 'I want you to see someone and start talking to them. You need to let this stuff come out. You need to talk to somebody. You can't hold it in all the time.' I was so depressed and lonely."

"I was an electrician and was always active, into sports and the outdoors. I helped people move. I liked to party and to have a good time. I was a people person. All of a sudden I was immobilized and lonely. I was at home all of the time. All of the people I knew were working."

Janiece remembered her first visit with Dr. Mitchell. "I felt safe with Dr. Mitchell. I was twisted in my desires with a girl, but I still felt safer with another girl than a guy."

"I remember that first therapy session with her. What do

you want? How do we do this? She said, 'Well, start talking to me.' I asked, 'About what?' She asked, 'Well, what do you feel? What are you thinking about?' I didn't know. You had to actually probe yourself to see what you feel. I hadn't thought about it, I guess. 'How long is this meeting anyway?' I thought."

Janiece continued, "This first meeting was primarily so that she could report to Dr. Dennis and say that I needed extensive care or I was okay, I should be fine. That's what he told me anyway. I'm going to have them check you out to see if you are up to this."

Mental Down Slide

Janiece & Deborah discussed the spiraling down.

Janiece started, "The mental down slide began less than two months after the accident. On October 10th, Dr. Dennis told me that he had a male and female psychiatrist and that I had to choose one of them. He sent me to both of them. I chose Dr. Mitchell. I liked girls back then, so I chose her."

"On the first meeting, she tried to get me to talk. I didn't know how to talk. I am supposed to be here, what?" Janiece said.

Deborah added a different angle to Dr. Mitchell. "Dr. Mitchell was a pediatric psychiatric doctor. She took care of children through the youth. Even though Janiece was older, 23 years old at the time, she was going through so much that would be in the developmental process, that they thought her practice was appropriate. She was starting over and learning to function again as far as her arm was concerned."

Janiece remembered the time vividly, "My emotions were a mess. I don't even remember a lot of it. I do remember that she was strong. She wouldn't put up with stuff and that really helped. You know, we need structure. Boy, did I ever notice I needed help and structure, more and more. I felt like a kid. I was scared and I started getting more and more paranoid through the years. Weird things were happening to and around me."

Deborah elaborated on Janiece's situation, "One of the things Dr. Mitchell told me, that really made an impact to me, was with the majority of people, almost everybody had the ability to imagine something and that was a release valve. For example: If somebody cuts you off in traffic, you could have this image of a police officer pulling them over. That's your revenge in your mind. She said that you were lacking that ability, right now. So, all of this anger was bottled up in you. You had nowhere to focus it and nowhere to put it. Most people have the ability to have images flash through their head like, they'll get their own. However, during that particular period of time, you didn't have that release. The anger was constantly in you with nowhere to put it. Dr. Mitchell felt like that was a big, big issue for you. She was very insistent that people just don't realize how many times a day they use that and it is not always in a negative situation."

Deborah continued, "As many times as things happen in my life, I'm glad I have that. I think of that very often. It makes a difference, especially when I am going through such a hard time. Then add to all of this, all of the lawyer's meetings and depositions you had to do."

Janiece looked at her in amazement, "It seemed like you did everything and that I didn't hardly have a load, from my perspective. I don't remember carrying anything."

Deborah helped her memory some, "You felt pretty loaded at the time."

Janiece interjected, "I knew it didn't take much to make me snap. 'I can't deal! I can't deal,' seemed to be my constant cry. I don't remember carrying the load, though. It seemed like I hardly carried anything. It's like, you all became my guardians and carried it."

Again Deborah corrected her, "Not for a long time! At the time the accident happened, you were so young. You were just twenty-three, just working, going home at the end of the day, hanging out with friends or whatever. You were just like every other young person. After that though, you were suddenly dealing with court, depositions, appear here and there, surgeries, healing, pain, medication, being in the hospital, being cared for at home and on top of it all, you were feeling overwhelmed and pressured. Then all the mental issues were added to that. I can't even begin to tell you all of the diagnosis that were progressively being pronounced over you, through the months and years."

Janiece began at the beginning, "It started as depression and clinical depression. Dr. Mitchell said I was just having post traumatic stress. It wasn't called a disorder yet."

Deborah added, "I don't even remember that. I just remember depression. She is depressed. She's been through a lot. From there you get, everything is schizophrenia, multiple personality disorders, there were so many. There were so many things and it finally got to a point where they're just guessing. We thought they knew what they were talking about, but then we realized that they were just guessing. They're guessing by a set of symptoms."

Trying To Work It Out

Performance Business Forms & Graphics

In all of the mental anguish and confusion, Janiece kept trying to go back to some kind of work. She didn't want to be a burden to anyone. From June 1983 through August 1983 she worked for Performance Business Forms & Graphics as a Printer's Apprentice in the bindery and warehouse. This is where she had the accident on August 12, 1983.

Because of the mental instability after the accident as well as all of the surgeries, she was having a hard time getting and staying with any job, for any length of time. On January 23, 1985, Dr. Dennis sent the letter to Dr. Mitchell, advising her of Janiece's mental condition and the need for her to monitor her condition as they progressed through the surgeries needed for the abdominal flaps. If things became too stressful, they would have to interrupt the surgeries.

According to records, she was admitted to Villa Rosa Psychiatric & Rehabilitation from November 16, 1984 through August 7, 1985 with Post Traumatic Stress Disorder. She was heading into some more traumatic experiences in the hospital that should have been avoided.

Mobile Gas Station

She worked for a while at the Mobile Gas Station on Culebra and Potranco from January 3 through February 5, 1986. She interviewed with her supervisor, Kay, and informed her of her condition up front. She wanted to be honest about everything. She didn't want to work the cash register. "Please don't put me on the register. It'll be too much stress for me, so I'll do anything else in the store. I'll clean everything that needs cleaning. I'll go and do whatever you want me to do, but please don't put me on the register," Janiece remembered telling her. They had to count cigarettes and cartons. She would count the rows, but because there were so many brands, she would get confused as she was counting. She would forget that there were separate brands and different categories within the brands. She was a smoker at the time and it was still hard for her. "It was just too overwhelming to just count the cigarettes," said Janiece. Some time later, Kay wanted her to do the drawer. "I can't do the register! I can't do the drawer! I can't do that!" said Janiece. Kay told her it was part of the job. She asked Kay to at least be with her in it or schedule their hours when she would be there too. She asked for the dog watch, nights. Kay agreed because it wasn't busy at all during that time. "Thank you!" said Janiece with gratitude. The busiest nights were Friday and Saturday. She was so scared to be alone, by herself in the store on those busy nights. "I am just scared and I don't think I can take the stress," she told Kay.

Also, nights lead into the morning shift where people are just starting to get ready to go to work. They are stopping in for cigarettes, gas, coffee, donuts and snacks on the way to work. That was a small store and all of a sudden it would be packed out and the lines would be long. The shift would be changing; they would be trying to count, all the talking, everyone at once. She felt like she was in a whirlwind every morning that she worked there. It was a stressful job. The pay was great. The only time it was real stressful was in the morning. It just got to where she began to break under it. She eventually had to quit that job, too. She had to go back into the hospital so often. She was in the hospital long enough, then came back out and worked, went back into the hospital, came back out and worked. She told Kay that if the register was short, she would pay for it. She was so conscientious about keeping everything right. She just wanted to be able to do something. She had enough money that she could replace what was short. She wasn't working for the money. Janiece told her. "I just need to work, to do something. Otherwise, all I got is sitting around depressed and suicidal." She had insomnia during this time, too. This was during the time of the surgeries and mental hospitalizations.

Pizza Hut

From February through August 1988, she worked for the Pizza Hut Corporation doing pizza delivery and on their downtime they all had to do prep work.

She thought it was cool working for Pizza Hut. She loved that place. She was a delivery person. She didn't like staying in and doing the prep work though. It was boring and tedious. She liked being in her own car, doing her own thing. She found out she could get more money if she put the plastic Pizza Hut sign up on her car, so she did. She ended up quitting because she was a basket case. She was in the mental hospital more than she was out. She had some little jobs like this where she was just trying to function and be out in public.

When she first started working at Pizza Hut, she remembered her interview with the manager. She told him that he couldn't go by her resumé because she wasn't that person right now. She wasn't the same since the accident and the injury to her arm. She told him she could do things physically, but that there were going to be some surgeries that might cut in on the job that would have to take precedence. She told him, "When the doctor tells me that it is time, I will have to go in. However, what will really mess everything up is if I have to go back into the hospital at Villa Rosa." He asked what Villa Rosa was. She replied, "Ok, it is a place where people who are unstable go to get stable." She also told him that she was on medications, but they wouldn't affect her work there or her driving.

She continued the interview with, "Because of the accident, I have been a big mess, off and on, off and on. I am real tender, so go real easy on me if you are getting ready to fire me. I can take being fired, but just be nice about it. So if you don't want to give me the job, I get it and if you don't want a nut case on your hands that's fine. However, if you give me a break, I am a good worker. I only need a few hours so I won't be bored. There may be times I will have to go into the hospital, all of a sudden and right in the middle of a job, but I'll be honest with you and sometimes I'm scared. If you look at me as being handicapped from the beginning then you won't be disappointed with anything ahead. Sometimes, I just need to go into the hospital, so they can get my medications adjusted and blood work. If you would be willing to bring me on again, I would appreciate that, but would not expect it." She worked at the Pizza Hut on the corner of Babcock and Huebner, next to the Volkswagon Beetle shop.

Shock Treatments

Janiece and Deborah discussed her time in the mental hospitals.

Janiece questioned her sister, "Why was it, that it would help me to have the ECT's, the shock treatments?"

120

Deborah explained, "I remember us going to a meeting with Dr. Mitchell and Dr. Clifton Barnhart, who was going to be administering it. This was in June 1985. They explained to us that it was not like the one in 'One Flew Over The Cuckoo's Nest,' anymore. They explained how they do it in a clinical setting. The reason they were doing it was that you were having visual and auditory hallucinations that were dangerous. It wasn't just the fact that you were hearing things at all, it was the fact that you were hearing these words, 'Injure yourself! Injure yourself!' They said something in her brain is just misfiring. We have tried the medications, the counseling and we cannot seem to get that from misfiring, so we are going to try and make it fire and get the electro activity back on track. At the time, it would be nothing for you to just sit there and burn yourself or to go up to a wall and just start banging it until you were bleeding. You would be saying, 'I am supposed to be doing this. Something is telling me to do this.' The visual was causing sleep deprivation and you weren't getting good sleep at night. You were exhausted. You were overwhelmed. They just didn't know what else to do. They said something is just zapping in her brain, so let's see what we can do. It was a full hospital setting."

Janiece said, "On the second time around, I do remember. They did the first twelve and it was like a year or two later, that I had another round of twelve. That one I remember."

Deborah questioned, "I don't remember another twelve."

Janiece was sure, "Yeah, because it was a series of twelve. They did it every other day or every two days."

Deborah said, "I remember it was outpatient to where we went there and sat in a waiting room."

Janiece reaffirmed, "I remember the second time, when I

was already inpatient on Cottage E."

Deborah was still talking about the first, "By outpatient, I mean like outpatient surgery. You weren't taken to a hospital and admitted for days. But they did it while you were already there. They had an anesthesiologist; you were given a shot to calm you. Everything reminded me of a general surgery."

Janiece continued on, "I remember that thing they gave me to put in my mouth, to bite down on. It is like that thing football players have in their mouths, but it had a tube that stuck out so I could breathe. They showed me how they were going to use the butterfly needle just to sedate me, that it wasn't anything serious, not to worry. I was going to have short term memory loss, not long term. I remember being put back on Cottage G and staying close to the nurses. I was in Cottage E the first time and then they made that into a drug rehab and then they used Cottage G for those who were depressed or just needed to rest from all of the stress of life. I met a lot of people who were only there for a weekend. I remember I'd walk over and they would walk me back."

Deborah went on, "After your shock treatments, they'd wheel you back, because you were sedated. You were acting perfectly normal, except that you were a little sleepy from being sedated. The treatments were really short and you still had the sedative working. But other than that, you would be chattering, kind of like is anything different."

Janiece added, "I remember being afraid after that because of the short term memory loss."

Deborah continued, "Yes, but it never stopped you talking."

Janiece said, "It seemed that when I was depressed, I wasn't talking much."

Deborah answered, "When you were really drugged, that to me, was when you would be quiet, I'd call Dr. Mitchell and just raise Cain. You'd be so drugged."

Janiece continued, "I remember sleeping a lot. I remember just wanting to lay down all the time."

Deborah said, "I don't remember what happened when you were on pass with anyone else. Here, you weren't sleeping. You didn't sleep here. Most of the time you were here was after all of the surgeries."

Another Blow

Janiece explained, "They set the second set of shock treatments up in ICU and then they also had an IICU. I remember having to stay on the IICU ward sometimes, because I had either misbehaved or something, got caught with a joint or whatever. That was so bad, because with those people, that is where I got hurt. I got raped and they checked me out. Mother remembered this too. I remember how angry she was, because that was allowed to happen to me. They checked me out to see if I had been torn and I was. I don't remember who it was. I was out of it most of the time."

Herd Of Elephants

Janiece remembered a funny story when the med nurse and she were shooting pool in the day area one evening. During the game, as Janiece was holding her cue in front of her, with one end resting on the floor, as she had both hands around it, she kind of spun around and returned to the same position. She exclaimed as she asked the nurse, "Did you see that?" He responded, "See what?" She said, "Did you hear that?" He answered, "Hear what?" She said, "I don't know what it was, but it sounded like a herd of elephants just went through here."

They both played pool together sometimes because they had fun together and were both skilled enough to be a challenge to each other. He looked at his watch and told her, "Let me go and see if it's time for another PRN, if you want one." She said, "Yes!" He said, "Come to the window and I'll look." He checked it out and it was time for some more Thorazine. She had been having hallucinations and this was one of them.

He placed a large bottle of Thorazine on his medicine counter. It had a medicine dropper in it, so that the drops could be measured correctly into the tiny cups for the doses to be taken. He took the dropper out of the bottle and grinned at her. He reached over, picked up a straw and put it down in the bottle. Then he lifted the bottle up, as if to give it to her and said, "I'm just kidding." Then he removed the straw and gave her the prescribed dose. They both laughed. They had known each other for many years, because she had been hospitalized there so many times.

Suicide Attempts

The following is a brief synopsis of her suicide attempts.
Janiece's dad filed an Application For Temporary Commitment For Mental Illness on April 30, 1987 for her to be admitted to the San Antonio State Hospital. The basis for this filing was because she had tried to commit suicide three times within the prior week and was presently residing at Charter Real. Her current diagnosis by Dr. Mitchell was Bipolar Disorder, mixed-depressed. Dr. Mitchell stated in

the document that, "She has been chronically suicidal and recently cut wrists in a suicide attempt last night. She feels suicidal and cannot control these feelings. She cut her wrist last night and reports no memory of the incident."

According to records by Dr. Barnhart, Janiece also tried committing suicide on December 4, 1987.

In April of 1988, Janiece tried to commit suicide again, according to Dr. Barnhart's records. She used an Ensure tab at the Medical Center Hospital.

On October 31, 1988, Janiece again tried to overdose. She took a bottle of Lithium, but vomited instead. Her friend Diana, who was staying with her at the time found her.

In December 1988, she was placed in Laurel Ridge because she was suicidal.

On September 7, 1989, she was admitted to Villa Rosa for fear she might hurt someone.

Guardianships

On May 7, 1985 Virginia Sue Turner was appointed guardian of Janiece E. Turner, a person of unsound mind. Some time later, Janiece was able to function again and this guardianship was dissolved.

On December 15, 1986, Dr. Elizabeth L. Mitchell recommended that Janiece E. Turner again be given a guardian to assist with the management of her financial affairs. On January 20, 1987 Bobby D. Turner & Virginia Sue Turner were appointed guardians of Janiece E. Turner, a person of unsound mind.

On May 11, 1989, Dr. C. C. Barnhart stated that it is his opinion, that Janiece has improved in her ability to assume responsibility for herself. "With this in mind, I am encouraging you to consider an alteration in the current status of her financial management. I would recommend that Janiece be given some gradually increasing responsibility for handling her own funds. Janiece should probably begin with some limited responsibility for check writing, having a monthly deposit and a budget to work with. Assuming that she handles this appropriately, I would recommend that more of her funds be turned over for major expenses. I believe that within a matter of a few months, Janiece should be able to demonstrate her appropriate level of responsibility. If all goes well, I would recommend the relinquishing of her guardianship and all financial responsibilities again becoming hers."

This guardianship was not dissolved as per his request and was still in effect in 1991 when she was placed in her sister's home.

(See Appendix C for Guardianship Documents)

Legals & Financials

Larry and Deborah Ursell took care of all of Janiece's financial records, because the guardianship required a bookkeeper. Larry is a CPA and it was the natural thing to do for her. It was another one of those things that seemed to fall into place, like the doctors who happened to be at the hospital when she was brought in.

Lawsuit

Janiece's lawsuit was filed in December 1983 and was

settled in May 1986. Her parents encouraged her to buy a house with some of the settlement. They wanted to be sure that her settlement could not be touched, so they placed a large portion of the investment into a homestead where it would be safe. They wanted her to always have a place to live, a home without large payments because they didn't know if she would be able to work again or to what extent she would be disabled. They knew she was going to have to deal with the emotional limitations that had presented themselves and were unsure of the final outcome.

"We hired the law firm where I was employed," said Deborah. "The reason Janiece ended up with Hornbuckle was because he was board certified in products liability. This was a products liability case. The main reason for the lawsuit was the safety shut off switch was not accessible. These were inset while the new switches were designed to stick out and could be hit at any angle. What's more, is that there was a previous injury on this particular machine before. It had done this same thing to someone else. It wasn't just this brand of press or even just this model, but this actual press."

Janiece said, "After the fact, Dad ended up designing a safety feature for this area of the press for the press manufacturer."

Bob challenged the manufacturing company over the safety device issue. They argued that a safety device could not be placed in that area of the press and were going to produce a witness who would verify this information. Bob said it could be done, designed it and proceeded to have it constructed and installed by Mike Fryar for that press. Their expert witness had been working for their company for approximately fifteen years. Bob had around thirty-five years of experience at the time and knew what he was talking about and had dealt with their witness before at another place he worked. They never brought the witness forth.

Again, as in other situations before, the law firm was right there for them. They didn't have to go looking for someone, they were already in place.

(See Appendix B for photos & sketches of the press)

Chronic Suicide Attempter

Janiece remembered, "I went into Charter Real and was transferred the next day. I had started shooting up, Methamphetamine IV, intravenously. I finally called Dr. Mitchell and said 'I think I got myself hooked on Methamphetamine IV. What do I do?' She said, 'Okay, I'll get you a bed over at Charter Real, they have a drug abuse program there and you can go in and get clean.' So I went in and they put me on the regular side, with people who are trying to come clean and later on that evening I started hallucinating. They didn't understand that hallucinating for me wasn't the same as hallucinating from the effects of the drugs. I needed certain medications that they couldn't give me on this side of the facility. I would have to be on the psychiatric side for that. I asked them if I could sleep in the galley area, where they kept the coffee and snacks, instead of staying in my room all alone. I told them to call my doctor, but it was too late at night so they wouldn't. The galley was next to the nurses' station and I felt safe."

When Janiece told the nurses that she was feeling suicidal and didn't want to be alone, they changed their minds. They told her that she couldn't stay in their unit and called her doctor to get orders to move her to the psychiatric unit.

Janiece went on, "Sometime during this time, I went off the handle, tried to slice my wrists and all. The next thing I knew a sheriff was called and he took me to the state hospital. They hauled me out of there. I felt like a criminal the way I got hauled out of there. I was so scared too. I was sorry I did this."

Deborah added to the story, "I had been at Charter Real with you right before this and had no sooner gotten home when I got a call and they said they were taking you to the state hospital. You had lost it. When I got there they were basically holding you down and had put a straight jacket on you. They had pinned you down because you were fighting, thrashing, screaming and hysterical. I followed them over to the state hospital."

Janiece talked about a suicide attempt, "Diana found me once. I was living at the Walnut Hill apartments. I thought for sure I had locked that door and chained it. By the time she got there to come over and visit the door was cracked open. I had taken a bunch of the lithium and drank a bottle of wine. I didn't hurt myself so they just administered the charcoal at the hospital."

Janiece continued, "One of the times at home I took a bunch of pills. When Dad found me after he got home from work, they took me to the hospital. Dad was so mad. He said, 'Next time just do it right,' because it wasn't the first time I had tried it around them. He didn't mean it. It was evident. You're killing yourself; it's hurting. It pulls them away from work and messes with their emotions."

Deborah said, "I remember once you called on the phone

and said you had taken a bunch of pills. I said get over to Bexar county and I'll meet you there. When I got there you were outside and you said, 'They wouldn't take me. They said I am a chronic suicide attempter.' I remember being so furious because you are either chronic and you keep trying or you are successful and you're dead. You know, we have to do something. It's like so what if you are chronic. What are we supposed to do from here? It was so aggravating."

"She was over at my place all the time. I would get her out on day passes," said Deborah.

Janiece shared, "It was so boring all day long. When I was starting to get better I had to get out and I wasn't ready though, completely. They had to make sure I was really ready to get out. So I practically lived here right?"

The Infamous Elevator Scene

Deborah continued Janiece's conversation. "When you were here, you would usually sit around dazed, watch TV, play with the kids, really just a myriad of things. A few incidents stick out though. I remember being in the living room and hearing a bunch of crashing in our bedroom, banging on the wall and cursing. Oh, my God, you could curse like a sailor. I ran into the bedroom and you're like, 'This g _ _ d _ _ _ _ _ elevator won't come!' and you kept just hitting this imaginary button on the wall. You were just livid that the elevator wouldn't come and just cursing it and hitting the imaginary button on the wall. I said, 'Why don't we just take the stairs?' and you said 'Okay.' It's a good thing the house had stairs. We didn't have to imagine the stairs. As furious and livid as you were, when I suggested the stairs it was like, 'Okay!' Redirect."

Deborah said, "We eventually had to tell you, 'No more overnight passes.' Day passes were okay because we were all up and around. We were seriously worried that you might successfully commit suicide and the kids would see it. You didn't try it here, but it was getting more frequent. You began talking about it really often. It had gone from an anger to 'I'm just sick of this,' to a hopelessness. It went from an anger to nobody gives a darn anyway, to really what's the point, deeper and more questioning. 'What's the point of life? Why should I even bother?' It was sounding more hopeless to where this might actually happen one day. We were thinking, 'No you can't stay overnight.' You said, 'Okay!' You were sad, but you understood. You were very coherent. You were saying that the last thing you would want to do is hurt the children. You said you understood because you felt the need to end it all. You were very sure about it."

The Break-Up

Deborah said, "I remember Diana being very angry at you when you were breaking up with her. She felt like, 'You're the one who got me into this!' It was during the time you had gotten real sick."

Janiece was touched, "I don't remember any of that. I do remember always calling her like I was always calling you from the hospital. I called one time and she said, 'I can't take this anymore. It's just too much. I can't take this, this on and off and on and off, the emotions and stuff. You call me at work all of the time. I'm sorry, I love you so much, but I can't take this emotionally myself, anymore.' And I said, 'You're not breaking up with me?' So I was scared. We were best friends by then. I wasn't even interested anymore in the intimacy so that didn't help matters either. To me, we were just pals. But, it was still too emotional and I was on the pay phone out in the waiting area. I was over in Cottage F at Villa Rosa. It was right before I got moved into Starr's house. Everything was coming to a head, losing interest, losing interest in drugs. Everything was culminating. Then I was getting moved. My car was taken from me, my driver's license, my money, everything! I didn't know why I was getting moved, other than I was too much of a burden. That's all I could think of. I was always thinking what a burden I was and I wish I couldn't be one. I didn't know how else to be what I was and being so needy all of the time. I didn't know how not to be needy either. This was my internal war."

Such A Burden

Janiece continued, "I used to apologize to mother. 'I am so sorry, so sorry I am such a burden.' I really started to realize how much of a burden I was when dad came to visit one time and brought me quarters. He said your mother is not coming up here anymore. I am not letting her come up here anymore during the week. She needs rest. That was when I realized it. It hit me. It finally just hit me and I sure didn't like that dad was coming up because I was always afraid of him. I didn't trust him. I was scared of him. I wondered, 'What did I do wrong?' But that was my years of feeling like I was always in trouble even if it wasn't true. I thought, 'Okay, I won't be calling home a lot to get something. Deb can you come?' It was then I realized mother needed a rest, and that everything was coming to a head before I was moved. I don't know how close it was to the end when Dad started coming. Mother would only come on a weekend if I was in there."

Deborah said, "With Diana her getting upset was more because it was more your idea. You convinced her to get into this lifestyle and then you just walked away from the relationship."

Janiece countered, "Well, the walking away part was because my feelings for her were just gone. The need or whatever it was that was driving me was just gone. I still wanted to be friends and I was so sorry. I just couldn't be anything else."

Deborah asked, "I wonder what her perception was during all of this?"

Janiece replied, "I have wondered that too. I have asked the Lord to watch over her, protect her, heal her, comfort her and to even bring her to a place to forgive me. I hope that she has a family and children. I just prayed that she was having the life that she always wanted like when she was a young teenager."

Deborah said, "We stayed in touch for a long time after that and then she quit calling. She needed to move on too."

Dire Straights

Deborah said, "I do know that out of all the incidents the hardest on me was the straight jacket. That and your five times a day phone calls were really hard."

Janiece defended herself, "I had to start calling you because mother was at work."

Deborah continued, "We got our first answering machine because of you. It actually got so bad that I wasn't coping well. It was affecting my life to the point that Dr. Mitchell told me that I needed to get some counseling. Your medical paid for it. It was just a couple of visits, but it was that doctor who told me to get an answering machine. There wasn't any 'caller Id' back then. She told me that I needed to take a break and I needed to answer the calls when I was able. We still talked at least once or twice a day though. I'd still go down and bring you quarters, cigarettes and all of that. I knew when you were calling. I could hear your voice and kind of brace myself from whatever was there. I am sure I dodged some calls, but I don't remember dodging calls. I did tell you that I had an answering machine and for you to speak up so that I knew it was you. If I didn't answer, it was because, most likely, I wasn't there. I explained to you that I got a machine and why. You didn't seem to have a problem with it."

"I remember the let's try this test, let's try this test, let's try this, this is new, let's try this medicine, we think this diagnosis, and the continual ongoing drama," said Deborah, still irratated by all the guesswork by the doctors.

Janiece said, "Before too long I had a bag. Every time I took a pass I had a bag of medicine, so many bottles."

Deborah said, "I remember them telling us that the EEG, Electroencephalogram, isn't going to tell us anything that's going on; the PET gives you some info, but the brain is a mystery." They tried so many different things to try find the problem and the solution.

'Round And 'Round We Go

One time, when Janiece was in the San Antonio State Hospital, her parents visited and were amazed at what they saw. They couldn't believe their eyes. All of the patients in the locked ward were walking around in a circle, one behind another in the day area. They were so amazed that no one was sitting down. Bob called Janiece over and asked her what they were doing. She responded, "I don't know, but I'm getting in with them. I'm not going to get my a _ _ caught in a sling." They thought that was so funny. Later on, she was asked to be the Marshal and round people up for group and for exercise. She learned later that the circle was for exercise.

A Good Samaritan

Sometime towards the end of her last mental hospital stay at Villa Rosa in Cottage F, a nurse by the name of Jim Autry was attending to her. During one of the times he was there, her pulse was racing about 120 which was usual for her when waking and off and on throughout the day because of the high anxiety and she could hardly breathe. She wished she could have even yawned. She couldn't even yawn. She was so tired and wanted to sleep. She couldn't sleep and when she finally did get to sleep, it was usually so close to the time of having to get up and get her vital signs taken, go to group, and/or get breakfast that she wasn't getting any rest. She was anorexic so she didn't want to eat. Everything was just misery. To top it off this particular morning, there was this nurse trying to talk to her and calm her down. "Like talking is going to do it. The only thing that ever worked was taking medicine," she said. She was on Xanax a lot and it was usually the best one that would work. Valium didn't work at all. Sometimes, they would give her an anti-psychotic because she needed it, but it would also tranquilize her. They also tried Busbar because it was supposed to be non-drowsy, but would still take care of the anxiety and depression. That didn't work either. They said she was in it for the high. She was like, "Yeah! Sure! I wake up from sleep with my pulse so high and all I want is to get high?" She needed help. Nothing was working and she was hallucinating all of the time. She was scared and paranoid. It was always something coming at her. She was either hearing it, seeing it and/or feeling it with the tactile hallucinations. It was like all of her sensory system was operating at peak levels. They were scared and genuinely worried about her. She was like, "Don't worry about me. See, I have flesh on my bones, way too much flesh on my bones."

On this particular morning, Jim was trying to talk to her. She didn't even know who he was. Finally, after a lot of questions, Jim asked, "Can I pray for you?" She looked at him with a face that probably shook him inside. She remembered the glare she gave him. She replied, "IF you HAVE to... If it makes you FEEL good... If this makes you FEEL good, you go right ahead! Like it's gonna work! I don't think so!" He was faithful though and he prayed for her. After a bit, she thought to herself, "Are you done yet? Take a breather, man!" In a way, she thought it was nice too, but she knew it wouldn't work. He checked her pulse again and it was still up there, so he went ahead and recommended the medicine. He was there to monitor her and to see if he could help bring the anxiety down without using the medicine.

Unbeknownst to both of them at the time, they would be attending the same church less than one month later where Jim operated the sound for the meetings.

A Peer To Help

Leslie and Janiece discussed a time in their life together.
Leslie Burke and Janiece were in Villa Rosa Hospital at the same time in June 1991. Janiece got out July 7, 1991 and

Leslie had been discharged a short while earlier.

Leslie told her, "I would come over and pick you up from the hospital to take you out for a while. I would come and check you out for day trips. Dr. Raymond Potterf, Janiece's psychiatrist, approved of the visits. We would go out and get drunk. She would take her pills and fall asleep in the car. She would tell me not to tell anyone because they wouldn't let her go back out on passes. She didn't really drink before I came along. I think I probably got her started drinking."

Janiece confirmed, "I didn't ever drink. I had even quit smoking pot by then. In those days we would go driving around in the car all day and do stuff."

"Yeah, you can tell she was a good example for me," Janiece teased sarcastically.

Leslie took it all in stride and responded, "Yeah. But back then the person I met was JJ. JJ taught me all about the lingo of lesbians too."

Janiece looked up with a question on her face, "I don't even remember that."

Leslie went on, "We would be walking through the mall and people would be looking at us, kind of strange-like. You would go, 'Oh, people think that you're my fluff.' I'd say, 'What's that?' You said, 'You have a female part.' You see, back then your body was built like a man, broad shoulders and a small waist. You were truly, truly, in front of God, built like a man. You had a man's haircut and a leather strap on her arm. You also had a tattoo showing on your left arm."

Leslie continued, "I remember my first day at Villa Rosa and you were so sweet. My family and I were sitting around this table outside. I was really upset and my family brought me a clock radio, an African violet and something to read. You walked over and had your radio and had your headphones on. You sighed and then you leaned down in between us and said, 'They will let her have the radio but not the one with the cord. They are afraid people are going to hang themselves with the cord. So you can't take that in there.' We kind of went, Oh, thanks. I thought, 'Okay, go away.' Then you walked around to the other side of the table and you go, 'My name is JJ.' You hung around the table and talked for a while. You told my parents what it was like there and all that kind of stuff. My parents were going like, okay."

Janiece added, "I always tried to help people and their families so they wouldn't worry and so the new patients wouldn't worry."

Leslie said, "That is how we met and then I just kind of kept running into her while I was there. Then we started hanging together. When I got out, I thought for some reason it was good for her to go on day trips with me."

Janiece said seriously, "They don't normally allow former patients to take patients out on day passes. Did we lie about it, because they just don't ever let that happen? It was policy. But you walked right up to the nurse's station to check me out, so we couldn't have lied. They would have known."

Leslie reassured her that it was real, "They would make me sign for you and give me your medicines."

Janiece said thoughtfully, "See, your name was down by Dr. Potterf. It had to be for them to allow you to do that."

Leslie went on, "Anyway, we did that for a while."

Time Is Running Out

Deborah said, "When the MRI became available, that's

what changed it all. When they used the MRI, (Magnetic Resonance Imaging), that is when they found out about the demyelination. They said, 'We are seeing something we have never seen before.' That was the first time we had heard the word 'demyelination.' That is when they explained that it is like having your house electrically wired with no coating on the wires and every time the wires touch, they are shorting out. That's what was going on. That's when they said there was no cure, no hope and not much longer."

Deborah went on with mixed emotions, "The thing that changed, when the demyelination diagnosis was given was that this journey was going to be over soon. All the emotional stress and hopelessness over all of the years was going to be over. They were going to quit messing around with her psyche and with medications. The nerves shorting out messed with the auditory and the visual so it would mimic other symptoms. It would affect any area where the shorting of the nerves occurred."

Deborah said, "I remember that after that meeting we talked and wondered, 'What now?'" She continued, "I just kept feeling like it's going to be over soon. They won't be drugging her anymore. That was just a big contention with me in the past. Dr. Mitchell and I had several cross words over that. It was nice to finally have a definitive answer, one that had some scientific backing, rather than we think it's this and we think it's that and it sounds like this. It's like how many mental disorders are there. I know your book's that big, but my goodness. I mean does she have to have every one of them? The only med, (medication), I can remember as a constant issue was Lithium. The demyelination has basically the same premise as Multiple Sclerosis, only it is not in the brain, but in the body. A person is basically losing the myelin sheathing over the nerves. They didn't say how it was happening only that it couldn't continue much longer."

"They told us that they were a psychiatric hospital and there was nothing they could do psychiatrically. Medically, there was nothing they could do either, so basically, the insurance was not going to cover her in a medical hospital. All she could do was go home and wait."

"By that point she was really bad. Physically she was not good. She had very little movement. I think they had her in diapers, because she was incontinent by then. All she wanted to do was smoke and have coffee. She was very zombie-like, very, very out of it. She was in a bad, bad shape at that point."

"When they moved her into Starr's home, that was the end of my doing anything to help her. Starr took over at that point."

Janiece provided a summary, "At that point, the doctors had come to a conclusion at a meeting at Villa Rosa hospital where I was staying. They had a meeting with my family and told them that it doesn't make sense why the brain cells aren't regenerating because it was normal for them to regenerate. They were dying off and it didn't make sense. The myelin sheathing was dying away from the cells. It was like a short circuiting going on in the brain. It was not that I was a mental patient as much as that these brain cells were dying off over a period of time."

Dr. Potterf described demyelination to Janiece by drawing an illustration for her: *"Demyelination is a breakdown of the cells, (feeder cells), that insulate the nerves, eventually causing short-circuiting between the nerves. Could be brought on by trauma, (mech. injury, head injury, etc.), viruses, high temperature, as a child or autoimmune."*

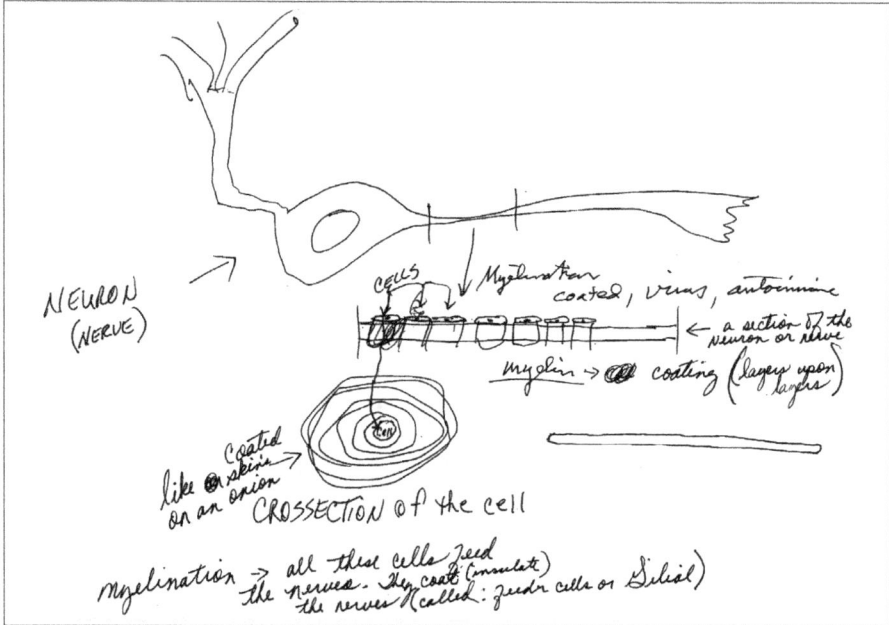

Illustration Above: Dr. Potterf's diagram he sketched for Janiece to explain Demyelination to her

Bob recalled the final prognosis meeting, "Gin, Deborah and I were all in the meeting. Dr. Potterf was the doctor. He was a renowned doctor in SA. He said, 'Her brain cells are just deteriorating and she will only get worse. She will never, ever be whole again. We know that this is what is happening.'"

"I asked him, 'Then there is nothing at all we can do?'"

"He said, 'Oh no, nothing!'"

"We ended up moving her over to Starr's house, because she was a caregiver who was taking care of people who were dying."

Stripped Of Everything

Prior to moving into Starr's home, Janiece gave her car to her brother, Bobby, because she was no longer safe to drive it. She no longer had a driver's license. She was under the guardianship at the time and no longer had access to her money. Her name no longer meant anything. She felt stripped of everything, including her dignity. She felt, "Like a nothing!" This feeling would stay with her for a long time, even through the years of healing and restoration to come.

Living Out Her Last Days

Janiece told this story about the anorexia.
"One of my favorite groups at the time was Metallica. There was a song I really identified with called 'Sanitarium.' A person that is lost like that, nobody gets it. You just want people to leave you alone. It was like, '**Sanitarium, leave me alone!**' I was always just wanting to be left alone, but don't leave me alone. It's like a kid's cry."

"I was always just outside for a smoke. I always had headphones on, because I was always hearing voices. They were always tormenting me, bugging me and telling me how bad I was. They were telling me that I needed to hurt someone, needed to do something! It's like, 'Just shut up! Just shut up! Just leave me alone.' So I would put on the headphones and listen to the music, you know, Pat Benetar singing 'Fire & Ice,' and all kinds of Rock & Roll. The music kept me from hearing their words and sounds. I was drowning it out. It was so depressing and tiring. I was on so many different medications for high anxiety, so they had me on Xanax, and anti-psychotics or psychotropic medications, including Thorazine, Meleril, and Haldol. I was on Phenobarbytol because they thought I was having little seizures. They gave me Chlorohydrate just so that I could sleep, two instead of one, because they didn't always work. I'd get tolerant to the medications and they'd have to change them. I was taking Lithium all the time, Synthroid, and Busbar. They tried all sorts of stuff, all of the new stuff that came out."

"I think I was still anorexic at the time because I didn't really want to eat. I didn't really want anything. I remember it being so bad that they took away my journal. I remember saying, 'Somebody please get my journal, my calories journal. I've got to have it. It has my records in it. I need my stuff. I need my stuff. I mean, you need to give me my stuff.' I would record every calorie that I took in even a Tic Tac. I knew it had one calorie. I would record it. I wouldn't let myself have hardly any calories because when I saw myself, I saw myself as fat, even though I wasn't fat. I was gaunt, not bony, but a little bit gaunt."

"I was in the hospital during this time, just before they moved me over to Starr's and was under a guardianship with my parents. They told me this is the doctor's orders; you have to have this or we are going to have to strap you down or something like that to somehow feed me intravenously or directly. I guess it was a tube or something. I don't know. That scared me because I didn't want anybody to bind me. I didn't like being strapped down. I had a straight jacket on once before and I didn't like that. I didn't like any of that stuff, to be strapped down and not get out of bed, bound at four points because a person would hurt themselves. It was all about harming themselves. One to one is the suicide watch. I always had a nurse watching me in those times. I was anorexic at the time and the Ensure was the only thing I would accept. I finally agreed to their demands, 'Okay, I'll drink the Ensure. How many do I have to have a day? How many calories is it?'"

"'You are not allowed to know,' they said. 'We are going to pour it into a cup.'"

"They wouldn't even let me know and that was so tormenting. I got to the point where, 'Okay, I'll have some mashed potatoes. Is that okay? Is that being good? You know, was I being good to do that? Can I have mashed potatoes, maybe once a day?' I was drinking coffee. I always drank it black so it was easy, no extra calories in that, no milk product. I was smoking two cartons of cigarettes a week."

Annual Family Gathering

Shortly after the meeting with Dr. Potterf and the decision to move Janiece to her sister's home, they had their annual family gathering at Bob and Gin's house. Most of the family were saying their last good-byes without saying a word. It was not a very joyous occasion at all.

Mother's Last Resort

Bob and Gin had exhausted every means to save their baby girl. They had walked with her through the asthma for years, through the dog bite, through the gender issues and especially through the injury and the suicide attempts during the mental slide. They never gave up. There were many people who also tried to help her over the years, including many who weren't family. Many prayers had been prayed, but they seemed to land on hard and dry ground, unanswered.

Janiece was now at her sister's house just waiting for the inevitable to happen. She was oblivious to the things around her as she continued the slide down into the depths and clutches of death. It seemed impossible now for most; however, one person in particular chose to go beyond her natural motherly instincts and take the ultimate step of faith. Just prior to that day when love broke through, her mother stood in her kitchen and wept. Gin loved the Lord Jesus so dearly, and she couldn't understand why He wasn't healing her. She had so many questions that seemed to go unnoticed and unanswered, but this moment in time was different. In spite of the agony and grief in her soul, she dared to lift up her hands. Bob was in the room at the time. From what I recall her telling me, it went something like this. "Lord Jesus, I place her in Your hands. No one else can help her. Everyone has done their best, but I know You can help if You will. So, here she is. You take her and do what You will."

Road To Death

The accident occurred on August 12, 1983 and she was placed in a home to die, in July of 1991, almost exactly eight years. This road was long and painful for Janiece and it touched everyone around her, especially her family. Everything was coming to a close and it seemed like it was going to be soon. They all gave it their best, sometimes working alone and sometimes alongside each other. The things they had witnessed had been etched into their memories. They had struggled to understand each diagnosis and then it would change. They questioned, "Why?" without getting any answers. Now, it all came down to this hopelessness. It was time to just sit back and wait for the inevitable, to prepare their hearts for their last "good-bye."

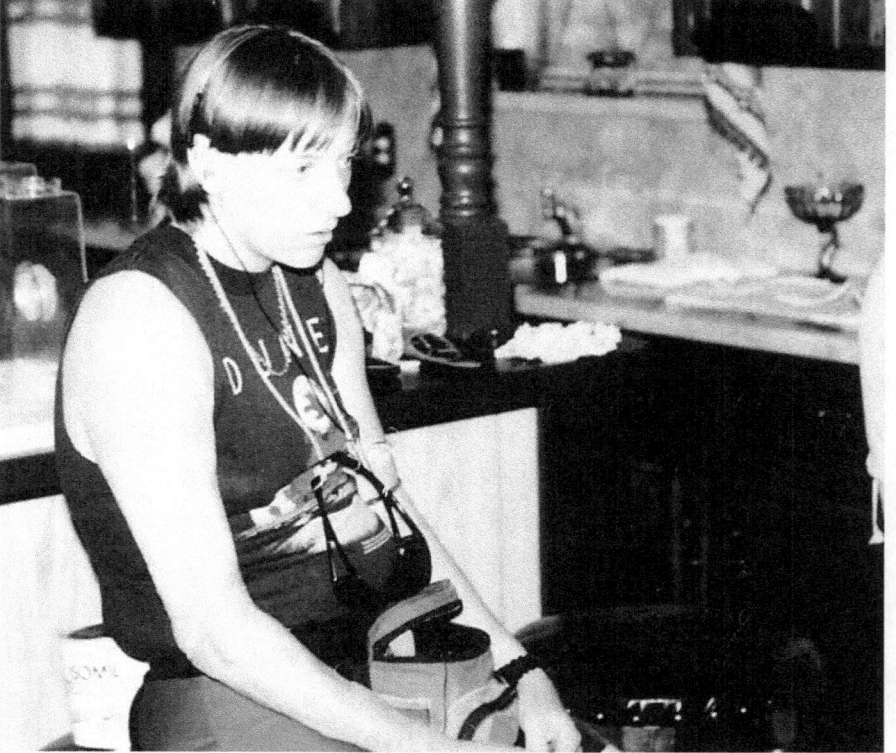

Chapter 8

Destined For Life

Love Breaks Through

This story ends on a rainy day in July of 1991 on the northwest side of San Antonio, Texas. The 'Sentence Of Death' had been issued and there was an eerie feeling of the certainty of its judgment in the atmosphere. A young woman, in her early thirties, is seen standing on the front porch of a home for the terminally ill. She is smoking a cigarette and listening to her headphones. Normally, she would be sitting out in the front yard with her smoke; however, today the rain has forced her to stay on the porch. Her gaunt, anorexic figure displays her state of mind. She was depressed all the time. Her constant cry is, "God! Will you please take me home? Just take me home!" She cried out over and over in her mind as she listened to a song by Metallica called "Sanitarium," trying desperately to drown out all of the voices inside of her head.

Janiece Elaine Turner had been through years of extreme pain and misery. She was tired, extremely exhausted, and

Photos at Left: Top: The infamous porch where Janiece was standing on the last day of her old life; Bottom: Janiece at a family gathering on July 6, 1991 just days before moving into the care home in the photo above it to live out her last days

she just wanted it to be all over, finished. The voices inside of her head would not leave her alone. Unbeknownst to her, she was getting her wish. Soon it would be all over, but it would not be the way she had expected.

After almost eight years of pain, surgeries, mental institutions, treatments, drugs, and medications, the doctors finally came to a new conclusion, aided by a new technology called the MRI (Magnetic Resonance Imaging). They told her family that the myelin sheathing around the nerves in her brain were dying and this was causing her brain cells to die. At the time, they called it Demyelinating Syndrome. They told her family there was no hope for her and asked them if there was a place that she could stay comfortably until she died because the mental hospitals could not help her anymore and, also, they were so expensive. Taking into account the doctor's advice, they decided to place her into her oldest sister's caregiving home for the terminally ill. The family was told not to tell her she was dying for fear that this time she would be successful in taking her life after all the numerous attempts she had made in the past.

There was something very special about this dreary, rainy day, however. This day was different. It was not like all the other days before. This day was special because it was the fulfillment of a promise from a long time ago. This was the day that death would be sentenced and life would begin to blossom.

As she continued to listen to the music and continued to smoke her cigarette, the front door opened and her sister walked out. Janiece pulled the headphones down to her neck so that she could hear. Her sister only spoke a few words, this time out of frustration and then went back inside. It was the same words she had heard from others over the years. "Do you want to stay sick forever?"

Something was different this time though. Something had changed. These same words that had brought condemnation to her before now had Heaven's glory all over them. This was the Lord's timing and His answer to all of the prayers that had been prayed over her all of these years. He had heard her cry over the years and in His perfect timing He was stepping in on the scene. He pierced through all of the confusion, the chatter of all the voices, and the hopelessness in her heart. Aware, for the first time in many years, she suddenly exclaimed, "No! No! I don't want to be sick forever!" As she was turning around to face her sister, she reached down to put the cigarette out; but by this time, her sister had already gone back inside.

Janiece opened the door and looked for her sister. She walked up to her. "No!" she exclaimed. "I DON'T want to be sick forever! Now what..."

Now What

Suddenly, Death was thrown down, violently to the mat and Life arose victoriously. She was Destined For Life and He came in His resurrection power, reached into her mind, and began the long healing process on the journey to a full recovery.

Janiece had heard these words many times before and each time she would question, "How do I not be this way? How do I not be sick? How do I not hear voices? How do I not be depressed? How do I not be confused? I am scared all of the time. How do I get out of where I am into somewhere else? I can't move me. I can't change me. How do I not be this? How do I get free?"

Janiece remembered, "But this time, when I heard it, it was like, 'No, I don't! No, I don't!' But Starr had already gone back inside the house. So I put out the cigarette and ran back inside and said, 'No, I don't want to be sick forever! Now what? What do I do?'"

"Starr said, 'What do you mean, now what?'"

"I said, 'I don't want to be sick forever. I don't! Now what do I do?'"

Her sister prayed for her and told her she needed to get in the Word, the Bible. She had all kinds of study and reference bibles, materials and even a concordance. She told Janiece that anytime she wanted, she could sit down at the table and do word studies.

Janiece asked her, "Well, what's a word study?"

Starr replied, "You pick a word that you want to understand and look it up in the concordance."

Starr showed her how to use it. They looked up a word, found the definitions as well as where it appeared in the scriptures. She saw how each word could mean different things in different passages and could also be translated differently in the different versions of the Bible.

Janiece recalled those times. "The Bible I always used was the King James. I never got rid of the thing. I was afraid to open it a lot of times. I would quake in fear to open it. In my apartment fear lived with me. It was an actual, physical, paranoid, terrorizing, presence there, that if I opened that Bible I was dead. But I never did get rid of that Bible."

Miraculous Healing

Sometime after the awakening on the porch that day, she had been asking the Lord if He was real. She had to know personally that He was real.

Janiece recalled it vividly, "It was during one night, while I was still in my sister's house and I was sharing a room with one of the patients, that all of a sudden the asthma gripped me. It awakened me out of a sleep with immediate wheezing. That could happen any time over those years. When it did happen, it was like both lungs were just squeezed and held. I wasn't allowed to breathe. I was fighting to get air in, even though the medical personnel always told me I was fighting to get air out. As far as I was concerned, I wasn't getting air in. It felt like I was drowning or being suffocated. That night, I was on all fours in the bed and I was trying my hardest to breathe. I remembered reading, 'Call on the Name of the Lord and you will be saved.' It was like, 'Yeah! Jesus! Jesus!' In between the wheezing, I would cry out and it stopped. I thought, 'Wow!' I thought, 'That doesn't normally happen.' It just doesn't normally stop and then there is breath. Normally, there is wheezing for another 30 - 45 minutes and that is with medication. I would still be trying to breathe and my chest would be tight. I would get so hot and sweaty and cough up stuff, the sticky mucous-like stuff. Well, that didn't happen at all this time. It was like I had never had the asthma attack. It just stopped. There were no left over symptoms, nothing left over. My head wasn't full of pressure. I went, 'Wow! Cool!' I was tired from that little bit of trying to breathe, so I went back to sleep. A little while later, still in the middle of the night, it hit again just like that."

"It was always so scary and such a bother. I hated the thing. Then I remembered that, 'By Jesus stripes I am healed.' So first off, I am remembering one scripture and then another and I went, 'Yeah! By Jesus stripes I am healed. If this is true then it's for me. If You are really real God, then this is true and it's for me.' I didn't even know what stripes were. As far as I knew, stripes were stripes. So anyhow, it stopped again. So, okay, God is real. I knew Satan was, 'cause I had seen the demons. I went, 'Attack! Wow! Asthma attack! So that was an attack.' Both times it was an attack and both times it was stopped by God. 'So, God You are real! I want to know You!' So I went on a quest. 'I got to know You. Who are You? What are You all about? And what do You want? Where are You at and how do I get to You?'" she said.

This was the first real healing that happened to her since she had the porch experience. This was sometime around August 1991.

For the first time, she didn't need her inhaler during the attack, nor a shot. She didn't have to lie down for a while because she was exhausted and needed to regain her strength either. She had gotten her rest and woke up early and refreshed. She told her sister the next morning, "He healed me and you know there is a devil, too. I saw that there was an attack on and he's been caught, too." She had seen a lot of demons, "They brought spooky with them, terror and paranoia. Their very presence does this, everything that makes you just want to crawl up under a rock and let someone else take care of it."

Word Studies

Janiece didn't know how to pray in the beginning. She knelt beside her bed on the concrete garage floor with her hands pressed together like a little girl. She would start out with "Now I lay me down to sleep…" and would ask the Lord to bless each individual she could think of as she called them by name.

"I just kept doing more word studies," she said as she fondly remembered those times. "The first one I remember doing was on 'Faith.' Then I found out there are other 'faith' words in the Concordance next to each other. It was 'faith, faithful, faithfulness, faithless, faithlessness.' I was like, 'Wow! We go from one spectrum to another.' I still have a lot of my word studies, even from back then. I look back at them every now and then. That was a big one."

Daily Changes

Sometime, soon after she started doing the word studies, she would wake up in the mornings and discover the Lord had done something new. She got to where she would start looking for something new every morning. "What did He do over night?" It is something she still does today. She'll look in the mirror and question Him. "What did You do? What is new today?"

One day, while still at Starr's, she woke up and was grossed out by what she saw. She thought, "I need to shave my legs and under my arms." Because of the way she thought she was for so long, 'a man's mind trapped in a woman's body, why shave, that's just not right.' So here she was, looking in the mirror and she had hairy armpits and hairy legs. She went and found her sister and asked her if she could talk to her for a minute. They went into her bathroom and Janiece said, "I need privacy." She was so embarrassed, even though she was wearing long pants and a long sleeve shirt. She was embarrassed just being awake. She was aware for the first time. She went on, "Do you have a razor, or two, or a few, or a miniature lawn mower or something?" Starr asked, "What?" Janiece replied, "I need to shave!" She was almost embarrassed to talk about it. Starr replied, "I'll get you a whole package." Starr got all excited and Janiece was just glad to have it all gone, finally. Everything was always so intense and dramatic. She went to bed one way and woke up different. It was like a switch was turned on in the night and she had been wrong. Little by little, the untwisting of her mind was beginning to unfold, as the Master skillfully untwisted each and every area of her mind.

Janiece also had scoliosis, a curvature of the backbone, making it into an 'S' shape. Even though it was only slightly curved, it caused her pain. She talked to Starr and Linda. Linda was Starr's friend. "Hey! Can we pray? Remember my back! I bet He'll fix that too, huh?" Starr said, "Sure! It says in the Bible to lay hands on the sick and they will be well." Janiece said, "Okay, let's do that." Starr said, "You have hands too." Janiece replied, "That's right!" So she put one hand down low behind her back and raised her other hand over her shoulder to touch her back. "All right!" They were all praying and touching her back. "Okay! Back get back straight. You are not supposed to be crooked in Jesus' Name." It was over and done that fast. Janiece went and put it to the test. She thought, 'I need to go find something and lift it.' Anytime she lifted something and started to carry it, she would feel a tug in her lower back. This time there was no pain.

Then she thought, "What else? What else?" Then she thought of the Fibrocystic disease that was in both of her breasts. The doctors told her she couldn't have chocolate or caffeine. She liked both so she thought, 'Hmmmm!' So she laid her hands on both of her breasts and prayed. When she found out she could lay her hands on the areas that needed healing, she went for it. Then she started thinking about other stuff, 'What else?' Most of this took place while she was still living over at her sister's house.

Goodbye Medications

She was still taking all of the medications too, at that time. Someone had given her a Crown Royal bag. She didn't even know what Crown Royal was, but she liked the beautiful purple velvet bag. She thought it was the coolest thing and she would put all of her bottles of medicine in it. She would carry that around with her, so that she could have her medicines near her at all times. It was real convenient for her because with certain medications she had to take them three times per day.

She started thinking about the medications too and how to start weaning herself off of them beginning with the Lithium and then the others. She had discovered in the Bible that the Holy Spirit was with her. "I'm born again and He is with me. We are palling around. We're buds and He's going to help me. He's my Helper, my Comforter, my Friend, my Teacher, my Guide. He leads me into all truth. He untwists my mind, because He is leading me into truth. Then I found out I have the mind of Christ."

Again she started talking to Him, "Okay, since You know everything, You also know what I'm ready for. I don't know what I'm ready for, but will You know it to me? Will You give me that knowledge? What medicines can I get off of now? Which ones should I start weaning from safely?"

At first she was sneaking around and not telling anyone, because Starr would have to divvy out the medications. She trusted Janiece to take them on time and as prescribed. (Synthroid, Lithium, anti-psychotic, Xanex, Chlorohydrate, Phenobarbytol, etc.)

Dr. Potterf was her psychiatrist during this time. She was trying to be discreet about backing herself off of the medications. She was just checking out Holy Spirit to see if it was cool. It seemed like it was so she continued on. It finally got to where Dr. Potterf started noticing something was going on because she wasn't asking for refills. She sheepishly admitted to him, "I've been sort of weaning myself off of my medications and I know it is NOT a good idea to do it all at once."

(Please note that this is how Janiece did things and we are not suggesting that anyone do this. Please use caution and wisdom when dealing with medications and drugs. Seek medical advice.)

Her doctor suggested they do some blood tests to which she agreed. Everything checked out and then he helped her continue the weaning off of the medications. He did tell her it was not going to be a good idea to get off of the Synthroid, the thyroid medication. Janiece told him that it all had to go, no more drugs. He did agree to it, stating she would have to be weaned off of it slowly so that she wouldn't stroke out. He told her that he was going to watch her as he was taking her off of the medications and that if he thought she needed to be on them, he was going to let her know and he would tell her sister, too, so that she could govern it and get her back on. He was going to be watching her behavior. It was all about her behavior and how it was there at home. She felt as if it was like she was slowly regaining consciousness after being out of it for years. All of a sudden, she was awake, alert, and sharp. She felt like a sponge. She was learning everything.

Need More Input

She was writing everything down and just absorbing it all. It was kind of like the little robot on the movie, "Short Circuit." "Input! Input! Need more input," demanded Number 5 in the movie, "Number 5 is alive!" He wanted to learn everything, and so did she. This is one of our favorite movies and we watch it together every once and a while. It is great to be alive. Walking with Him, in His Kingdom, on a daily basis, is a continual adventure.

She had to find out, "Who is God? What is He all about? What's His business? What does He want? What's His whole purpose? His purpose, not mine! What's He up to? Why is He even?"

There were so many years when she was so confused and she was asking, "Am I just a figment of someone's imagination? Am I just in a movie? Am I even real?" So much of the time, she just wanted to know that she was real. She couldn't tell if she was even real and sometimes she would burn her arm with a cigarette. She would be smoking and would take the cigarette and burn herself and think, "Okay, I can feel that. I must be real, I guess." Sometimes she would cut on her arms with razor blades. She didn't like pain, so she didn't go very deep. Some people cut themselves for different reasons, but for her it was just to determine if she was really here. "Am I really here? Am I really real or is this someone else's show?"

There were also times she would just go catatonic. She explained it like this. "It was like someone just flipped an off switch, nobody home." She could hear people talking to her and she would say, "I'm here! I'm here!" but no one could hear her because there was no ability for her to talk. She couldn't move her mouth nor make a noise. Sometimes the tears would stream down her face, but it was like she couldn't do anything. She couldn't function. Just as suddenly as it started, after a period of time she would come back. It was so weird to her. She didn't have any control over it.

Once she was born again, none of these experiences ever returned, even to this present day. It was like it had never happened. When scripture talks about becoming a new creation, it really happens.

Once, when we were living in Dallas, the asthma tried to come back. She said, "No way! Not happening! No, you're a liar! I found out you're a spirit. No way, I'm not letting you in again! We're not buds! Get out of here!" It would try sometimes when we played racquetball. She said, "I understand that maybe my body can't handle this activity right now, but I'm not receiving asthma." She would have to continue to stand, sometimes just so that we could enjoy a game or two of racquetball together. Now, we're able to play basketball for even an hour and a half where she keeps going strong without any wheezing. She can run now without wheezing. When the Lord exposed it, it was exposed. It couldn't hide any longer. What she had attacking her from the time she was eight weeks old had been defeated and she was free.

Just A Patient

Deborah and Janiece reminisced again.

Janiece said, "By Christmas, I was feeling better already and I wanted to get gifts for everyone. Starr had this Maxim membership where she could order gifts. Mother and Dad said, 'Okay, only a little bit though.'"

Deborah said, "I only went over to this house once. By that point though, I was glad to let someone else help, too. I was exhausted."

"Leslie would bring me Bartles & James," Janiece recalled, "And I would sit on the curb and complain to her how bad I was being treated, like a patient. Even my nephew, when someone once delivered a package said, 'Awe, you can't talk to her, she's just a patient. You need to talk to my mother.' That was when I first started praying, 'O God, please fix that. Please, can I be a person. They don't even let me come into the living room and have family time. I am not family even here. At 8:00 p.m., patients should be in bed. I had a TV in my room, but I couldn't watch it."

"Sometime, before I moved into Starr's, I had stopped smoking pot. I would take a hit off of it and get scared. I got to where I was afraid of it," Janiece said with reluctance, because she really liked the taste and smell of it.

Leaps & Bounds

"The next thing I knew, literally, it was just

improvement, improvement, improvement in leaps and bounds," Deborah added.

Janiece began, "Starr and Bob weren't real big on the church thing back then. They were big on the counseling and marriage counseling."

Deborah added, "They were involved in that one church. It was San Antonio Christian Fellowship, but is now called Oasis International Christian Center."

Janiece said, "The reason I didn't go all the time with them was because they didn't always go."

"The lady that always visited Nanna was Debbie Alder. Nanna was her grandmother. Nanna was my roommate in that home and that is how we met. I would ask Debbie if I could go to church with her. She went to the same church. She started out with, 'I don't know,' but ended up taking me when she could. Her children were real nice to me. They treated me like a person. I felt special with them. I didn't feel it where I was staying though. I was simply a patient there, treated that way, and not as a family member at all," said Janiece sadly.

Deborah said, "I remember we had phone calls, but I didn't go over there. One day, you told me you were born-again."

Deborah continued, "When you were at Mother and Dad's, I remember you telling me you quit smoking because you didn't come back to life to kill yourself. You were as clear as day. 'I'm done with it. I didn't come back to life to go and kill myself with cigarettes.' It was just like, 'Wow! That's really cool.'"

Deborah continued down this vane, "Then, I remembered getting irritated at you because as time went on and you were really into the born-again thing, this was one of those, my moments. We were talking and I was going to tell you something. I don't remember what, but I started saying something to you and you said, 'I don't gossip anymore.' I'm like, 'I'm not gossiping, I just wanted to tell you this.' And you asked, 'Is it about somebody else?' I said, 'Yeah!' You said, 'Well, that's gossip.' I was like, 'Okay! So, what are we ever going to talk about? I was so ticked off.'"

Janiece jabbed at her playfully, "I might as well have slapped you right?"

Deborah kept on, "I said, 'This isn't gossip!' You said, 'Yes it is, if you are talking about somebody else.' I asked, 'Well, what if it is just information.' You replied, 'If it's about somebody else, I don't do that anymore.' I thought, 'It's like, fine!'"

"I was like a little kid in the beginning," said Janiece thoughtfully.

"You were exciting and irritating, a little of both," Deborah began. "It was really amazing watching you. It was like getting your spirit back, your heart back, your soul back and your brain. It was everything. Because I wasn't there to see it and our conversations not being everyday but once every few days, they were like leaps and bounds between those times. Even down to meeting Joseph."

Deborah continued, "Everything was just like amazing to see and then trying to convince people that you were okay to be around now." She even had to rethink things because the years of pain had been so engrained in her mind.

"Here is an example," Deborah was on a roll. "Talking about y'all going to Estes Park here recently. There's part of me that wants to remind Linda and Richard that you are sane and safe to be around. Now, how many years has this been, seventeen? I don't need to remind them. They know what's going on in your life because they are always asking. Part of me still wants to reassure them that you are okay to be left alone at their house for a month. There is really a part of me that really feels like I need to reassure people that you're normal again. For so long it was the other way."

Janiece agreed, "Eight years is a lot of years in that mental degradation."

Reaching Out To Others

Deborah went on, "Families dealing with someone with mental illness need so much help. They need information. They need support. They need financial help. And yet the ones who are in the middle of it, are too busy dealing with it to really be helpful and once you are out of it, you never want to go back. You don't want to look back. You don't want to go to the state hospital and help those people. You don't want to go to Charter Real and help those people. You are so far from it."

"That's how I feel also. Gun shy!" admitted Janiece.

Deborah said, "But while you're there, you're like, why isn't any one here to help? Why can't someone be here to help? It would be difficult to make the effort to go into those situations to reach in to help. You're not wanting to volunteer yourself. They need someone for that, to go run an errand or something. They could use someone just to sit with them through one of the suicide attempts. While you are there, you can't do it, because you are so busy dealing with it yourself. Afterwards, no, I'm not looking back for anything. It's like glad, over, done. I remember thinking so many times, 'I wish somebody could just help. I wish somebody had answers. I wish somebody had one place, rather than us having to go here and there. Where is she going to live next? If she is not in the hospital now, none of us can have her, where does she live? She can't live by herself.' The constant question was, 'Why can't we get help?'"

Deborah continued, "We weren't always privy to each other's information either. I mean, I couldn't call Mother and Dad and say, 'She has her motor skills back because she can roll a joint.' We didn't always trade information. Sometimes, because I know they're wiped out, I would think, 'I'm handling this.' There's no reason to bug them with that if it wasn't going to affect them dealing with you. I am sure they did the same with me."

Wow! Curves!

Leslie and Janiece looked back and discussed some of the times they spent together.

Janiece began with, "I went to the apartment to clean up and then over to Starr's house. I stayed one night at the apartment and that was it." This was the time she was moving into her sister's house to live out her last days.

"I remember you basically worked at Starr's," said Leslie. "I mean, you were there as a patient for a while and then you started getting well. Then you started doing things."

"I had to do something before I lost my mind," Janiece said as she laughed. "I was doing electrical things. That's funny, lose my mind. I went in there without my mind and then had to work to keep from losing it."

"I was really being taken advantage of while I was living there, but I don't remember a whole lot of it. God's pretty slick and He's smart. Once you've forgiven someone, it is so wiped out, not even the memory is there. It makes it real easy to not have a grudge."

Leslie added, "Even if you did know the whole thing, you might not feel emotional over it, but not hold a grudge."

Janiece explained, "I couldn't hold one now, because there were no feelings attached to it, because I had released it all through forgiveness. There would have been, if there could have been. You know as far as a human being."

Leslie went on, "You were so dead set on helping other people, even when you were sick. That was such a core part of who you are. That transcended all of the illness."

"I know, it was really odd," Janiece said, as she agreed. "It didn't make sense to me. I'd be so miserable, but I'd come out of it to help someone else. You're right! It was so weird."

"That's the true nature God put in you," suggested Leslie. "Everyone has a true nature. I mean, I have a faith. People struggle for faith. You have this core desire to make people happy. It's not a bad thing."

Janiece remembered the times people used it to their advantage and stole from her. "Before it was in the hands of God, others could take advantage of me."

Leslie wanted to continue her thought, "But, all of us come down to our basic nature and your basic nature is goodness. That's how you really know how someone is, when you see them down. When you see them when they are nothing. When the only thing they are existing on is when God has this little marionette thing going on."

"That is how I used to put it when I was a babe in Him, using me like a puppet," said Janiece. "That was long before He reached down and grabbed a hold of me. I am sure glad

He gave me a lift."

"When you started going to that church, San Antonio Christian Fellowship, with Dennis Davis," Leslie said. "Yeah, Starr was going there and she got you to go there because you wanted to get out. You wanted to get out so you started going to church."

Janiece's argument with Starr about going to church concerned her dressing up. Starr reassured her that she didn't have to dress up.

Janiece remembered, "During the first worship service, I went out to smoke. Boy, Starr got upset when she found out I went outside to smoke during the service. And it's like, when I came back in, 'So!' You know, it's like in the middle of a movie. Go out! Have a smoke! Come back in! Did I miss anything?"

"You were so happy," Leslie smiled as she remembered the change in Janiece.

Janiece quipped, "Even to have a quarter in my pocket was exciting!"

Leslie was serious, "But when you started going to that church, it was like, in a matter of three weeks you started transforming. It happened like that. At first, it was like, 'Yeah, you know.' Then you started getting excited about it. The weeks went on and you started getting more excited and I started going there. I'd pick you up and take you when Starr and Bob didn't want to go. Before I knew it, this woman, this person was changing so rapidly. Before this all happened, you went by JJ. Then I walked in one morning and asked, 'Where's JJ?' Starr went, 'Her name is Janiece.' From then on we called you Janiece."

"Then one day I went in to church and you were doing

this play on the stage and you were so good," said Leslie. "It was incredible. This woman, that used to lay passed out in my car for hours on end, was doing this incredible acting job. You played a demon and you played it very well. Everything in your face and actions was like, I am going to get this guy."

Janiece was so serious, "I prayed for help with this, because I didn't have it in me."

Leslie remembered, "Even Dennis got up and said, 'Janiece, thank you! You played a perfect demon.'"

Janiece laughed, "I told him, 'Thank you! That is real encouraging.' I was being sarcastic. The experience part is going to be deliverance and I don't want to go there. Being there for someone who needs to go through it. Ministering to others. I don't have the guts for it. Father and I keep going 'round and 'round on this one. I saw all of those things in the spirit, especially when I was in the hospitals."

Leslie questioned, "That's one of those things, that if Father is wanting you to do it, why struggle with it?"

Janiece responded, "That's one of those things He is still fixing inside. Fear! I saw so much and they called it hallucinations because they didn't have a better word for it. But, when you have a demon staring you in the face, pointing his finger at you and saying 'You're mine!' and things like that are happening, it is scary. You see someone walk through a wall, kind of half way in and out, it affects you. Those aren't pleasant memories."

Leslie encouraged, "Yeah, but God's not going to put you in a position to do that, until you are fully prepared to do it."

Janiece said, "I know that, but at the same time I've been

in some positions where, 'Joseph, that person is staring back at me.' It is not a picnic and in the moment I am scared and Father is going, 'It's okay.'"

Leslie continued on the play she had done. "Fear makes you search your emotions. Yeah, but you were a mischievous demon in the play. These are down right dirty demons."

Janiece laughed, "Yeah! You dirty old demon."

Leslie changed the subject. "You and I hung out for a while and then Mike came into the picture. Mike was my doctor during that time."

She continued, "Remember the time something happened. You called and Mike and I came over to Starr's with two, four-packs of wine coolers?"

Janiece remembered, "Oh, yeah, I just kept wanting to leave. I wanted to go home, to get out of there."

Leslie went on, "It was really nice when you moved out to your parent's house. It was much more convenient."

"It was immediate freedom," said Janiece with relief.

"It was like a transition. It truly was," Leslie added.

"Kicking out those tent pegs, stretching it a little more. I didn't have a car yet," said Janiece.

Leslie countered, "Then you got that little white one."

Janiece said, "Dad and I went looking for one. They had started trusting me with their car. I was freaking out that they let me do it. 'Are you sure you want to do that?' I asked."

Leslie said with a smile, "It was incredible. Your parents were wonderful."

"I remember," Janiece began, "when they first started coming over to take me out from Starr's house. At first they were afraid and it was only for an hour, then two hours, then weekends. It was like, 'Wow! She's not so bad.' They were afraid. They were so afraid to get too involved with me again after what they had been through. Plus, they figured I was dying, but all of a sudden I was resurrected. It was like, wow, these are real changes."

Leslie looked at Janiece, "Your body is perfect proof. It has changed from the male physique to a female one. It's the physical part of it and internal transformation. It's incredible. You're pretty special, a miracle before your eyes. It was more than a favor, it was a miracle."

Janiece responded, "That's a good word for favor, 'cause when He gives favor to us, it is always a miracle. Did you realize that?"

Kasi Turner, Janiece's sister-in-law, remembered the miraculous physical changes in her body. "She was shaped like a guy. Her hip structure, her waist and her chest were all masculine looking. After the miraculous change in her mental and spiritual condition, her physical body also changed to feminine. Her hips, waist and everything changed and the curves were there. The Lord actually took her body and remolded it. Every change she was going through was impressive, spiritually and mentally, but the physical change was the most impressive to me of all of the miracles."

Jerry and Lu Tipton shared, "Something we remember about Janiece is how God changed her whole countenance. Her facial features were changed to totally feminine in just a few short months. It was awesome to see God in action."

Tell My People I Love Them!

Chapter 9

Take Off The Grave Clothes

Lazarus Comes Forth

At SACF, we had a lot of prayer times scheduled during the week, including each weekday morning. By this time, we had begun to pray for the Lord to send a Lazarus to us. Little did we know it wouldn't be long in coming, at all. One day, in walked Janiece and none of our lives would ever be the same again.

During one of her first services at SACF, when Dennis Goldsworthy-Davis was ministering, Janiece went up to the front after the message and to kneel down before the Lord. As she was kneeling, there were other people crowding around her and she was getting scared because her back was to everyone. She kept asking the Lord, "Don't let just anybody touch me. Please God! Please don't let just anybody pray for me or just anybody touch me." Then she felt this hand on her and she tensed. Then she remembered what she had asked and she was immediately okay. She thought, 'That's right, not just anybody can touch me so this person must be okay.' She doesn't remember who it

Photo at Left: Two and one-half years after the porch miracle at her mother's birthday party in January 1994, Janiece, her dad, and her mother all hugging, so grateful at the chance for another life together

was at the time. She still feels the same way today. She doesn't want just any one to touch her or pray for her, not unless He has sent them. She says it this way, "If He hasn't sent them, I am not up for grabs. Not just everyone is up for just anyone to pray for them. Certain people need a certain ministry in any given time." She was so scared to have just anyone touch her. They did a lot of that in the mental institutions and she also had a lot of that with all of the trauma and surgeries. Then, she was always questioning in fear, "What are they going to do to me? What this time?"

She did know that for God to talk to her, it must be a safe place to be. She kept wanting to come back because the people were nice. They didn't care what she looked like. At the time she came in, her hair was cut short in a boy's hair style. In the beginning, she showed up as she was, no special clothing, generally just jeans and a T-shirt. She was dressed like a guy because that was the only kind of clothes she had to wear. She carried a big wallet in her back pocket. She had a braided leather bracelet around her left bicep, just under the tattoo. At one time, she wore an earring which consisted of an upside down cross and a skull. She thought it looked cool. It didn't have any significant meaning to her; it just had a cool look. She didn't realize that it was contrary to her belief. She had a couple of shirts that her sister told her she might want to get rid of. She had a black T-shirt with a cobra's head boldly showing its fangs. She also had one with 'fists of steel' that had spikes extruding from the knuckles. She wore those mainly to keep people at bay, but she thought they were cool, too. She hid behind a lot of the strength she had in her muscular build and the tough exterior, so that people wouldn't try to hurt her inside.

God Loves You

Janiece remembers vividly, the day a prophet, Eddie Traut came to SACF. She was sitting about eight rows from the front and offset a bit to the left of the center. Eddie walked up to her. Janiece was still all broken inside and was just starting to come out of the mental dungeon she had been in. She was still worldly and had a lot of things that had not been cleansed out by the Lord yet.

So, Eddie walked up to her and simply started by telling her, "God loves you." Her tears began to stream down her face. She was wondering, "Why did he pick me out?" When he mentioned the suicide spirit following her around just waiting for her to mess up, she thought, "Boy, is that an understatement!" There were so many times she had tried to get off the planet. Now, here was this man that she had never met, and even from another country, South Africa, and God's telling him to let her know that He loves her, over and over. He told her, "Don't you know you were born for such a time as this!" This wasn't a question to her, but rather a statement of truth. He told her, "You will live to proclaim His glory. God chose you." Those few words in a row like that are a part of her foundation.

Janiece knows this for certain. "I am certain that He loves me. I am certain that He started this thing. I am certain that He gave me life and chose me and that I am here to proclaim His glory, to tell all about it." That was one of her first beginnings in this new place. "It's like, 'Wow! You picked me out of this whole crowd to tell me, God loves me!' That's big!"

In The Kingdom At Last

On June 21, 1992, Eddie Traut was speaking at SACF and he spoke these words to her:

"Janiece, God loves you. You don't believe it, but God does. The suicide spirits followed you a couple of times around. I want to tell you he's just waiting for you to make the mistake, but God says, 'You're gonna live and proclaim My glory!'"

"You're a blessing! God loves you. You are not a mistake. You weren't born by accident. You are not a mistake. God let you be born at a time like this."

"Yes, you've made mistakes. Yes, you've been weak. Yes, you've been frail, but He's come to give you life. He's come for your benefit, and you're not gonna feel like you're no good anymore and you have no right to breathe. Yes you do. Yes you do. You're God's child. He has chosen you. You didn't choose Him. He chose you and He loves you and He's never gonna let you down!"

"You've been searching for love for a long time. God says, 'Don't look around anymore, look to Me! I'm the One that loves you. I've loved you ever since you were born. I've loved you desperately, even before you were born and I will not let you down. I will not let you down.' You've been let down so many times, abandoned so many times, but God says, 'No more! No more! Come to me, hide in me and I won't let you down!'"

Father's Little Girl

Janiece had always wanted to be just like her dad. Whenever he would go to do something, whether it was

174

just working on the truck or doing something else, she would want to be with him. If he was working on the engine, she would sit on the inside of the fender on the wheel well under the hood to watch him. She wanted to be in the mix.

Her mother would say that she would follow so close behind him that if he would stop she would run right into him. She just wanted to be like her dad and hang out with him. Then she found out she was real good at things, putting them together and taking them apart. She loved going to the print shop where he was working. Her mother would take her dad something to eat and the girls would get to go along. She and Deborah were able to fit in between the skids and play. They had a lot of fun there and she loved the smell of the print shop as well. She always loved the smell of the ink. Although the sound was loud, it didn't bother her at all. They would have to raise their voices in a shout to be able to hear each other over the sound of the operating equipment. These are precious memories for her. She just wanted to be like her daddy.

Her dream did come true. She did get to be a printer like her dad. She got to be his helper and that was the biggest dream. That was her dream, to be her daddy's helper. Now, in addition to that, she also wants to be like her Heavenly Father.

Guardianship Dissolved

On July 21, 1992, Dr. Raymond D. Potterf recommended that Janiece E. Turner be returned to full competency as she no longer required intervention in handling her personal and business affairs.

On August 25, 1992, Janiece Elaine Turner, Ward, was adjudged to be a person of sound mind by Judge Polly Jackson Spencer.

Janiece had hung on to the scripture in 2 Timothy 1:7 for a long time and it had finally been upheld, even in a court of law, *"For God hath not given us the spirit of fear; but of power, and of love, and of a <u>sound mind</u>." (KJV)* She was so happy to get her life back.

Even The Little Things

While Janiece was still over at Starr's house during some of the new transformations, her mother and dad were still reluctant to take her out for short periods of time due to all of the traumas, suicide attempts and stress from the past. They had become so exhausted over the last eight years of ongoing events. Remember, they had placed her in this house at the doctor's request, because they thought she was terminal. Now, they were hearing reports contrary to this, but things had a history of being up and down with her, a lot of roller coaster rides over the years.

Her requests to her parents went like this: "Will you please, please take me out of here for a while? Please? I'll be good. I'll be good. I'll do my best to be good." The hard part was convincing them that something had changed and it was not just another religious kick like in the past.

She wasn't trying to get into His Kingdom anymore, rather, He was the one who snatched her and brought her in this time. When she found in the scriptures, that the Lord had pulled David out of a pit, Psalm 18, she so identified with it. The Psalms were so right on with what she had been through and experienced with His love and

176

acceptance. She could identify with almost all of them. Talk about a pit. No one could reach her even though many had tried.

Janiece said, "I couldn't reach me. I couldn't get me out of there." Her dad would tell her to pull herself up by her bootstraps. "How do I not be this way? How do I not be depressed? How do I not be anxious? How do I not be suicidal? How do I not be hearing voices? Tell me how not to be this way and I'll stop. I promise! How do I not be like this?" She struggled so much to change during those years, but it was always outside of her grasp.

When her parents finally thought she was doing well enough, they took her to a bar-b-que restaurant that had picnic tables set out to eat on. That was the first time she remembers being able to hold the fork correctly with her right hand. It was one of those special moments for her. Janiece recalled telling them. "'Mother, look! I can hold my fork now just like you taught me.' I know it doesn't seem like much to others, but it is a huge deal to me. He cares. He cares about the smallest things. It makes a difference." After all of those years of multiple surgeries and hours and hours of physical therapy, a miracle occurred and her wrist and hand flexibility increased. Up until this time, she would use a spoon and have to hold it in her fist like a shovel. She also had not been able to use a fork, because the side effects of the medications had caused her hands to shake too much. But this day, not only could she hold and use the fork correctly, but the shaking was also gone. She was off of the medications by this time, too. Before this day, she was always nervous, a nervous wreck. Now, she was calm and collected.

Talk To God?!?

Before the Lord lifted her out of the pit she was in, Janiece had always tried to protect herself and had the headphones on with heavy metal music, trying to drown the voices and just trying to exist. Now, she still put her headphones on and listened to music, but it was the Hosanna Integrity type of songs. These songs brought her peace because they used the scriptures as lyrics. They were peaceful melodies that helped bring peace to her soul. She would put the headphones on in the midst of some of the gatherings of her new church family because she was still so tender. She still couldn't take a lot of stimuli. She said, "All I could think of was to keep on pouring in God stuff. God stuff! I still had to find out that He was real, more and more. I was on a quest for truth and still am."

When she found out that God talked to people too, she just had to find out more. Another quest! So, when she heard someone say, "God said…" she determined that she would go up to them and ask them, "How do you hear God?" Some would answer, "I don't know. I just do." She would say, "That's not good enough. What do you mean, 'You just do!'?" They would say, "I just know!" She would come right back with, "How do you, 'Just know!'?" They would respond, "Well, I just know!" She would counter, "Well, that's not working for me! How do you 'Just know!'?" They would say "I don't know!" Again, she would ask, "How do you know?" Sometimes they would say, "Well, I have dreams." That opened a whole new conversation,

"What do you mean you have dreams? What's that all about? I have dreams and I have nightmares. Boy, do I have nightmares."

People were telling her things and then she would go and get in the Lord's face and tell Him, "I want that! If they can have it, I can have it!" Dennis had preached, "If someone has something you want, ask the Lord to give it to you too." She was like, "That's simple! Okay, cool! Okay, I want to hear God. I want to hear You. I want to know You. I want to see You. I want to be with You. I want to chat with You. I want to walk with You. I want to talk with You. I got to have You! Nothing else is going to do!"

She is still like that. If she doesn't get to have Him in the morning, "It's just not fair." She feels like she's been robbed. She just kept bugging Him. "It's like, I still don't hear You. I still don't know You."

There was a time she was reading the Bible and it just seemed like He was talking to her from the scriptures and it was so real to her. "Okay! Wow! Wow! I just got wowed! Wow! What was that? Wow, that's real! That's deep!" Sometimes she would have questions and then she would find the answers. "Wow! Instruction manual! Cool! Wow! This teaches me how to live. I didn't know this is what this was." Then there were times that she would listen to the radio, to find messages that would teach her more about Jesus, or God the Father, or more about who Holy Spirit was. She wanted to know about God's history with His people. She had never cared about it before, but something had changed. She didn't understand it before either, but now things were starting to make sense to her.

She had a King James version of the Bible and thought

it was kind of a trip that she could understand Old English. "That was a whole different language. It was enough that the Bible was a whole different language, but then to have both." She shared.

He Repented Me

One day, she was listening to Charles Capps on the radio, during the time a friend of hers had a problem with alcohol. This friend had told her that she wished she could overcome it. It seemed to rule her and yet she loved the Lord. It had ruled her so long, that it got to the point to where it was almost tormenting. Janiece had been praying for her and now she was listening to Charles talk about it. He was saying that the beginning of change was a choice to repent. But when Janiece heard him say repent, it had more to do with smoking, and she was still smoking at the time, about two packs a day. Janiece heard him say, "Repent." She got so offended at him that she turned the radio off. She thought, 'That was a cheap shot!' because he was talking about alcohol and she heard smoking. She was trying to figure out when he switched. The whole subject was about alcohol, so she turned it off.

Next, she thought she'd read the Bible. "That's what I'll do," she thought. So she opened the Bible and it opened right up to the book of Matthew to where it said, "Repent, for the Kingdom of Heaven is at hand." This was not going well and she was upset. "It's like, ahhhh! That's just wrong! I don't know what repent means, but I don't like it. Something is wrong here."

She thought, "That's not right!" So, she thought she would open it to another place. She opened to a place where it said, "The body is the temple of the Holy Spirit."

She thought, "So that is where Charles got it from. That's a cheap shot! Now, I can't even serve You, 'cause I'm trashing the temple of the Holy Spirit! So, now I can't even serve You?" She cried as she realized what this meant to her. It hurt her so deep. She had finally found God and now she couldn't serve Him because she had an addiction. This is what that moment was like for her.

Then she realized there was nothing wrong, evidently, because He's not wrong. She meditated out loud, "Why am I hearing... I'm actually hearing! Oh, God... Okay, so You want me to repent." She didn't know what repent meant. "What does repent mean anyway? Okay, I repent!" she said with her teeth clinched. "I don't really want to repent. Whatever it is, I don't like it. Okay, that's not real. I'm not being real with it." She even got on her knees, thinking maybe that would help her. "Okay, I repent. I don't 'feel' sorry. I don't mean it. I'll just do this thing already. I'll just do it. I repent, so there! I repent! Now what?" She had tried so many times over the years to quit smoking with no success. "I can't do it! I can't do it, okay? I can't do this. I can't make me quit. I've tried. I need You to repent me! You've got to do it! Okay? This has got to be Your thing then because I can't do it. You have to promise me that You're going to do it. I can't!" She said in tears and with a broken heart, "I don't have the strength to do it."

After a while had passed, she regained her composure some. "All right then, I repent," she said in a calm and collected voice.

She sat there for a while and then said, "Will You forgive me for trashing the temple of the Holy Spirit? And clean it then. It needs cleaning. Fix it and clean it out then. And just make it a good place for you, that this will be Your temple. I want to be Your temple. I want to serve You, but You got to take this away, 'cause it's had me all of these years. Now, I want You to have me all these years more. I want to be Yours."

"My dad said that when he quit, he kept one pack of cigarettes unopened and a lighter. So, I'll get rid of all the others. Is that cool with You?" She wasn't feeling bad about it anymore. Something had already changed by now. So she kept a pack on hand, just in case. She was never interested again. Sovereignly, He took the addiction and desire away. It was just gone. It was like it never happened. There was no draw, no pull and no addiction.

In that moment, He was taking her through it and then out of it. She gives this illustration of it. "First, He pulled me into the knot hole and then He was pulling me through it. He's got me with the word 'repent.'"

She didn't tell anybody about it at first because she didn't think they would believe her anyway. She thought they would think, "Yeah, here we go again!" So instead of being mocked, she thought she would keep her big mouth shut.

At this point, Janiece was living with her parents again. Janiece and her mother used to smoke together in the kitchen. Her mother noticed that she wasn't smoking with her and said something about it. Janiece finally told her. "I kind of had a talk with the Lord about it. Actually, He had a talk with me about it." Her mother was always safe for her to talk to about anything. She could also talk to Jane, her mentor. They were safe to be around, as she continued this new journey into the realms of His Kingdom. He continued to show her how Sovereign He was and how much He loved her. She had been through so much, more so than a multitude of people would ever go through in a lifetime, but He was making Himself known. This one person, who seemed to be lost in the ranks of this continuous line of humanity through the ages, was not forgotten, nor lost. He was watching, waiting, and ready, for the pricise moment, to reach in and show those around her, and those who will hear this story, the power of His love.

Which Bra

One morning, Janiece awoke and was aware of her breasts. She remembers vividly, "They weren't very big, but I never wore a bra. I didn't really have to wear one. All of a sudden though, my mind was changing." It was like someone was going through a house and turning on the light switches, only it was her brain and things were working again. She thought, "All of a sudden, oh my goodness, this isn't right. I need a bra. I don't know how to pick out a bra." She was a teenager the last time she had worn one and now she was thirty-two. She didn't know how to pick one out or even what size to get. She was totally oblivious to the how-tos of a bra. "Oh God, what am I going to do? Mother and dad are at work and I am home alone."

She was allowed to drive and use her car by this time. Over time, they were seeing the changes and were starting to trust her more. She wasn't on medication anymore. She was now clear-minded and focused. She was very alert and intelligent. She could actually understand things. She didn't have comprehension problems anymore.

She prayed, "Holy Spirit, I need You to go ahead of me and prepare the way. I'll go to the Walmart in Boerne, because no one knows me there. Lead me to the one that will fit me right off because if it doesn't fit, I am not taking it back. It goes in the burn barrel. This is hard. I am embarrassed and I'm scared. Will you please protect me, go ahead of me and comfort me. Just be here! Please? I need You!"

Now, it's hot in San Antonio during the summer, but she grabbed her sweater and put it on anyway. Then, she went to the store into the lingerie section and pulled the first one off of the rack that she sees that looks like it might fit. "It was like a 32AA," she recalled. "I was just coming out of anorexia too at the time, so my body was really small. I got home and put it on and it fit. I just started crying and saying, 'Thank You! Thank You! Thank You!' That's how I got to know Him and that He cares about stuff. He is always with me even if I don't know that I hear Him. Evidently I am, because He is coming out of my mouth more often than not. Everything I was reading during the day, on any particular day, someone needed to hear it that day. It's like they are going through that very thing, that day. I'm thinking, 'Wow!' I just read that in the Bible. It's in the Bible. I would tell them, 'Check it out! I just read it and it says, this, this, and this.' Then I'd go, 'Isn't that cool? Wow!' That is always how He has wowed me. It's like we were mouth-to-mouth. It's like He always had someone in mind and I was clueless. All I did was show up on the scene and just yakety-yakety-yak. They go, 'Thank you!' I go, 'For what?' You don't know if you don't know. 'Don't know' is kind of cool sometimes."

The Best Gift

"I was always asking for all of the gifts of the Spirit, because I heard that you could ask for them." Janiece had heard in a church years before, that anyone could ask the

Lord for a gift. She decided she would think about that one for a while because she didn't want to ask for just anything. She went searching through the scriptures for a gift. "A gift! What's the best gift? What do I ask for? What do I want? What do I need? What would work?" She remembered she had read about David and Solomon. "Solomon asked for the best thing of the Lord. That's what I want! I want wisdom. 'Cause if I have wisdom, wow! Nothing else really matters, because it is all in that. I didn't know until later that He is wisdom." He gave her wisdom to even ask for wisdom. She still asks for wisdom, knowledge and depth of insight. "In the New Testament, it is all about asking for wisdom, revelation, knowing who He is, all about His Kingdom, having everything uncovered and knowing what His people need. It is so cool to be in partnership with Him."

The Untwisting

Janiece had felt like the Lord started the process of unscrewing/untwisting her from that time on the porch through her beginnings at SACF. "It was like he was untwisting the threads on a screw, even to such a point that I was naive about life. He, (the Lord), wouldn't let me read just anything or watch TV." She spent the next three years in her room, outside of coming out to eat and drink, and going to church and prayer at SACF. She couldn't watch any of the shows her parents watched on the TV. They were too battering on her. "I felt like I was raw and I can't take it. It hurts. It was like new brain cells were being put in. I didn't know that I didn't have that many to work with." Her family had not yet told her the whole story about the last days in the hospital, the doctor's prognosis, and the real reason she had been transferred to her sister's home.

"It was neat how the perversion left me. It left me with an innocence. I was just so naive. If someone talked about something, say for instance sex, I didn't get it. It didn't register. Nothing seemed to hit home. I was just oblivious to a lot of things and curious. It was so neat, literally new. My body was becoming more new, even physically. There were so many healings. Where I had been so anxious and wired all of the time, such a wreck and nervous, and fidgeting, I was finally at peace."

"I just wanted to hide in Christ. I still visualize how big He is behind me and if I back into Him anytime I get scared, I know He's got me protected. I am totally surrounded by Him and I am okay. He's my comforter. He's my shield, my buckler, my God in whom I trust. He's my fortress, my stronghold, the place I run."

"When I can't deal with something and if I'm not backed into a corner, I can actually get with Him and then I'm okay. I get strength and I can come out. If the phone would ring at my parent's house and I didn't want to get it, I'd say, 'Please help me Holy Spirit. Please help me! Please help me! Would you please not let just anybody touch me with their words or anything? Please!' Sure enough, either they forgot why they called or they would just call back later and talk to my parents. It is really interesting how He shields me and protects me. He hides me. He strengthens me when I am scared."

Flooded House

On one occasion, Janiece received a phone call from her renter about a problem with her house. Their clothes washer had overfilled and flooded into the kitchen and into the dining area, getting the carpet wet. Janiece replied matter of factly, "Okay, that's fine, no worries." She always had peace now, because she knew that God was in it somewhere. "Where are You at in this? Where is the blessing for me? You got something good for me in this, so where are You at in this? Yeah, it may look like it is a bad thing, but I'm not buying it." She found out the details from the insurance company. They told her to go pick out a new flooring and the carpet that she wanted and they would cover it.

She found a flooring company and went and picked out the linoleum and carpet. She also had a verbal agreement with the owner of the company concerning certain specific wants that she had requested, that he had agreed to do. After they had completed the installation, she found that it wasn't according to what she was told. She asked him about it and he denied the conversation. While she was at drama practice one day, Deborah Nazami Lewis, one of her mentors and drama leader, decided to pray about it. She prayed that out of his mouth, in front of witnesses, he would admit to not telling her the truth the second time. She got all excited about the prayer, "Ooooh, that reminded me about a story in the Bible with that Balaam dude!" The next time she went over to the flooring place, she took her dad with her and sure enough, he admitted the truth in front of her dad. He couldn't help himself, but tell the truth. She thought to herself, "Way to go Lord. You are so cool. I am going to use that all the time when people are trying to lie about something to get by with it." In all of this, she was learning about God with us, Emmanuel.

Quick Work

Janiece went through many healing sessions with the healing teams at SACF, but mainly with Mike Paxton, Bonnie Braun, Jane Aguilar, and Alyce Alcock.

Jane became Janiece's mentor, too. She was always over at Jane's place and would even call her at work. Sometimes she would lay her head on Jane and just cry. She felt so much comfort. If Jane had a corrective word for her, she always asked the Lord what words He wanted her to tell Janiece so that she wouldn't get hurt in the correction. It was always about bringing healing. Janiece was always asking the Lord for a quick work. She wanted to be healed. She wanted to be fixed, to be whole.

She went through a lot of personal ministry with Papa Mike Paxton. Over a period of time he became like her papa. She called him, "Pappa Mike." He was a very safe place for her. She knew he heard the Lord, because he couldn't know the things he spoke to her without the Lord personally telling him. She got to where she could hardly wait for the next healing session to come.

Sometimes a session would last three hours and she would exclaim, "What do you mean we're done?" Then she would remember, "Oh, that's right, you guys have families." This was where she learned what the real gifts of the Holy Spirit were. Two of them would generally be in the room with her, while another would be on the outside interceding. They read her mail, (knew what she had been through because Holy Spirit told them), listened to the Spirit's leading, timing and His healing flowed over and over again, catapulting her forward in more wholeness and freedom than she had ever known. Mike Paxton likened her heart to the rose bud, closed up, yet beginning to open more and more.

She learned how important it was for others to receive from body members. Whatever gifts were flowing through these people, whether it was prophecy, words of healing, words of knowledge, words of wisdom, etc., wherever there might be error in her life, she could be brought back on course. She got to the point, when there were altar calls, she was already asking, "Okay, what do I need?" She was ready for more of His goodness. She was like a dried up sponge that took in every drop of water it could get. "I know something is wrong here, let's fix it. Wherever I am out of order, here I am Lord. Put me right. I wanted the works. I want to be whole."

When she was at home or away and the Lord showed her something that needed fixing, she would add it to her list as He would show her things. She would take that list to Mike and he would tell her to schedule a healing session for the next Saturday. Sometimes, she would get dreams concerning the body, the church, and would write them out and take them to Dennis. Most of the time, the dreams were very accurate and informative to things going on in the body that she was totally unaware of. More than anything else, she wanted to be free and whole again. It didn't matter how hard a word was for her, or who she needed to forgive, or whatever, she always pressed through on it. It was life to her and she didn't want to exist the way she had for so many years before. She had found a treasure and she was not going to let go of it. She equates times, when she would go up to individuals including me, to pray about something for her and to help her get through it, as feet washing. She said that

Jesus told the disciples they were already clean, they just needed the effects of the day to day stuff to be washed off. She said, "We wash each others feet as we help them with the things like this."

Unsound/Sound Mind

One day, she read in *2 Timothy 1:7, "God has not given us a spirit of fear, but of power, of love and of a sound mind."* **(KJV)** She was still under a guardianship at the time and at the top of that court document it read, "Janiece Elaine Turner, person of unsound mind..." When she found this scripture, she said out loud, "You have not given me a spirit of fear, but I'm still a scaredy-cat. I'm afraid of my own shadow, sounds and noises in the dark, and still cowering and cringing in fear, breathtaking, terrorizing fear." She could feel when the darkness was around her. "I can't see it, but I know you're there." It wasn't just paranoia, because when she got delivered from them, they had left. They weren't around her anymore. Now, when she felt their presence around someone else, she knew who they were. They couldn't hide from her anymore and now she could pray for others. The Lord gave her the power to overcome. "I am an overcomer now with the power to say, 'Shut up!' and they have to obey. 'Cause Father told me, 'Use your mouth and I'll take care of the rest.' Concerning that sound mind thing, I want to be whole more than anything."

"On getting a sound mind, I white-knuckled that one. That was like right in the kisser to my enemy. I found out I could smack him in the mouth every time with God's word. Jesus used the words, 'It is written!' Cool, I can do that too."

"I wanted for everybody on the planet, that they could

know Him personally, know how real and precious He is and hear His voice, comfort, hugs, to know Him this close. I want them to feel His hugs and know that He is hugging them!"

Pointing Fingers

One Saturday she went up to the church and no one was really available to minister to her because she had not set up an appointment. She went looking for one of the elders, but couldn't find any. Bonnie told her that Brent Scott was upstairs in his office. She thought for a moment and remembered that these guys seemed to know and hear God really well here. So, she walked up the stairs and went to his office. He was at his desk. He looked up and asked her, "So, what's going on?" She went in and sat down on the sofa. He seemed so far away at his desk. After a moment, he came around his desk, grabbed a chair and sat down in front of her.

Janiece began, "I am having a problem with something."

Brent listened to her and then he replied, "Well, I don't see a problem with that. You are okay with that, but there is something that you need to do."

She said, "Okay, what is it?"

He replied, "Take your finger and point it towards yourself." She did and he continued, "Now say, 'Janiece, I forgive you.'"

She immediately said, "I can't do that!"

He said, "Okay! You keep it then. Just keep on like that."

She questioned, not wanting to believe that was all, "That's it? You're not going to pray for me?"

He replied, "Nope! It's on you."

She responded, "Oh, okay. Okay!" Again, she pointed

her finger at her chest and then she said, "Janiece, I forgive you." Buckets of tears streamed down her face. It was a breakthrough for her. She could hardly believe that's all it took to break free in that area. It was like the alabaster box in the scriptures had broken open. She still uses the pointing of the finger for herself and when ministering to others. She says, "Thanks, Brent Scott!"

That was huge for her because it does break it open. You have to forgive yourself too. God's already done it and others have too. When you have asked forgiveness from others and not given it to yourself, you lock yourself into it. You have to get yourself out of jail now. That was the key that unlocked that particular issue for her.

That's My Bear

One personal ministry session that stood out from some of the others was the time Alyce gave this word to her. Alyce had a dream and it had something to do with a big, pink, stuffed bear. Janiece immediately started crying. This word broke open a period of time in her life where she had closed off.

Her brother, Bobby, was a baby at the time and Janiece was about nine and a half. She had a stuffed, pink bear and her parents made her give it to her brother.

First off, as far as she was concerned and from her perspective as a nine year old, the boy was finally born. The Turner family name will finally carry on. Her parents had three girls and her dad finally got his son. She felt like, "I lost my place as the baby of the family," which she thought was a very special place. She had been the baby of the family and suddenly, now Bobby is the baby of the family. "He's the son, yeah! The favorite one, now!" This was how she perceived this time period in her life. She felt like a throw-a-way. Her struggle was wrapped up in, "'She was too big for it. Let's give it to Bobby.' But it's mine! Y'all gave it to me." That just added to the fact in her mind at the time, that she was not important. She doesn't matter. She even had thoughts that she must have been adopted. She loved her brother dearly, and they had many fun times together over the years, but these broken places in her heart wouldn't let her get past the pain.

She used to pal around with her dad and they also played catch with the football and baseball. She just liked being everywhere he was. If he was cutting down a tree, she wanted to do it too. If he had a hammer in his hand, she wanted to know how to do it too.

This ministry time was very special because she had to forgive her dad, her brother and she had to let everything go. It was one thing to say the words, but she also prayed for them. Through these sessions, she learned how to pray for others that had once hurt her, even unknowingly. She decided that she wasn't going to just ask that they got what she just got, but that Father would give them double of the goodness she was receiving. She thought that would fix things well. "Give them double of Your forgiveness, loving kindness, mercy, hug on them, make Yourself real to them, and give them double good," is what she prayed.

Faces Of The Past

Every time Holy Spirit would bring up a face to her of someone she had hurt, she would immediately ask forgiveness. She would ask Him to make any words she had spoken, that they would come to nothing. If it was someone who had hurt her, she would forgive them and ask that He would forgive them too and bless them. "Don't hold anything against them. Instead, bring them in, heal them up, and make them Your own. Let everything be okay, and just make everything right, please."

During these first three years, a lot of faces came up before her, including the doctors, nurses, people in the previous churches and others. One time, when she was alone with the Lord, He brought to her, the remembrance of some incidents from a previous hurt by some of His people. She responded, "Yeah, but they hurt me!"

He replied, "Okay! So what are you going to do about it?"

She thought, 'I know what to do about it.' She asked, "Take me through that again."

He did and told her, "By the way, that's My bride. So anytime you got a problem with 'The Church,' just remember, that's 'My Bride' you are touching."

Janiece thought, 'This must be You, Jesus. You're talking about Your bride, not Your daughter. I'm talking to Jesus.' She said, "I'm sorry! Will You please forgive me? I forgive them. They didn't know what they were doing. Will you hug on them and love them to life, just like You did with me? I'm so sorry."

He replied, "Right or wrong, She's still My bride, not for you to touch."

She said, "Yes, Sir!" She knew she was experiencing the fear of the Lord.

She had learned Who Father was, Who Holy Spirit was, and now she was learning a little bit of who Jesus was. "I knew Him as Savior and now I wanted to know Him as my Husband. I knew Him as my Lord, as my Friend, as my Brother, but I didn't know Him as my Lover. That is what we are doing now, all these years later."

"I know Father is loving, kind and will kick you in the tail until you get right because He loves you. He will let things happen so that you will wake up and go 'Oops.' Where am I off? I want to see."

"What Joseph didn't know, before we got married is that I was always asking for a 'quick work.' I still am to this day. Even before a message I always ask, "Will you let Your word come in on good ground. Let my ground be good ground. My garden, make it ready. Let Your word take deep root on good ground in Jesus' Name. I always want His word to take deep root on good ground. I don't want to miss out. I want everything He is saying, to have good fruit and for everything to be life for me. That way I can pour life out to others."

Comfort Your Dad

There was a tremendous time of healing that took place between Janiece and her dad. It started after she had left her sister's house and went back to live with her parents. One day, they decided to watch a show together during the day. He had just recently severely injured his wrist at work, so he was staying home during the healing process. Janiece had been helping him do things during this time. Holy Spirit had been talking to her about not being rude by staying in her room so much. She spent a total of three years set apart to him in that room, except for coming out to be with the family of God. She needed to come out more and visit with her parents more. She had been in her room so much because she just wanted to hang with Him all the time. She didn't want to be in the living room because she didn't feel safe. The shows they watched were scary to her. She felt her dad wasn't always very nice. She was still afraid of him. She didn't trust him with her heart. He had a way of hurting her. One thing he used to say to her when she was younger was, "Awe, you're going to just run to your room and cry." She would cry herself to sleep after most of those moments.

When she had moved in with them, he told her, "I'm going to try not to hurt you. I am going to be more thoughtful. It's safe to talk to me."

"Yeah, well, I'll have to see that one to believe it," she thought to herself, very hesitantly, "because he's always right and that's just how it is. He is never wrong. He has never asked anybody, in my hearing, for forgiveness for anything. He has never said, 'I'm sorry.' Everybody else is always wrong."

He was hot natured physically and generally had the air conditioner set really cold while he wore shorts and a short sleeved shirt to stay comfortable. So, they sat down to watch TV and the air conditioner was on 'ice age.' She could hardly concentrate on the show because she was so cold. After a little time had passed, Janiece got up and said, "I'll be right back." She went and put on a long sleeved shirt, grabbed a blanket and came back and sat down.

He commented, "Oh my goodness! You're cold?"

She was thinking, 'You really didn't just ask me that, did you?' She answered, "Yes sir, and I don't think this one is enough."

He replied, "Oh, here you want some more blankets?" He started teasing her. "You are just always cold, aren't you?"

He just kept going on about it and teasing her. She felt the mocking and she felt pressed and pressed and pressed by it.

She was so tender. She was brand new inside. She thought, 'And you said you weren't going to do this.' So she got up, took off the blanket, went to her room and threw herself across her bed. "I tried to be with him, Father. I tried!" she exclaimed as she was lying on her bed in her warm room and throwing a tantrum. She was crying, "There he goes again. I feel like a little gnat between the hands, splat! Here, trust me! Trust me! Trust me little bug. Gottcha!" That was how she felt and she kept going on. "How long? How long, Father? How long have I got to go through this? How long? How long? He's so mean. Why is he always so mean? Why can't he just be nice for a change? How long do I have to go through this."

She was crying and crying and crying. She told me, "I finally shut up long enough that I could actually hear Him say, 'Are you through?' It was like you could have dropped a pin on the carpet and I would have heard it. It was one of those moments."

She replied, "Yes sir!"

He said, "I want you to go out there and comfort him."

She exclaimed in total shock and disbelief, "Comfort him? What do you mean comfort him? I'm the one he squashed! What do you mean comfort him?"

He continued on, "Well, you got Me. He doesn't."

She was taken by surprise, "Oh! Wow! Yes Sir!"

He said, "He's out at the garden."

She asked, "He's at the garden? What's he doing at the garden?"

He replied, "You go comfort him."

Her whole attitude had changed by now. "I ain't going alone. You go first. I can't do this. I don't have the guts to do this. You got to give me the guts to do this because I don't want to do this either, by the way. I don't want to do this. You got to protect me. Okay? Please, give me guts and protect me. You go first and prepare the way, please."

So, Janiece got up off her bed, opened the sliding glass door and started walking out to the garden and just like the Lord had told her, her dad was in the garden. With each step, she was thinking, 'I'm dead! I'm dead! I'm dead! This has got to be you or I'm dead. Oh, please, please, please! Do I have to do this?"

Her dad had his back to her and while she was still a few feet away from him, he turned around. Her whole body went into a frigid mode and she didn't know if she could take another step. He said, "Sweetheart, I'm sorry, so sorry."

It was like time stood still for her. 'Something happened,' she thought. 'Wow!' She couldn't say anything but thought, 'Okay?'

He continued on, "I don't know why I do this. I didn't mean to do it. I didn't want to do it. Will you please forgive me? My heart must just be hard."

She thought, 'He doesn't' read the bible. How could he know it?' It dawned on her then, 'Holy Spirit, You did talk to him! He couldn't know that a heart being hard is why things like that happen, so easily, so naturally. It's been closed off.'

She replied to her dad, "Yes Sir!"

He looked at her and asked, "How do I get what you have?"

She thought very slowly to herself, 'Sounds to me like you already got it.' She replied, "I don't know."

She thought, 'You already have it. Just ask for more.'

She said, "Yeah! Seems to me, Dad, you already have it. Just talk to Him more. Spend time with Him and read the Bible. Ask for more. Ask for more of Him. Just keep bugging Him until you got Him."

He opened his arms and she went and comforted him. It felt safe. That was when the hugs began again between them. She felt safer. It was now a comfortable place. That's why she hugs on him all the time now, when she can.

Chapter 10

Up To A New Level

Jane & The Shepherd's Staff

Jane shared her thoughts about Janiece, April 2011.

"I remember the first time I met Janiece," Jane began. "I was in church and was deep in prayer. It was one of those times when a deep intercession had come over me and I was praying, sobbing and just full of anguish. Then I felt this hand on my shoulder and she said, 'It's all right. God loves you.' I looked up and thought, 'What a sweet person.' She had no idea what was happening. All she saw was someone who she thought was in pain and she wanted to comfort me. It brought such a refreshing to my spirit. That was my first impression of her and I liked her right away. There were other times we would just talk through things and she reminded me of a very tender girl. She had that same vulnerability of spirit as my daughter. I was very happy to become her friend and become her surrogate mother. She felt safe with me and I would be able to comfort her in the way a mother would. It was just beautiful because I knew that was what she needed. It is so refreshing, because there is nothing about her that

---

Photos at Left: The Four Musketeers at Fiesta Texas in San Antonio. Top: Joseph, Christa Edwards, and Janiece; Bottom: Joseph, Janiece, and Greg Allen

is phony. She just accepts what the Lord gives her and sees herself free."

"Now, I've come back here after ten years of being away, and see that she's grown a lot."

"I remember when Joseph and her met and watching it. They went from being acquaintances, to friends and then they were getting closer. I was wondering when they were going to realize what was going on."

Jane continued, "Janiece didn't realize how tender she was. Sometimes, I would get a word for her, but then had to ask the Lord how to word it for her so that it wouldn't come across the wrong way. She was in a constant state of untwisting, an unraveling of the grave clothes so to speak, and deliverance became a natural part of it. With each thing that came off, the more free she became."

"The Lord did things sovereignly with her, through dreams, and also through others. She wanted a quick work and she was getting it. He was giving her the picture of the True Father. He was grooming her to be able to show others Who He is from first hand experience."

Jane was someone who Janiece felt safe with, as with her mother. She didn't have the attraction to her, that she had to some of the other women. She still had to fight this spirit of perversion for a period of time in the natural, until gradually it became less and less. Additionally, some of the perverted dreams continued way into her years of our marriage. It had been so much a part of her life and was so ingrained in her mind that it simply took time to work through it. She would wake up from the dreams asking the Lord to continually wash it from her mind. Gradually, it became less and less.

Feminine Attraction

Once Janiece confided in Jane about a lady she was really attracted to and was dealing with serious thoughts. Jane asked her more about it. Janiece said that this person always dressed well. Jane got a revelation from the Lord.

Jane said, "I know why you are attracted to her."

Janiece asked, "Why?"

Jane replied, "Because you have trouble with accepting your own femininity. You want to be able to do the things that woman is doing, but you can't accept that, so it's being turned around in your head to be attracted to her, because that's who you want to be, or at least to be somewhat like her. But you can't accept that, because of the lie you believe about yourself. My gosh, how many other people are dealing with homosexuality, when this is really the issue. They are attracted to people they want to be more like and instead of believing there is a way to change they follow the lie and accept it."

Janiece shared that she couldn't be with any lesbians or homosexuals, because it was so embarrassing to her. In her mind she had a man's mind in a woman's body, not that she was happy being a woman in a relationship with a woman. She felt "That was just appalling, it was just wrong." She had a relationship with one lady for ten years. It was during this relationship that she decided to get some counsel from her doctor, to proceed down the path to getting a sex change.

The deliverance from the spirit of perversion had happened over such a long period of time and had been so sovereign, that she doesn't know exactly when it happened. She just changed. She went through a lot of inner healing over the years with the healing teams at church. She kept coming back for more, because she wanted to do whatever it took to be totally healed and set free.

A couple of months after Jane and Janiece had this conversation, Janiece remembered her mother telling her the same thing, almost word for word. Janiece, as an early teen, was infatuated with a girl she knew at school. She had typed out a page for her journal that told the whole story and forgot to take it out of the typewriter. Her mother found it and her parents confronted her with it. Her mother ended up telling her, "You are not in love with this girl, rather you look up to her and admire her."

The Cop & The Nun

Janiece told the story of her and a traffic officer. She was traveling down the road on her way home one day, when she saw an officer on the other side of the road, parked facing the opposite direction. She was speeding at the time and promptly pulled over to the shoulder of the roadway and stopped.

She must have really been a sight to see. She was wearing a sleeveless T-shirt, that had an image of the "Fists of Steel," had a boy's haircut, an earring that had a skull and an upside down cross, and had a marijuana leaf tatoo on her left shoulder.

The officer saw her stop, so he did a U-turn and parked behind her. He asked her why she pulled over. She told him that she was speeding and wanted to save him the trouble of catching up to her. As he was writing, he was asking her the questions on the ticket. He asked her what her occupation was and she answered "None!" After she got home, she looked at the ticket and next to "Occupation," he had the word, "Nun!"

How funny! People laugh everytime she shares the story.

All The Drama

"The first time I met Janiece I was on the stage doing a drama," said Deborah Nazemi Lewis. "I went up to her and asked her if she wanted to be a part of the drama team. She told me 'No way!'"

"My heart really went out to her and I wanted to find a way to draw her close to the people who could help her," Deborah continued. "It was really slick how it all worked out. The Lord arranged everything. She agreed to be a part of a drama."

The drama had to do with Jesus going to the cross and Janiece had been doing a lot of word studies. She happened to be doing one on the word 'scourged' at the time. Jesus was scourged or beaten. She had looked it up in one of the Bible dictionaries and saw a picture of the Cat Of Nine Tails. She thought she would just draw it and give the drawing and the short write up on it to Deborah. She thought that's how she could be a part of it without having to do anything else. She took it to Deborah and told her that she wasn't staying, but just wanted to drop it off. She was so nervous. Deborah convinced her to stay a while.

Janiece gave her the drawing and told her about it and how they fashioned the whip and used it.

Deborah listened and then told her they were going to go into the sanctuary to pray and convinced her to come with them. They asked for prayer requests and finally Janiece told them the story about the guy who installed carpet in her house and was not honorable to do everything he had told her he would do. So Deborah started praying and asked the Lord to have him speak out of his own mouth, in front of her and her dad exactly what he had promised to do. Later on, when they met with the guy, he did exactly that. It was like he wanted to shut his mouth but couldn't, so he ended up doing that which he had promised in the first place. She got to share the story of prayer with her dad, and he got to witness it first hand. Also, she got to bring a praise report from answered prayer to the next drama practice.

Deborah kept coaxing her gently and gradually she came around. She tried to pick a role for Janiece that would draw something out of her that was in her heart or even the opposite.

One time Deborah convinced her to play the part of a demon. Janiece was like, "I'm just coming out of all this stuff. I don't want to play a demon. No way! I can't do that! I don't want anything to get on me just because I was acting a part in a play."

She did agree to play the part and Dennis told her afterwards that she was the best demon he had seen played. That scared her some.

Deborah had told her that playing the role of the enemy also helps us to see his schemes. Janiece thought she was just snowing her to get her to play the part, because no one else would do it.

In one drama she even played the part of a demon getting cast out of someone. She had prayed to do the part effectively and she did. She took a dive right off of the stage and it looked really real. The fear of acting these parts had left her and she gained a new boldness.

Bringing Conviction

"Janiece used to come over to our house a lot," said Deborah Lewis. "She was always so pure in her faith and so hungry for God and taking Him at His Word for every step. It was so much so, that every single time she came over, I was convicted about something, just by her being there. I had been a Christian for twenty something years then and she was coming in here all pure and awesome. She draws love out of people because of the pureness in her."

"There are some people who are real needy and they never change. They always want someone to pat them on the back and say 'You're okay! You're okay!' and they come back the next day for more," said Deborah. "She wasn't that way. She wanted to change, to be healed and to be whole."

Terry Lewis recalled, "The thing I remember most about Janiece, is that it reminded me when Jesus said, 'This is the way the Kingdom of God is, child-like faith. Just look at these children.' That is exactly how she was. She was so without guile. If it was in God's Word and she got one of us to talk about it, it was a done deal. She was going to run with it. She might even fall down, but she would get right back up and do it again, just like a child."

"She was one of those, that a spiritual mother or pastor just loves to be around. She was so hungry. She would grab the Word, eat it, and then just go and tell somebody else," said Deborah. "And then she would change! She was constantly changing and growing. It was really such a joy, to not only watch, but to be a part of it."

"I remember going over to Deborah's home," Janiece began. "Sometimes, she would pull out the harpsichord and I would just sit there. I would start bawling and bawling, just taking Jesus in. Those were good times."

She continued, "I'd call Jane up and ask her if I could come over after she got off work and she would say, 'Okay, pick up some noodles or something.' I would drive from Boerne all the way into San Antonio just to have dinner. It always turned into personal ministry whether I was at Jane's or Terry & Deborah's home. I was always just wanting to grow. I had this phrase I would always use, 'Eat crow and grow!' Where am I off so we can cut this off and I can grow some more because it hurts so good. I just wanted it over with, so I could move on from wherever I was at the time. It was and still is such a joy to be alive. It was and still is great to be a part of, not apart from. I was always apart from the body of Christ for so many years. Then it was, 'They like me.' My next thought was, 'What do they want?' And it was like, 'But yeah! If you knew me, you wouldn't like me.' Love broke through, though. They loved me to life."

"This is my passion, to say God is on the planet. He really is real and He cares about the littlest things!" exclaimed Janiece passionately.

Jane Help

While Janiece was still at her parent's house, it had gotten to the point where she would put a sign on her door to let them know if she was in prayer, praise and worship, or doing something else, so as not to be bothered unless it was important. Her room became her sanctuary. She didn't even want to come out of it to eat. The Lord kept revealing things to her during these special times with Him.

There were times, however, when she had to call Jane

from inside of her room, sometimes even after midnight. One time she called and told her, "Jane! Jane! What do I do? I'm so scared!"

Jane answered, "What are you talking about?" She had just been awakened out of her sleep.

Janiece replied, "There's something in here! I heard it come down the hallway and now it is in the bedroom next to me. Mother and Dad are asleep! I feel so much, so much fear! It's big! It's real big!"

Jane replied, "Calm down! Calm down!"

Janiece kept going, "I can hardly breathe. It's so big. What do I do? What do I do?"

Jane demanded, "Hush, so I can hear!"

"Ok! Yes, Ma'am!" Janiece said as she started to calm down a bit.

Jane directed, "Father says to sing Him a love song."

Janiece questioned, "Sing Him a love song? What love song does He want?"

"I don't know. He said sing Him a love song," Jane replied.

"Do you know any love songs?" asked Janiece.

"He just said sing Him a love song," Jane repeated.

"Okay! Okay!" replied Janiece, calming down some more.

Jane continued, "I'm going to go back to sleep. You go on and do as you're told."

Janiece replied, "Yes, Ma'am!"

After Janiece hung up the phone she thought, 'I got nothing. I hardly even know the church songs. What love song is there? I don't know any love songs. I don't even have a tune in my head, not even tunes I grew up with.' She closed her eyes real tight and asked, "Holy Spirit help me? You're my Helper. Help me please with a song?"

He gave her His own song for her to sing back to Him. Here is the song.

"Father! Oh Father! Oh Father I love You! Father! Oh Father! Oh how I love You! What father would leave his daughter alone? No father would! Oh no! Father! Oh Father! Oh Father, I love You! Father! Oh Father! Oh how I love You!"

She sang this around and around to Him. Before too long she wasn't only just crying because of His loving presence but she was now totally relaxed. There was nothing around her now except Him. She turned the light off and drifted off to sleep.

Again, Jane Help

There was another time she called Jane in the night. "Jane, there is something in the house again and Mother and Dad are asleep. It went down the hallway again and it's in the bedroom next to mine."

Jane was awakened again out of a sleep, "Hold on a minute. Let me ask Him what He's doing and what He wants this time."

Janiece said quietly, "Okay!" There was silence on the other end of the phone. "Jane! You there?" She paused and it was still quiet. "Jane! You there?"

Jane went, "Shhhh! He wants you to speak to it."

Fearfully, Janiece was thinking out loud, "He wants me to speak to it?"

Jane replied, "That's all I heard. Speak to it."

Janiece was trying to get it together, "Okay, what's He

wanting me to speak to it?"

Jane again replied, "He didn't tell me. He wants you to speak to it."

Janiece sheepishly responds, "Yes ma'am!"

Jane continues, "I'm going to sleep. I'll talk to you tomorrow."

Janiece says, "Okay! Okay!"

Janiece got off the phone and was really scared, "Help!" she said quickly to the Lord. She closed her eyes again as her whole body was shaking in fear. "I'll just back into You. Okay! What do you have for me?"

Immediately the Lord responded, "Tell it, it has no rights."

Janiece spoke towards the room next door, "You got no rights! Be bound and get out of here in Jesus' name. Be bound and get out of here in Jesus' name!" She looked back towards the Lord, "Thank You! Thank You! Can I have some of Your peace?"

He responded, "Of course!"

The entity, the presence, was gone. It had left. She learned that the same things don't always work all the time and in every situation. She asked Him, "So I always have to ask You what You're doing?"

He replied, "Well, yes! That is a good rule of thumb."

Janiece continued on, "Okay! You're not always the same, but You're the same yesterday, today, and forever."

He said, "Yeah! Just ask Me."

She said, "I can't hardly think though when this stuff happens. You know, I just freak out and ask for help."

He chuckled and said, "Yeah!"

Much Afraid

One time Christine Davis gave Janiece a ride home to her parent's house after a meeting. Janiece asked her to come inside the house and tell her what she sensed. Janiece was wanting some confirmation of some things she had felt in the house. Christine could tell where Janiece's room was. She could sense there was a lot of prayer in that room. She felt it was really rough in the rest of the house.

Usually when Janiece got home late from either a church function or a get together, she would be afraid of going into the dark house by herself when her parents were already sleeping. Sometimes, she would go to turn on the light switch and Holy Spirit would tell her, "Don't be afraid!"

She would reply, "Okay! Now I'm afraid!" After a period of time of this happening often, she finally asked, "So how come You are always telling me 'Don't be afraid!'?"

He answered, "Because you are so afraid. You're scared."

"Oh! Yeah! That makes sense." She replied thoughtfully. "So, what's coming? What changes are going to happen?"

She finally got to where, before she would enter the house, she would say, "I'm clothed in Christ. I've got the armor of God on me and I'm just hiding in You. As I walk through the place everything just bounces off. It can't touch You, so it can't touch me. Where ever I go, there's a bright shining light. Whether I see it or not, there is light, lots of light. You are a wall of fire around me. You are so bright that You blind your enemies as you come through." She would force herself to go into every room of the house and dance in the Holy Spirit. She would say, "You've given me this place and every place my feet go is the nation of God. So here comes the nation of God. Look out all you other nations, be gone." She knew, that if He didn't protect her, she wasn't going to survive. This is how she was able to live in the house during this time until changes began to happen with her parents. Eventually, the whole atmosphere in the house changed.

Janiece is still hidden in Him. "I am still clothed in Christ. He's the only safe place to be, so if I come across as a little kid I don't care, I got the goods. I know how to hide in Him, because when I hide in Him, I can step out in everything. 'Cause I ain't going alone."

How Big, Father

One night, after her parents had already gone to bed, Janiece was propped up in her bed with her back against the wall. She had her arms lifted up and was just loving on the Lord. She asked Him in that inquisitive, child-like manner of hers, "How big is Your Kingdom anyway? Can I see? I want to see. How big is Your Kingdom? How vast is it? What does it look like?"

All of a sudden, it was like space was all around her, like on Star Trek. It took her breath away. It was such a shock that it was like the breath had been sucked out of her. "Oh, my gosh! There's no end!" She exclaimed fearfully. The next thing she knows, she is in a cave. She sees this big stone-like chair off to her right. An arm comes around her and she is aware that Father has His arm around her. He said, "Walk with Me." They walked away from the chair as He still had His arm around her. He asked her, "What do you see?"

She said, "The mouth of the cave."

"Well, what do you see?" He asked again.

"Well, it looks like space out there, a bunch of stars and black," she continued.

He goes, "Now, what do you see?"

She answered laughing, "I see a really big eyeball."

He soothingly replied, "See, I am ever with you. I am always watching. I am always with you. You have to go back now."

"I don't want to go back. It's nice here with You. I don't want to go back," she said as the tears fell from her eyes.

"You have to go back," He gently repeated. "You got to go back. You can't stay here, but I'll always be watching and I'll always be with you."

Lady Of The House

In her early days, Janiece would to go to the Lady's Prayer meetings when the church was on West Golden Lane. It was called San Antonio Christian Fellowship at that time, and later, the name was changed to City Church and is presently Oasis International Christian Center.

They would start out talking about the Bible for a while and then start praying. Christine Davis always remembers, "Janiece always had a million and one questions. She would also critique people when they prayed. She had questions like: 'Why would they pray that? Why are they saying that?' She wanted to know. I would stop the prayer and then we would talk. It was like she was trying to put together the mechanics of prayer. 'Why this? Why that? How does that work and fit? When this happens, why are you praying that?' She was so bold because she didn't really care about how she looked, she just wanted to know and to learn. Sometimes we would sit and talk for up to an hour after the prayer time and she would ask questions."

Hannah Davis Uribe recalled, "For a new Christian, she

really wanted to know and understand this new life she had been given and it was really neat watching her."

"She wouldn't take anything for face value," Christine went on. It was like, "No, that's not good enough. Tell me! I need to know and understand." Then we would explain what had happened.

"She was very sincere and had to know the truth," interjected Hannah.

"We did that every week for maybe a year," Christine continued her story.

"When Janiece had come in, she had all the effects of what she had gone through in her past. We watched, over time, as the effects were slowly washed away," said Christine. "The more she continued in her new walk, the more her countenance was changing. She went from being tormented, to being filled with joy. She had hope. It was like she was determined to hold on to this for her very life. She was not going to let go."

Christine went over to Janiece's house a few times and they would sit and talk with her mother at the kitchen table. Christine and Gin really got on well.

"I had to know that God was really real and I found out right away through asthma," Janiece said. "When it gets cut off from me in the middle of the night, with no one else around, simply by His Name, there is something to this. I have to find out Who He is and what He is all about."

"I remember how hungry you were and never accepting 'no' for an answer," Christine continued. "You were very forthright in what you thought. It was so encouraging to me, to see someone that hungry. It was so encouraging to others too, to see someone come out of that environment and be so inundated and on fire to know the truth, on a search for truth and not settling for second best. 'I have to know for myself. I'll listen to what you say, but I'll process it through the truth.'"

Which One?

Anything that Dennis taught on Janiece took it and ate it like a scroll like the prophets did in the Old Testament. That was her sustenance. She remembers one story in particular. "Dennis had been preaching on Elijah and Elisha and their anointings with Elisha having the double portion. At the end of the message he asked everyone to stand. She said, "I got up, walked to the aisle, then started walking up to him to ask him a question. As I got near, he covered the mic and whispered, 'Not now.' He had the lapel microphone on and it was being recorded. I asked him, 'Which one do I want, the Elijah or Elisha?' He whispered, 'You want the second one.' I whispered back, 'Okay, okay!' and returned to my seat." She was totally oblivious to the fact that she had interrupted the message.

Where's The Teacher?

Another time, after the service, Janiece was just spending some quiet time with the Lord up by the altar. All of a sudden, she just knew she was supposed to go find the teacher. Everyone was at the back of the church by then, having coffee and refreshments. She went running to the back and over to Dennis. "So, Dennis, are you the teacher?" she asked. "I'm supposed to find the teacher."

Dennis said quickly, "No, I'm not the teacher! You need

to go back and pray some more."

She responded hesitantly, "Yes Sir." She went back to the front of the sanctuary and prayed some more. "So, who's the teacher?"

She heard, "Holy Spirit!"

She thought, 'Oh! I knew that, gosh.' So she got up and went running all the way back to Dennis. As he saw her, she could see he was hesitant to hear what was coming next. She went up to him excitedly and said, "It's Holy Spirit. He's my teacher."

Dennis exhaled in relief, "Yeah!"

As far as Janiece had been concerned, Dennis was her teacher. She was getting so much from him. She purchased every message on cassette tape and then took it home and listened to them, some over and over again, even while she was driving, until she got it.

Sometimes she would say, "Holy Spirit, I don't get it. Will You teach me what this means? I don't get what this means. It's like a whole different language to me. What does this mean anyway?" He would give her revelation on it.

There were times she would tell Him, "Wow! I can't keep up with You when You're teaching. You're too fast. I can't write fast enough. I can't even think as fast as You think. Can You slow it down a bit, please?" Sometimes she would feel Holy Spirit bubbling up inside of her and wondered, "How do you keep a lid on this? It feels like an explosion is fixing to happen inside, like a geyser. How do you keep an order when you feel like something is going to pop a top. You can't help but talk and it comes out and you're thinking, 'Wow! That was huge. That was God! That was a God thing.'" She found out later that was called a prophetic word. This happened in her early walk and then later it changed to her needing to rely more on faith to step out. He would give her a word or a few and then she would have to speak out in faith and then He would continue to give her the rest. It was easier for her to share when she felt it. It was much harder when she didn't and felt like she was sticking her neck out there for someone to cut it off.

Chains Unbreakable

She had a lot of dreams during these times, that were very vivid. Some of these dreams had to do with things happening in the church body in areas where she had no knowledge. It brought confirmation to the elders.

Sometimes she would see words and visions. One of the visions she saw was that Jesus' Name was like chains unbreakable. She saw these monster chains around a big demon once and the Lord told her, "This is My Word. It is like chains unbreakable. That's what the Name of Jesus does." Later, she found it in the scriptures. She was so excited to find out that what she saw in a vision, also lined up with scripture. She would tell the Lord, "See, I know it's You, now!"

Feminine Overlay

Once, the single's group went out to a restaurant, Souper Salad, after church. While she was there, during this particular time, the others around her were cutting up a bit and laughing. She drew into herself and was meditating on the morning's message and was just spending some time with the Lord. As she was talking to Him about some things,

He told her, "Look over there!"

Janiece replied, "Okay! What do I see?"

The Lord continued, "Now! Look again!"

Janiece was somewhat taken, "Oh, now that's weird. What's that about?"

The Lord replied, "Well, what do you see?"

Janiece said, "Well, I see a guy that looks gay, you know, homosexual. He's real feminine looking."

The Lord responded, "Now, what do you see?"

Janiece answered, "Wow! What a good looking guy! He has these really sharp, chiseled features and eyebrows. He looks real manly and handsome. Okay?"

The Lord continued on, "Look again!" Janiece looked again and He said, "What do you see, now?"

Janiece replied, "Okay! Now I see, kind of like a transparency of femininity covering up the masculinity that's really there? Is that what I see?"

He said, "Yeah! Kind of like a transparency! That is what a spirit of perversion looks like. That is what it does to a person that's normal without it."

Janiece said, "Wow! Okay, that's an eye opener. I didn't know it was like that."

Almost every Sunday after a meeting, a group of people would get together either at a restaurant or would bring food over to someone's house and they would eat together. Usually Deborah and Terry Lewis were there too, and in the midst of the group milling around and doing their own thing, Janiece would go up to Deborah and start asking her questions about the service. Sometimes Deborah would pull her harpsichord out and sing Janiece a song. Janiece

SENTENCED TO DEATH, DESTINED FOR LIFE

would sit on the floor, lean against her and let the music and healing flow into her heart. She received so much healing this way, too.

Stammering Away

One really neat thing the Lord did for Janiece was in changing her ability to read. She used to be so nervous, when called on to read out loud in school that she would stammer through the whole thing. She would be embarrassed. Her body would get hot, and she would be teased about it. It also happened when she was alone and would read out loud. During this time of walking with the Lord, the stammering went away. She said, "He just took it away. Being so much more in His peace, the nervousness isn't there."

Photographic Memory

While on Evers Road, City Church had a School of Ministry. Janiece enrolled in it because she was so hungry to know more about the scriptures, church history and the Lord's Kingdom. She had not counted on having to take tests, especially after all of the years of being out of school. She had very poor comprehension problems and that had been a big part of her problems when she was in school.

Rick Turner was teaching one of her classes and one day he announced that they were going to have a test. All of a sudden she got all nervous. She didn't do well with tests. She talked to him about it and he reassured her that it was not going to be a problem. She had taken excellent notes according to the outline he had given them.

That evening she went home to study. She prayed

and searched through the scriptures to desperately find something that was going to help her. Then she remembered in the Bible it said, "We have the mind of Christ, and that He knows everything." She asked the Lord, "Since I have the mind of Christ now and You know everything, will you remember it to me." Rick had told her that everything was in the notes and that if she could remember them she would be okay. So she asked Holy Spirit to help her see her notes. To her amazement, as she was taking her test she was able to see her notes in her mind. The Lord gave her a photographic memory. Sometimes I wish she didn't remember things so well. It can get annoying, but it is great most of the time.

Tell My People I Love Them!

One night, when Janiece was asleep, she heard these words, "Janiece!"

She responded half asleep, "Not now, Lord. Not now." It was so good for her to be able to sleep at night. She used to have to take medications to sleep and now she was sleeping great at night and it was so precious to her.

His voice spoke again, "Janiece!"

She begged, "Oh, please! Not now, please! This sleep just feels so good."

The Lord spoke again more urgently, "Janiece!"

She responded quickly, "Yes Sir? I'm sorry. Did you want something?"

The Lord said, "Yes!"

It finally dawned on her what he had said. "You called me Janiece." She had gone by the name, JJ, before that. With the sex change, she was going to change her name to Jonathan Jay. Those around her were already calling her JJ or Jay. The

Lord had just called her Janiece. She said, "You know, it sounds real pretty coming from you. I'm taking my name back, Janiece. Okay! Janiece it is!" She paused for a bit and then continued on, "What did you want?"

The Lord replied, "Tell My people I love them!"

She grinned and chuckled, "Aw, they know that."

He responded matter of factly, "No! They don't!"

She said, "How can they not know? They're Your people! You know — They're Christians!"

He said, "To whoever I say, tell them, 'God said to tell you He loves you!'"

She said, "They are not going to listen to me! They're all big. They all know. They're not going to listen to me!"

He said, "Don't you worry about that. You just do what I tell you to do and I'll take care of the rest. By the time you've turned around and walked off, they're going to know it's Me that said it. It's not up to you to carry out the word. It's up to Me." Later, Janiece found the scripture, *"So shall my word be that goeth forth out of my mouth: it shall not return unto me void, but it shall accomplish that which I please, and it shall prosper in the thing whereto I sent it." (Isaiah 55:11 KJV)*

She said, "Yes, sir! I'll do that." This was her first mandate from the Lord.

Mouthpiece - A What?

Some time later on, He told her, "You are going to be My mouthpiece!"

She responded, "Oh cool!" Then she questioned, "What's a mouthpiece?" She didn't find the meaning of that word for several years.

One time she was at Dennis' home group. She felt special, because she got to be over at his home and yet, she also felt so out of place and like she didn't belong. She always felt like she didn't belong, especially with the big boys. She had such a level of respect and a fear of the Lord for leaders and still does.

During this particular meeting, everyone was sitting in a circle on chairs. Going around the circle, Dennis asked each one individually to tell what they thought they were called to do. One by one they answered until it was Janiece's turn. As she was called on, she felt like a 'deer in the headlights,' like a 'basket case' and felt she had nothing. After a moment she responded, "God's mouthpiece." She didn't say it very loud and Dennis asked her if she said, "preacher." She said really quick, "I didn't say preacher. I did not say preacher. I said God's mouthpiece."

Dennis said, "Okay," and moved on.

She didn't know at the time the two terms meant basically the same thing.

Photos Above: Top: Janiece & Joseph at the Turner family gathering in July 1994 as they announced their engagement; Bottom: Janiece & Joseph as they announced their engagement to his mom, Lily Richter

Chapter 11

Special Friendship
(Joseph)

Sound Boards

Sometime in early 1992, while I was working the sound at SACF, Dennis made an announcement for me, that we needed some help in the sound booth. I was the only one working it at the time, and had been for a very long time. (Sounds like Elijah, huh? "I'm the only one.") Seriously though, I was at a point when I did need help running the sound and it had been impossible to get anyone to help. If you made a mistake everyone knew it, believe me, so it was one of those 'someone else can do it' areas of ministry. This particular time, however, Janiece answered the call. Interestingly, Jim Autry, the same guy who had prayed for Janiece in the hospital, had asked me to take over as he had been doing it by himself for a long time.

After the meeting she came back to the booth and asked me if she could help. She said she had been an electrician, so she thought this was something she would be able to do. I agreed to train her and this started a new journey for both of us. Later on, she would refer to me as her sounding board. Really funny, considering the fact that we worked on the sound boards, making sure that everyone could hear during the meetings.

I didn't really know Janiece well at this point. I had seen her walk into the church months before and knew she had been through a lot. Several years before, I ministered with a group called Exodus SA in San Antonio. I had been the leader of a half-way house, where we helped bring teenagers out of the occult. In my time with them, I had seen many deliverances, demonic manifestations, and angels as well as many healings. I was a quite familiar with mental problems, as I had seen this in some of the kids. I was not eager at all to get back into that realm.

Our friendship began almost immediately and so did the ministry. I think the biggest part of it was just being a friend. She would talk about what she was going through and we would pray and just continue walking on. In fact, she ended up telling me about everything...really everything. The Lord's love, grace, and mercy are never ending. When we confess something and repent, He simply pours out His grace abundantly to overcome any situation and bring healing. I marveled at the rate she was growing in the Lord. It was like she had been this dried up sponge and was being saturated in the water of His love and His word. I had never seen anyone this hungry or willing to do whatever it took, to not only be free, but also to be made whole. She was always asking Him for a quick work.

She was so afraid of almost everything. However, if someone got in her face about something and she felt cornered, that was another story. She was a survivor, in spite of herself, on some occasions. She had a desire to know how every knob on the sound boards worked. What was its purpose and how did it connect to the microphones and instruments on the platform? If she could understand it, then she got it. If she was going to do something she was determined to put forth the effort to do it right. To some degree mixing the sound and tweaking it was very similar to the adjustments the Lord was doing in her life. I saw this fragile, young lady start to blossom into this beautiful, strong person through this time. Little was I to know, the Lord had bigger plans for the two of us.

Over the course of several months or so, she progressed to where she could operate it all by herself. She reminded me of what Jesus talked about in the Gospels. *Matthew 18:3, "And He said: 'Truly I tell you, unless you change and become like little children, you will never enter the kingdom of heaven.'"* (NIV)

On Her Own

In the fall of 1992, I contracted to do a job in Montrose, Colorado. I told Janiece I'd be gone for a short while and then I'd be back. She was not happy at all. Her comfort zone was leaving and she would be all alone with this complicated sound system. It was another time to grow. Even though the job didn't work out as planned it opened up a season for me to live in Colorado for a few months that next spring so that I could get away and seek the Lord.

During my second trip to Colorado, Janiece felt like I had abandoned her. I had trained her and now I was leaving her all alone to deal with the upcoming change of events. The church had moved out of the building on West Golden and began to meet in hotels again. Janiece was having to set up the sound before each meeting and tear it down after each meeting. The only person who helped her during this time was John Lightfoot. He would take part of the equipment home with him in his truck and she would take the other part with her in her 'little white chariot,' as her mother called it. It was her white Ford Escort. She went from being a trainee, to becoming totally involved in every aspect of the sound. It was her domain. She was in charge. The Lord was stretching her and training her through all of the stress that came with it. When everything is working perfect with the sound no one notices, but let there be a hint of feedback and it is incredible how some people's faces change from being very loving to angry and upset. It was like, 'How could you let that happen?' Loud sounds disturb most people immediately. It is a natural reaction, but she was having to deal with it and let Him cover her with His grace.

This second trip became the foundation of "Destiny Path Of Life," a revelation of a path for me to walk, the first book I would write, and an art print He would illustrate to me. At one point, I actually thought I was going there to live, but the Lord had something else in mind and would send me back in one of the most peculiar vehicles, an AMC Pacer. It didn't make the whole trip before breaking down. That was a story in itself and for another time.

Christ Being Formed

During this time, she felt like she wasn't perfect enough for some of the worship team. If you have ever worked with musicians and singers, you know that some of them carry a chip on their shoulders, you know the ones who have 'finally arrived', the 'kings and queens' so to speak.

She was so grateful for those who were understanding and humble. John Lightfoot, Greg and Kathy Marshall and Tammy Zimmerman helped her tremendously during this time.

One day, she determined she had enough. She figured she had been squeezed 'about as much as this grape could be squeezed, stomped on and pulverized.' She had already been thinking about leaving the sound altogether. One person had agreed to help her, but he would show up late after everything was already done. He would tell her he was sorry every time, but would continue to come in late. So, this particular day, while she was in the sound booth, Dennis happened to walk by the open window in front of her and simply said, "So! Christ being formed in you, huh?" and continued walking on. Immediately she thought, 'I ain't done yet! Father, if that is what You're doing, I want more of the Christ being formed inside of me, so grace to me. Help me, because I'm about ready to pop my cork here. Christ being formed inside of me, huh? I want more of that. I want more of Christ being formed inside of me. Evidently He's not done yet.'

The sound system has its own way of forming a servant of the Lord. It's almost as if the person is never seen unless something goes wrong. They are there to support those who are seen and help lift them up. It is a humbling place to be and it will help develop character in those willing to journey down its path. A well-mixed sound has a wide range of volume capability before it becomes noise, while a badly mixed sound is immediately noise, no matter what the volume threshold is.

Queensize?

At one point, while Janiece was still at her parent's home, she opened a Sam's club magazine. In it was an RV motorhome. As she looked at it, Holy Spirit told her to ask Him for it. So, she did. Then, she saw it had a queen size bed in the bedroom. She questioned, "Why do I need that? I sleep alone. Why do I need a queen size bed?" Then she left it alone and continued on. Later it would be brought back to her remembrance.

The Wall

At the beginning of one meeting, Janiece was in the sound booth, when this big man walked up and stood directly in front of the window with his back to her. She couldn't see anything, because his body took up most of the open area. She said to him laughingly, "Somebody want to move this wall? I can't see."

He turned around and she introduced herself, "Hi! I'm Janiece. Who are you?"

He introduced himself, with a smile on his face, "I'm Stephen Bundra."

She told him that she ran the sound back there.

He replied, "Oh, that's a joy."

She said, "Oh, well, it's got its moments."

Lifeline Of Sanity

I moved to San Antonio and became a part of San Antonio Christian Fellowship in May 1991. I stayed with my uncle for a while and ended up working for him, restoring antique autos. I had been divorced once, and was in the middle of a separation in my second marriage. I had two daughters, Desiree and Krystal by my first marriage and one daughter, Lauren, by this second one. Divorce was never acceptable in my sight, but there had been nothing I could do to prevent it. I tried my best, but in the end I realized that it only takes one person to end a marriage. I was crushed during the first divorce and by this time, I was totally devastated and my heart was ripped to shreds. I was so broken and torn that I wasn't sure about anything anymore. The foundations in my life that could be broken were. I knew the Lord loved me and was so real to me, but in my eyes I was a total failure. How could I be losing everything again? Am I really that bad? I was at my worst the day I entered the doors of SACF.

A short while later I began to be a part of the single's group, even though I felt that I didn't belong, because I was still separated from my second wife at the time. The trauma of this separation was more than I could bear. If it weren't for some of the people at SACF, I seriously don't know what I would have done. They were my lifeline. Like Janiece, they took me in, accepted me and helped me regain my life.

Well, the single's group helped me quite a bit. In all honesty, I really didn't let them too much. My shields were up and the feeling of not belonging was really strong. I felt like, "You don't understand! You can't see me where I am!" I was in a crowd of people and even among friends, yet I was all alone. Larry Larsen took me in and would let me stay at his place during the daytime on the weekdays. Many gave me words of direction, but they fell to the ground and withered, because I felt as if they didn't understand. I wanted someone to understand me. I needed someone to help me sort through the mess and make some understanding of it. Night after night I would lie in bed and just cry. My foundation was being tested. That which was not of Him simply crumbled to the ground in a terrible mess and it brought down any structures I had built on it.

Weeping Endures For A Night

When I arrived back from Colorado the second time, I continued working for my uncle, restoring and painting antique autos. I also became a part of the worship team, playing my guitar and later on, playing the baby grand piano. It was a dream come true. Janiece continued to work the sound and did an excellent job.

At one of the single's meetings Jane had me sit in a chair in the middle of the group, so that they could pray for me. A few people had already prayed for me when Jane looked over at Janiece. She was crying. Jane told her she had something for me. Janiece looked at her with disbelief and told her, "I don't have anything." Then she remembered that Jane always hears from the Lord, so obediently she came over to me. Janiece had been crying and didn't know why. She couldn't stop crying. Jane looked at her after a while and said, "The reason you are crying is because Joseph ran out of tears." Jane had her lay her hands on my back and pray for comfort.

I had almost become totally numb inside, emotionally. I didn't like it, but that is where I was emotionally. A person can only cry themselves to sleep so many times. The only thing I knew to do, was to hold on tight to the Lord. He had gotten me through everything before, and He was my only hope.

Boy, You Missed It!!!

Sometime, during this season, Adam Michael Gomez, he went by Mike, started a Spanish speaking church, at what was now City Church and was located on Evers Road. Janiece would run the sound for his group, but on one particular evening, Mike asked her to come up to the front, because this was going to be a prophetic night. He asked her to just put in a cassette tape and let it record. When she got to the front, he told her she would be first. He placed a chair out in front and had her sit down. She didn't like these kinds of things, being the center of attention, especially having to sit while she felt like everyone was converging on her. She would say, "So many people think they have a right to place their hands on someone and pray. How about they ask Father first, to see if He is giving them anything to speak. Some people are so tender, they might not be able to handle too many people around them."

She was already gun shy, expecting all these hands on her, but it ended up being only Mike and a couple of others that prayed for her. Mike said, "It's because you haven't wanted this or even asked it of Him, that Father wants to give you a husband." Janiece was thinking, 'Boy, did he miss it. He totally missed it! He doesn't even know me! Well, I heard prophets can miss it. Okay! No problem! I'll cut him some slack. Boy, this one goes on the shelf for sure, because I ain't seeing this happen.' Others started adding to what Mike said like, "You don't need to be looking for it." She's thinking, 'Oh, brother, I know you are not even listening to the Father now. I am not looking for it period! It's not happening. I don't do men and I didn't do men. I am just happy with being alive. Now that I've got a Father, He's all I need. He's mine. He's my Father. I'm just happy to be alive. I'm satisfied. I got the family of God. This is good.'

David Had Sheep - But Cattle?

Sometime in April 1994, Janiece was taking courses in the School of Ministry at City Church. Dennis was preaching on the kingdom of David during this time, so she was getting a lot of teaching. She had likened herself with the young David. She was also doing some personal studies at home on David. She was reading in Smith's reference book about how shepherds would oil the sheep's coat to keep the pests out. She thought, 'I want that. If the anointing is all over me then the enemy can't get to me and pester me that much.'

As she was thinking about the sheep she thought about the shepherds and that if she could learn what it was like to care for sheep maybe she could understand things better in the scriptures. She thought of Rod Reagan. He didn't have sheep, but he had cattle. When they were calving a lot, which was during this time, he had to be there to make sure everything went well. She wanted to talk to him right away, about possibly staying in the house on his farm and helping him with the cattle. She thought that hands on training, helping with calving, would help her understand more of the scriptures. The only problem was that Rod had gone on a ministry trip to England with Dennis and would be gone for about two weeks. She also wanted to talk to Dennis and run it by him first. She wanted to make sure that was the direction she should be going. She didn't want any Ishmael's created out of her own desires, rather than what the Lord desired for her. She really didn't want to wait because she was eager to hear what he would have to say.

Out Of Her Own Mouth

However, by the time Dennis and Rod got back from England, a whole new scenario presented itself. It was at that time, I started looking for a way to sell my car, the infamous Pacer. I had started restoring it, but it developed a crack in the exhaust manifold and had a few other problems that would not pass inspection. It was going to take too much time and money to bring it up to specs, so I went over to Janiece and asked her if she knew of anyone who might buy the car. She grew up in San Antonio, so I figured she might know of a place that bought used cars.

She immediately said, "Yeah! The southside on Military Drive and Zarzamora! That is used car lot city."

She got into her car and I followed her in the Pacer to the southside of San Antonio, to the neighborhood where she grew up. We went place to place, searching for someone to buy the car. It was a running and driving car. Someone must want it, right? No! No one wanted it. I don't think I could have even given it away for scrap metal.

After we had talked about it, in total shock that no one wanted it, she asked me a simple question. "Did you even pray about this?"

I thought for a moment and said hesitantly, "Well, no!"

She continued, "So you don't know if you are to sell it,

keep it or give it away?"

Again, I had the same answer, "No!"

So, we decided to go over to the Bill Miller Bar-B-Q parking lot to talk. When we got there, I got in the car with her, because her car was new and it had air conditioning in the hot Texas sun.

We started praying to find out what the Lord was saying in this situation. I felt impressed that I needed to give the car away. Close to the end of our praying the prayer took an unexpected turn.

I looked up at Janiece and spoke these words as they just rolled off my tongue, "I think I understand what it means in the Word, when it says, 'I love you, my sister, my bride.'"

Before Janiece could even think, and without skipping a beat, she replied, "I think I understand it too, except for, 'I love you, my brother, my husband to be.'" Then, realizing what had just come out of her mouth, in shock, she placed her hand over her mouth. She thought, 'It's already too late! It's out!' That is how the Lord continually speaks through her. It would come out of her mouth before she had a chance to analyze, scrutinize and hold it back. She had asked Him early on in her walk with Him, to use her mouth. She was getting more practice in being 'His mouthpiece.' This time it was a life changing thing.

This particular scripture reference is found in Song Of Solomon Chapter 4:9-11,
  "You have stolen my heart, my sister, my bride;
    you have stolen my heart
  with one glance of your eyes,
    with one jewel of your necklace.

10 *How delightful is your love, my sister, my bride!*
   How much more pleasing is your love than wine,
and the fragrance of your perfume
   more than any spice!
11 *Your lips drop sweetness as the honeycomb, my bride;*
   milk and honey are under your tongue." (NIV)

Janiece couldn't believe that the Lord wanted to marry her off. She felt like she had finally gotten close to Him and now He was pushing her away. She struggled with this even into the first few years of marriage. The abandonment issue really went deep.

Dennis Gets The News

Dennis and Rod finally arrived back from their ministry trip to England. We had already scheduled a meeting with Dennis as soon as he got back. During the meeting, we told him what the Lord had told us. It shocked him, but he knew that it had to be the Lord for Janiece to even begin to think that way. He made the remark, "See what happens when I go away!"

I had been thinking that we needed to get married in August of 1994. Since we got the word I just wanted to get on with things. I also felt like the Lord was moving us into ministry together.

The elders had a different plan, even though Mike Paxton and a few others already knew. They had known before we did and had been waiting for the Lord to tell us. They wanted us to wait a few more months though, just to be sure this was of the Lord. So, we decided to set the date for December 3, 1994. The way I was able to help Janiece remember the date after we were married, was to simply remember, 1-2-3-4; 12/3/94.

One thing I found interesting in all of this, was that a big move of God started at the church in 1994. It was so big, people came in from all different parts of the world to get touched. There were people rolling on the floor, laughing uncontrollably, losing their stoic composures, crying, shaking and all sorts of manifestations. The greatest thing about it all, was that they were in His presence and were being healed physically, emotionally as well as spiritually. We were married in this outpouring. What a time to be married.

I was always ready to go and do. If the Lord said to do something, I was like, "Hey, let's get it done." I didn't want to miss His lead, because of all of the pain I had already been through. There was a fear there that would sometimes drive me to go too fast. My dad had left us when I was three and I didn't see him again for twelve years. I thought I had done something wrong. Somehow, this translated over to Jesus. I didn't want Him to leave me behind or walk away. If He said something to me I was ready in a moment's notice to go with Him. It took a long time to understand His timing and I still struggle with it some today. Sometimes I think, 'Why would you tell me something, if You aren't going to do it now?' Mostly, it is to prepare us and get us ready for that which is to come. Then, when He opens the door we are ready to walk through it with Him, fully prepared to handle the situations before us. It reminds me of the story of Joseph's dream, His family and all he had to go through before the dream became a reality. (Genesis 37)

Open What?

Monday nights were prayer nights at City Church back in 1994. During prayer, Janiece would usually feel certain types of pain in her body and knew there was someone there that needed prayer for that specific thing. She would tell Rick Turner and at the end of the prayer time, they would pray for that person and the pain would leave her.

One Monday night though, was different. Earlier that morning Janiece was making her bed and just thanking the Lord for different things and before she realized it, out of her mouth came, "Father, while You are at it, will you open up my womb?" After she realized what she had just asked for, she immediately asked, "Why? Why do I need my womb opened? I don't need a womb opened. Do I need my womb opened? That's not fair."

That night at prayer she started feeling some cramping in her lower gut. It got really intense. She told Rick about it, but he didn't do anything this time. She was wondering why. Finally, he came up to her and told her that he believed it had more to do with her, than any one else. She asked him what he heard. He said he didn't know. About this time I came over with Greg Allen. One of us said that it had something to do with the female area, and the other one said it had something to do with the ovaries. We were getting these words during the prayer time and had come over to her to share the words.

It was then, Janiece told Rick what had happened earlier that morning. He said, "We are not going to pray that He stops what He is doing then."

Janiece said, "Well, okay."

Rick said, "But we will ask Him to take the pain away."

To Janiece it was a sign that the Lord did exactly what He intended, from the word He spoke through her that morning. He had heaven and earth agree through her mouth again, bypassing her brain, to open her womb. She thought He was smart and sneaky the way He did it. If He had told her to do it, she probably wouldn't have or at the very least would have had a fit about it first. After it was already done, it was over. Not much else a person can do but agree, at least if you wanted to do what He desires. He slipped a lot of things into her life this way.

Biting The Bullet

At the July Turner family gathering, we decided to announce our engagement to the rest of the family. They were videotaping each family with what was going on in their life at the time. The gathering was at Bob & Gin's home, northwest of San Antonio, close to Boerne. It was a hot day and swimsuits and the pool were definitely on the list for refreshment.

Janiece and I were just hanging out with each other as usual, only this time with the family. They sat us down in a certain place to do the interview. Janiece kept asking me if this was a good time to make the announcement and I kept telling her I didn't know. She was dealing with trepidation, butterflies in the stomach and she was starting to get hot from her nerves. Finally, Janiece said, "The Lord told us we are going to get married to each other." We didn't know what to expect next. Everyone was so glad to have Janiece back from the dead, so to speak, but they never imagined this happening with her. It took everyone by surprise. They were shocked, to say the least.

Her mother and dad didn't even question it. They knew for Janiece to even think that way it had to be the Lord. They had seen so many miracles happen in her life since she was awakened by the Lord. They never thought they would have grandchildren through Janiece. Their baby girl was being totally healed before their eyes and it touched them so deeply. They were in such awe of the Lord and His love.

David Koresh?

I asked Deborah recently, "How did you feel when you found out we were getting married?"

She responded, "Oh, that was easy. Actually, I didn't have a whole lot of thoughts about Janiece. I had more thoughts of you. Well, it was more of that you must be an incredibly patient, loving, and forgiving person. Janiece told me, 'He knows everything. I'm not going in hiding anything of my past and what I've been through.' I just kept thinking God really sent her an incredibly patient and loving man. He did. Then there's that selfish thing on my part, I just think married and having kids is the way to go. Anybody that hasn't done that, is missing out on something in life. I thought, 'Yea, she gets to really experience life.' As narrow minded as that sounds, that's kind of it in a nutshell. It's like, 'She's going to get to experience the best of life. How cool is that?' It's a God thing."

Deborah started down a different path. "Of course, when we met you, we thought, 'Okay! He looks too much like Koresh. Really, really bad. Oh yeah, 'cause your hair was really long, like David Koresh and it was during that time when all those things were happening with him. I thought, 'Okay! Now we know God sent him, but man alive, this guy looks like him."

Janiece added her input, "The thing I told Joseph before he came over, was Dad used to say, 'Before you can date him, you have to cut his hair.' I thought, 'I'm bringing a hippie home.' That was my first thought with all of the hair and beard."

Deborah added, "I had a friend, Bobby, when we were young and we had to sit on a curb to do homework, because he wouldn't cut his hair to come over to do his homework. We weren't even boyfriend/girlfriend. He was just a neighbor. We would be doing homework in the heat, on the curb, cause daddy wouldn't let us in the house because of his hair."

Janiece had some fun, "Yeah! Then this guy, that looks like a hippie! I warned him ahead of time. I said, 'I don't know how he is going to receive you so don't be surprised if it's not pretty.'"

"Always the baby girl," Deborah added with a smile.

Tell My People I Love Them!

Chapter 12

Two Become One

The Courtship

During our courtship, I would be over at Janiece's house, many times into the wee hours of the night just trying to communicate. Words that meant one thing to me, meant something totally different to her. Sometimes we would spend hours on just one word or sets of words. She was a city girl and I was a country boy. I think there was a song about that.

As we started to get more emotionally involved, we didn't want to get too close in our physical relationship before our wedding, so we would buy bags of Hershey's chocolate kisses. Every time we wanted to kiss each other, we would go and get a few of them out of the bag and give each other one. We saved our first kiss for our wedding.

California Rings

We were engaged in April 1994 and in May we decided that we wanted to go on a ministry trip with Dennis and Hardy. The only problem was that we didn't have the money to fly, so we asked them if they had any problems with us driving

Photos at Left: Top: Janiece, Desiree, Joseph & Krystal; Middle: Christa Edwards, Janiece, Joseph & Terry Lewis

out to California together, especially since we would need to share the same hotel rooms. Well, with Janiece's background, that was not a problem with anyone. They didn't have any concerns in that area whatsoever. In fact, when the Lord told Janiece that she was going to be married, she told Him, "Boy, You got a big job on Your hands now. I don't even think that way." She didn't do men. She had gone from wanting to have a sex change to being glad just to be alive and with Him. She had no desire to be with a man and was definitely not thinking about sex. Because of the miracle the Lord was doing in recreating her brain cells, in some areas she was like a child, naive. Even though she had been through some of those other scenes before they were so far removed from her that it was like it had never been. It was as if it had all been erased.

The trip took us from San Antonio, Texas to Los Angeles, then north to Fresno, Selma, Santa Clara, San Jose and back. Since they were flying, we had to cover a lot of ground on the road quickly. We ended up driving straight through to Los Angeles and then up to Selma before we even got a room where we could sleep. We took turns driving and sleeping in the car. It took about 24 hours of driving to get there. Of course, we ended up having a number of special things happen along the way. As we approached Los Angeles, we decided to go all the way to the Pacific Ocean. I-10 ended at Highway 1 and we ended up going north towards Malibu. That is an amazing highway and we kind of got caught up in the romance of it all. Finally, we had gone a ways, and we decided it was time to turn around and continue back on the journey. The place where we turned around, was Charlie Brown's, a seafood buffet restaurant. They had more choices on the buffet than we had ever seen. The restaurant was right next to the ocean, so it was a fantastic place to be, so romantic. It was one of those special memories we cherish.

Dennis was ministering in Selma, Fresno and Santa Clara on this trip and we didn't have much time to spare, so we headed north and caught up with them in Selma and then followed them by car to the other meetings. We had some extra time for the Santa Clara meeting, so we decided to go sight seeing and ended up in Los Gatos. There was a shopping center there that had numerous small shops. At one point, I needed to find a restroom, so we stepped into a jewelry store, Panache Jewelers, to ask for the nearest one. We ended up talking to the jeweler about rings for our wedding. He had developed a new process, using a type of sandblasting effect in his new designs on rings. He told us that if we could fax him a design he would be glad to make our rings for us. We ended up doing this and have some very special wedding rings that we designed ourselves. We received them in the mail from him, the day before our wedding. Talk about cutting it close. This was a very special thing for us. The design we chose included the Greek letters for the word "Adam" on each ring. Our theory behind it was that in the first Adam, woman was separated from man. In the second Adam, Jesus, we could be rejoined as one.

It was good for us to experience what it was like going into other churches and seeing the different ways Dennis ministered. We knew that one day we would also do the same. One of the churches we were in was not free to worship in dance. Dennis told us to be watchful to see where others were in their relationship with the Lord and to respect them in this way. At home we were free to dance in worship, but out of respect for them we didn't at this place during the beginning part of the service. After the worship time Dennis ministered on freedom in worship and when he finished we had another worship time where we were able to dance. It was the first time we ever saw Hardy dance. He actually moved his feet. It was great. Even though we teased him some about it he knew we were encouraging him. He is a dear friend. Our group didn't believe us at first when we told them that we saw him dance because he was so stoic at home.

The Wedding

Alyce Alcock volunteered to sew Janiece's wedding dress. It was made out of 100% brocaded material that Janiece had picked out. It was a heavy gown. Because of the injury to her right arm, Alyce had to do some special alterations to the sleeve of the gown, turning it some, so that the point of the sleeve came over the center of her right hand. That was quite a feat and Alyce was awesome and so patient with her.

On our wedding day Janiece felt as if she was being pulled in a hundred different directions at the same time. Everyone wanted something from her. She tried not to hurt anybody's feelings, because everyone seemed to be on edge emotionally. Usually it is the other way around. There wasn't too much normal about the way we did things then and it hasn't changed.

Dennis Goldsworthy-Davis was our officiating minister. My best man was Terry Lewis. Janiece's maid of honor was Christa Edwards. Desiree Hartmann, now Desiree Valdez, was our ring bearer. Pete Zimmerman and Elias Collas were our ushers. Gregg & Kathy Marshal, John Lightfoot, Deborah Nazemi Lewis, and Gloria Sandford Hansen performed and sang the songs for the wedding. Deborah Ursell and Adriel

Ickler took photos and video footage. Gregg & Kathy wrote and sang a special song for us during the ceremony.

The Honeymoon

Lake Tahoe, California

Our honeymoon trip to Lake Tahoe, ended up being an experience, to say the least. I had been through Lake Tahoe once over the years and had actually stayed there overnight on a trip to California. We decided we wanted to go there for our honeymoon, so we started looking for a honeymoon suite. We started looking through vacation brochures and publications to try and find a room. We found one that had a hot tub in the room and it was really reasonable, so we booked it for three nights. Being December, it was going to be good to have a hot tub in the room.

Prior to our wedding we purchased a 12 volt coffee maker for the car. Janiece had a brand new Ford Taurus at the time. A day or so before the wedding, we went by Sam's Club and got a few snacks and food for the trip. We got a big roll of summer sausage, some garden crackers, and a couple of cans of Cheeze Whiz, among other things. We were not thinking that much about our diet on that trip. We took turns at feeding whoever was driving at the time. One time Janiece would slice the sausage, place it on a cracker, add the cheese and then give it to me as we drove down the road and the next time it would be me feeding her. It seemed like it took us forever to get there. We just seemed more tired than normal on this trip. I enjoy driving and we had just made that trip to California back in May, in less than half the time this trip took us. But, it really didn't matter that much, we were having fun. We had praise and worship music playing along with a new CD we bought, "The Best of Bread." Mile after mile we talked, prayed, enjoyed each other's company and the countryside. We didn't have a lot of money for the honeymoon, but we did have each other and it was great. We took Christa's video camera along and filmed some of the trip. We were so glad to have that camera for all of the memories as we watch it again and again.

Everyone thought we were leaving town after the wedding, but we didn't. We were one of the last to leave the reception and even helped clean up some. We stayed overnight at the house to get rested up for the trip and left the next morning. It was quieter that way. We left San Antonio that morning and headed for El Paso, Phoenix, Los Angeles, then up to Sacramento and over the mountains to Lake Tahoe.

On one of our trips, we had the worst time going through New Mexico. We don't remember if it was this one, and think it might have been. It was really stormy weather and overcast, but there was also a strange, dark demonic presence. We could feel it close around the car as we were traveling, but we were inside in a bubble of peace. It started as we crossed the New Mexico state line from Texas and ended when we crossed into Arizona. It was so weird. It was like a presence following and watching us all the way.

As we went through different areas and towns along the trip Janiece was so sensitive to the Holy Spirit that she could sense the demonic strongholds in each area. We would pray with each other as things came up. It was good getting to know one another and when you are in such close quarters for that many hours, it was easy. Our route would take us over 1,800 miles and five days to get there.

Mirrors Everywhere

We finally arrived in Lake Tahoe about 9:00 o'clock and it was already dark. We drove over to our hotel called Secrets. Our room was a honeymoon special, but the hotel didn't really look that special at all from the outside. It was really like a motel. They even had a bottle of champagne for us at the front desk to enjoy. Janiece wasn't excited at all. In fact, we asked the manager if we could go and look at the room first. He agreed and gave us the key. Janiece freaked out when she walked into the room. There were mirrors on the ceiling above this giant king size bed and mirrors on the wall. There was also a red, heart-shaped jacuzzi for two against the back corner of the room. She made a U-turn out of the room and said, "Nope, not happening!"

I told her that I didn't know what it was going to look like. They didn't have any photos we could look at, nor even a brochure. We had already reserved the room, too.

Then she got this amazing idea, "How about we go see what else they have available in town? Can we do that?"

Here it is already dark and we are tired from the trip and she wants to go and look for a different room. I should have seen that coming, but I didn't.

So we went back to the front desk and talked to the manager. He told us that was fine with him, but that we wouldn't find anything else available. Everything was booked and that we certainly wouldn't find anything for this price.

Janiece was thinking, "All right then, if we have to, we'll be back."

Sure enough, we couldn't find anything and now it was later and colder too. Some of the places that had vacancies were out of our price range and everything else was booked.

We paid for the room, grabbed our bottle of champagne and went up to our room. We really didn't care for the champagne, but that was the tradition, so we shared it.

Getting hot water for the shower was difficult. The hot tub was not hot either. The water was warm, but then the bubbles that came through the tiny jets were cool. Janiece found out that she likes mirrors and is still waiting for the day we get our own home, so that she can have mirrors in the bedroom. It was another time of facing fears, embracing them and coming out victorious. What had been a dread turned into a lot of fun and laughter for us. We could have missed this special time and never experienced it had we found a different room. What a difference our choices make. We are looking forward to the time when we are able to go back with the money to really enjoy more of the sights and things to do.

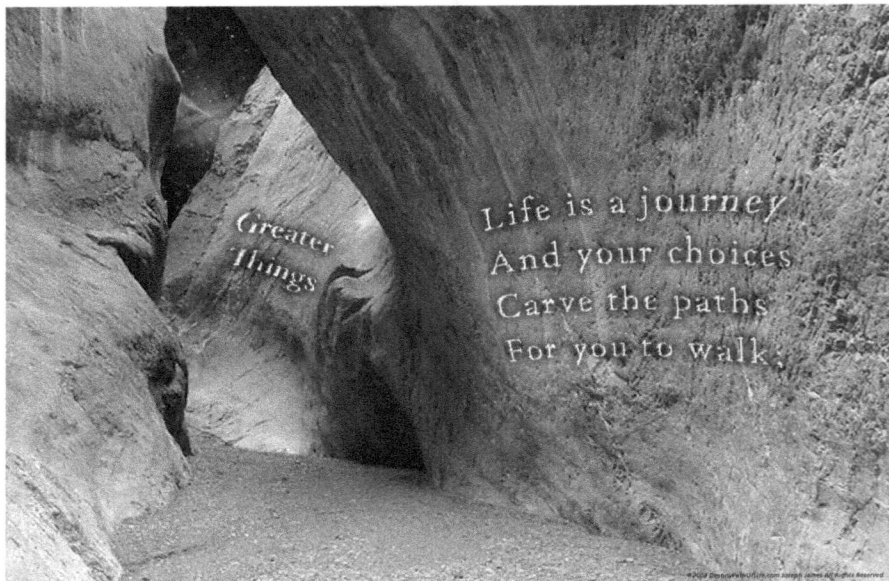

Greater Things

Life is a journey
And your choices
Carve the paths
For you to walk.

We had a lot of fun in Lake Tahoe. We didn't do the casinos, but did some window shopping and exploring around the lake. We took an awesome video of our trip around the lake. The Lord provided some amazing scenes with the clouds, the sun, the snow and the water. She didn't play fair, however. I was doing the filming with the camera and she chose these times to pick snow ball fights, like I could really do something about it.

On the north slope of the lake was the area where they filmed the Ponderosa for the old TV show "Bonanza." It was mostly covered in snow, but it was great to see. Seeing the tiny island with the English tea house on it was really neat. It was like a place secluded from the rest of the world. The lake was surrounded by the mountains and it was kept full of water mainly from the melting snow in the spring.

We were on a real tight budget for the trip, so there were a lot of things we didn't get to do. It would have been nice to go skiing and to have bought a few things during the trip to have more memories, but it was our honeymoon and it was special.

Changing Our Ways

During our courtship and into our marriage, I would open the doors for Janiece. Her thinking was that when we were friends, she opened it just fine. She would actually get upset with me, so I stopped. Later on in our marriage, this too would change, but it was hard getting back to it.

Of course, to be fair to her, was the fact that I didn't open the door for her when we were just friends. When we got the word to be married, I changed too.

We have to remain open for the Lord to daily change others. Just because someone acts or does something one way today, doesn't mean they will do or act that way tomorrow.

Photo Above: This photo of Janiece & Joseph was taken by Paul & Bunty Collins. Janiece is wearing her Aussie hat

Chapter 13

Wolves In The Midst

Danger In The Flock

After we arrived back from our honeymoon, sometime around December 18, we noticed right away that things had changed at the church. Evidently something had happened during the two weeks we were away. There was a noticeable distance between us and others, those who had been very close to us before. There seemed to be some friction between people, possibly division that wasn't there before. We don't remember any details, but that it was just different.

Janiece was like, "Where did my family go? What happened? What happened to the sweetness and the joy?"

People weren't as trusting anymore. To further verify this feeling, we were asked to return our keys to the building. Someone had broken into the tape room and erased a bunch of them, deleting masters of some of the messages. It was malicious, whatever it was. They didn't know who did it, so they ended up taking all of the keys back and changing the locks.

Janiece started experiencing the same feeling she had before she was born again. The walls went up inside of her. She felt like she wasn't trustworthy anymore and she didn't understand that. She didn't know what she did wrong. Even though she didn't do anything wrong, she had these feelings and they were overwhelming her. She had been such a big part of the group and now she was feeling like an outcast. It was hard for her to fit in. She felt as if she had no place anymore and it hurt. It didn't have anything to do with getting married, but rather it had to do with something that happened there. This was close to the end of the "Times Of Refreshing" movement of the Holy Spirit. It was so painful.

Australian Tag Team

November 5 - 11, 1995 - Paul & Bunty Collins

In November, Paul & Bunty Collins arrived in San Antonio from Australia. These two would totally impact our lives in a unique way. They were the first and only husband and wife preaching tag team we had seen. We knew we were going to minister together and they were a model we could see with our eyes. They were so full of life and they totally enjoyed each other. We were privileged to be able to be their escort around San Antonio during their stay.

Paul would be speaking for a while and then Bunty would get something. She would get so excited and motion to Paul. He would come down and sit and she would go up and continue on. Then he would get something, get so excited and she would sit down and let him continue. Sometimes she would only be up for a short while and then he started bouncing in his chair with excitement. One time she said, "I am not through yet." It was so neat. They were so adorable.

We felt privileged to take them out to the mall and the outlet malls in the surrounding area. On one of our trips through Ridgeway Colorado, we had stopped in a shop and bought Janiece an Aussie hat, similar to the Crocodile

Dundee style. She was always wearing it and when we got to North Star Mall, Paul decided he wanted to have a photo of us. So we sat in one of those instant photo booths and took two photos. He gave us one and he took the other one back with them to Australia. He had me write a short segment on her testimony which their son, David, later put on a web site from Australia. That was in 1995 and it is still there today. They were the first ministry to urge me to write the whole story and we never forgot. Even though we haven't seen them since, we write to each other occasionally. Those wonderful memories often come up in our conversations and thoughts. It is amazing how one meeting with someone can be so revolutionary to others, even years later.

Trepidation

During this time, the church moved locations to Louis Pasteur Drive in San Antonio. There were many changes, personnel changes among others. A school was also being built in the building. The worship team leadership changed too. Some leaders and people who had been loving and giving before were now watching each other out of suspicion.

It was also during this time, I was playing the baby grand piano on the worship team. We would go up there during the day and I would play the piano, she would pick on her guitar and we would worship the Lord together. There was a lot of hurt and broken hearts and finally people started leaving.

One meeting Anthony Chapman was the visiting minister from England and he prophecied over Janiece concerning the trepidation in her heart. He said that Daniel would be like John the Baptist in that, while yet in the womb, he would have the Holy Spirit. This brought confirmation to her since the Lord had already told her this.

Later, during the time of her pregnancy, and even for a while after Daniel was born, she felt like she was always under the microscope. She didn't want to come in, because she didn't feel safe anymore. Because she had been in charge of the sound and recording the tapes in the sound booth in the past, she kept feeling like others were blaming her for the destruction that had happened with the tapes. It was a very hard time for her. Sometimes I would go to church and would have to leave her at home. She would come with me occasionally to see if things had changed. She kept hoping. She remembers the timing, because she would nurse Daniel in the cry room and dance with him on her shoulders during the worship time.

Gift Of Peace

Stephen and Julie Bundra were at the conference when Anthony prophecied over Janiece. We volunteered for them to stay with us at our house during the conference. Some time later, we went to Corpus Christi where they lived and spent some time with them. We became friends during this time. They came over again from Corpus Christi and went with us to Arkansas for a conference at Paul Doherty's church, Victory Fellowship. Talk about Julie's Puerto Rican cooking, it was second to none. That was truly a gift to us and we enjoyed every bit of it. Thank you, Julie. We all stayed with Randy and Jill Wipf at their home in Little Rock, during the conference. We had a great time together. It was a reunion with Randy and Jill. They had been with City Church and had moved to Little Rock because of Randy's job.

On the way to Little Rock from San Antonio, we encountered a very severe thunderstorm and hail started coming down on the rental car we had rented for the trip. At the moment it started, the Lord had me command it to stop hailing and to speak peace to the storm. It stopped as quickly as it had started. The Lord had given us both authority over storms and we've continued to do so since. Sometimes, however, a storm is supposed to run its course and we need to be sure to listen to the Lord so that we don't end up being on the opposite end of His will. Thunderstorms are great tools of His. They regenerate the atmosphere and clean the air. They have a good purpose. He does, however, keep us safe in them.

One night, while we were at Randy's house, Stephen, Julie, Janiece and I were sitting at the dining table. Stephen was having a hard time because the Lord had given him a strong word that he was going to have to deliver at the conference, prophetically. He was trying to get his peace back because he was wanting to be sure of the right timing for the delivery. He told us he needed to get peace first, so he could hear the Lord.

Janiece immediately offered to pray for him.

He replied, "Oh, I don't know about that."

He looked over at me and asked me if she should pray for him.

Janiece got offended right away. She thought that was a new one. She had never heard that before. She thought 'Well forget it, I don't even need to be praying for you if you're that skittish. Gee whiz! I've got mistrust going on at the church and then this. Forget it! I don't want to pray for you now.'

I had responded to him, "Oh, yeah! She can pray for you, definitely."

Then he looked over at Julie and asked her, "Well, what do you think?"

Janiece was thinking, 'I can't believe he's doing this and right in front of me too. That's just plain rude. If you don't want me praying for you just say so.'

Julie said, "Oh yeah!"

By this time Janiece was back tracking. She didn't want to anymore. She was so offended, she had to take a moment to get her peace back. Once she had taken care of her attitude and Stephen agreed, she walked over behind him, as he was seated at the table, placed her hands on both of his shoulders and prayed for him.

She prayed, "Father, You've given me a bunch of peace, will You give him Your peace too and that You would just help him and make it clear." Then she kept her hands there for a bit, while she let the Lord minister through her quietly. When she felt He was through, she lifted her hands and walked back around the table. She got her peace back during this time too.

The Lord taught her early on to be still, quiet, invite Him to come, and He would give her words. That is how she would pray for anyone.

After a short time, Stephen looked up and said, "I bet you are wondering why I asked Joseph and then Julie about you praying for me."

She nodded yes.

He continued, "I've watched you. You are so tightly wound. I couldn't see peace coming from you."

Janiece was thinking, 'What's it got to do with me

anyway?' She didn't understand.

He continued on, "So while I was sitting there, the Holy Spirit corrected me."

She thought, 'Wow!' It really touched her deeply.

He kept on, "He told me, 'You should see her without My peace.'"

That was a revelation to her. She didn't know that it was always His peace that held her together.

She was to learn that vividly later on, when we lived in Dallas for five years, that it was a gift and that everything she received was a gift. She desperately needed Him, because without it, she didn't have any peace or rest or faith. She only had a little bit of hope. She said, "It is wonderful what the desert and wilderness can do for you, and to show you about what is really real." She got to find out that she was totally undone without Him, had nothing and could not function. She found out how really broken she was. When He pulled back and let her see that it was all His gift, she could see. Before, she had just run around in His glory, never even thinking about it. She was so caught up in Him. It was like a constant celebration and party. Being the miracle was different, because she couldn't see it, she was in it. She experienced His peace and wondered why others didn't have it. She wanted everyone to have it. Concerning faith, she couldn't understand why they didn't just believe. She hadn't gone through her desert yet. There was like a self-righteousness going on inside of her, because she was naive that it was all gift.

He had poured out all of His goodness on her and until He pulled back, she wasn't able to see it. She had no idea how He clothes each and every one of us.

One mature lady in the Lord, was going through some things and Janiece couldn't understand why she didn't have the faith. She was just the new kid on the block and didn't get why people just didn't believe. The Lord was protecting her while He was introducing Himself to her. She was wearing all of His clothes and attributes at the time. However, when she went through the stripping process, she understood how vulnerable she was without Him, a 'basket case' again. She was privileged to see what she was like without Him and His raiment. This process was necessary for her to get rid of the self-righteousness, pride and arrogance that had come alongside. It helped her to appreciate Him more and not have a stinking attitude. She was able to have compassion on people. It cost her everything, but she gained understanding in certain areas. She began to understand His goodness and mercy. She wants to hide in His goodness and doesn't want to stray from Him.

Commune With Me

One evening, as I was playing Ken Witt's music keyboard that we had borrowed for our meetings, and we were worshipping together in our living room, we sang the song, "Commune With Me." Here are the words to the song.

"Commune with Me, Commune with Me, Between the wings of the Cherubim, Commune with Me. I'll meet you there, I'll meet you there, Between the wings of the Cherubim, I'll meet you there."

After we finished singing in His presence, He told Janiece, "Don't worry about the finances. I'll meet you there." She said, "That's cute Father. We were just singing that." He replied, "Don't worry about the finances." She replied, "I'm not worried about the finances." When she shared it with me, I said, "Oh, that's for me." She said, "Okay! Great!" He meant that He would meet us when we needed Him, in every situation. It wouldn't be until we were there, at that place where we needed Him. He always has. It hasn't been boring, but an adventure that reminds me of a roller coaster from the heights to the depths, sometimes holding on for dear life and other times enjoying the mountain tops and the magnificent views. Over the years, He would bring this back to our remembrance over and over again to encourage us to go on.

Giant In The Land

During one evening, sometime in the beginning of our marriage, I faced a foe I hadn't seen in years. It's name was Rage and it took me totally by surprise. Janiece and I were in the kitchen talking when I said something to her. Keeping in mind that I was from the country and she was from the city, our vocabulary didn't always mean the same thing. Whatever it was I said, it caused something inside of her to react. She was standing with her back to the corner of the cabinets and counter. She had no where to run. She looked up at me with rage in her eyes and proceeded to slam her right fist down onto the counter. It was loud and the reverberations resonated through my soul. I was thinking, "Gee what did I say now?"

She was so angry and so I started asking the Lord what I needed to do in this situation, because this was not looking good at all. My mind had gone all the way back to the time I was the leader of the halfway house for Exodus San Antonio. I did not like to be in this situation, but here it was again in front of me. "Lord, I could really use Your help about now."

He said, "Speak My peace, like you've done before."

So I did, I looked into her eyes and said, "Peace, be still!"

Immediately, her head dropped down and she was no longer looking at me.

I asked the Lord again, "What do I do now?"

He said to hug her.

I was thinking, 'You've got to be kidding, she's not going to like this at all. This better be You!'

So I asked her, "Can I hug you?"

She looked at me and said in this stern, challenging voice, "If you HAVE to! If it makes you FEEL better!"

I knew that I wasn't talking to Janiece and this made it worse. I was thinking, 'Okay, now what's going to happen when I hug her. I had already patched some holes in the walls when she had gotten angry and punched through with her fist. This is my body and I really don't like pain.' The Lord told me to do it, so I knew it was up to Him to protect me, so I went over to her and hugged her. What happened next was shocking.

The spirit had lost its grip on her and she remained at peace. I prayed for her, she gave it up, asked for forgiveness, deliverance and healing to that area of her life. We prayed for her ancestors, asked forgiveness for them, cleansed the bloodline and all that good stuff. Suddenly, our attention was drawn to our back yard. The curtain to the sliding glass door was open and Alteria, her dog, was acting really strange. Janiece raised her voice and said, "Don't you be messing with my dog. No, to the dry lands you go in Jesus' Name." She remembered when Jesus had cast legion out of the man and they went into a herd of pigs. Well, this one was not

264

going to mess with her dog.

We opened the door and went outside to check on Alteria and she came up to us and we spoke 'peace' to her. It was like there was a storm had been going on because of the way she was reacting, but there wasn't. It was a still, clear night without any clouds.

It was then that Janiece heard and saw something. She looked at me and asked, "Did you hear that?"

I smiled and said, "Yeah!"

She replied, "Well, you couldn't have heard what I heard. What did you hear?"

I said really joyously, "I heard the cooing of the dove."

She was thinking, 'At night?'

She exclaimed, "That is not what I heard! What I heard and what I saw on that fence line over there was like black in black, with huge black wings and the sound of huge black wings going 'whoosh, whoosh' as it started to fly away." She was obviously terrified of what she saw by the shakiness in her voice and the fearful look on her face as she continued. "I believe in this stuff, but I don't even want to be seeing or hearing it."

It was amazing that we were each seeing and hearing two absolutely opposite things. The Lord showed us that night a revelation into the deliverance from a spirit of rage. It is still as vivid in our minds today as to what we saw, experienced and heard that night. Was it a sign of what was to come and the path that the Lord had for us to walk together?

The dove is representative of the presence of the Holy Spirit and He wanted us to be sure, that we knew He was with us in the midst of this powerful and formidable spirit of darkness. The Lord's light had come and exposed this thing that likes to hide in darkness, in the hidden and locked places in our hearts. Janiece was now free and feeling a wonderful peace in this area of her life, even though it would take some time for the habitual triggers to lose their hold on her. The power that they invoked though, left her this night.

She used to be proud in her earlier years of how she could stand up for herself and pin the boys against a wall, or even win arm wrestling contests. It was her protection and with it came a supernatural supply of strength to her delicate frame. We would wrestle occasionally before this night, and she could always out wrestle me, but after this night she lost that strength. Slowly, or quickly as it sometimes was, we were both being changed by the things we walked through together.

She was so worn out and tired the next day that she spent most of the day sleeping. One thing we have to realize is that spiritual deliverance is similar to physical surgery and many times there needs to be a time set aside for rest and recovery. Think about it this way, the scriptures say in, *Hebrews 4:12-13, "For the word of God is alive and active. Sharper than any double-edged sword, it penetrates even to dividing soul and spirit, joints and marrow; it judges the thoughts and attitudes of the heart. 13 Nothing in all creation is hidden from God's sight. Everything is uncovered and laid bare before the eyes of him to whom we must give account." (NIV)* The word of God cuts and surgically removes those things from our spirit man to bring healing and freedom from bondage, burdens, and sin.

Terror In The Night

One night, Janiece woke me up. She had dreamt that we were sleeping and Terror was in the room. She felt its presence and woke up in the dream. She saw a sliding glass door in the room. The door was closed, but the curtains were blowing. She reached over and awakened me. I sat up and said, "Yes, it is here." We rebuked it and commanded it to leave, to never come back and it left. Then she awakened from the dream and did what she saw in the dream. She woke me up, I sat up and said, "Yes, it is here," just like in the dream. We rebuked it, told it to leave and never come back and it left. Then I prayed for her and peace returned.

Years earlier, while she was a teen, she watched "The Exorcist" and that is when the fears that were around her, changed into terror. She was so afraid. A presence had invaded her life and would stay with her for years, until this night. Now, she was free.

Years earlier, on a sunny day during the eight year mental downslide, Janiece was in her apartment bedroom. Suddenly the room went black as night. The darkness was so thick that it was pitch black. Not a glimmer of light could be seen. All of a sudden, she could sense terror all around her. She was sitting on the edge of her bed and suddenly she saw two green eyes glaring at her. Then a black figure took shape in the front of her. It was as tall as she was as she was sitting. It pointed its finger at her and scowled, "You are mine!"

She felt like she had been bound and paralyzed. She was unable to move or speak and could barely breathe by this time. It was then she remembered that if she called on the Name of the Lord, she would be saved. If she could only say, "Jesus!" it would have to go. She tried with all of her might, but she couldn't get her mouth to work. She was shaking her head and struggling to get the words out, but all that came out were some faint sounds. Then, she knew that if she closed her eyes, so that she couldn't see it, maybe that would help. So, she closed her eyes and tried again. She was able to say, "Jesus, save me!" As the terror and paralysis eased, she noticed that she could see light through her closed eye lids, so she timidly opened one eye to see what was up. After she saw that light had returned to the room, she opened her eyes and relaxed. The presence was gone.

The Big Black Panther

One of the things that happened from the time we became close friends to early in our marriage, was the fact that Janiece was constantly changing. One day things would be one way and the next it was different. I couldn't count on her ways being the same as when we were hanging out and working with the sound.

After we got married I continued to write, get my first book ready for publishing, perfect my art print, "Destiny Path Of Life," wrote new and continued to practice my songs, and began to work on two new inventions. I was constantly busy and had too many things going. In my mind, I didn't have enough file cabinets (none) nor the area to keep things really neat. I was determined to push forward in these areas, so that we could get a nice income established. I reminded myself as being like someone who was so focused they forget to carry an umbrella in the rain, or just have things scattered everywhere. In this organized mess was some kind of organization. I knew where things were, but it was really becoming a major problem to her.

Well, this didn't fly at all with her. God is a God of order, and He was making order in that brain of hers, so disorder was really, really starting to bother her, to say the least. The sad thing is, I wasn't changing as quick, you know, that 'quick work' prayer of hers. It was so hard to keep up with all of the changes.

Prior to her coming into the Kingdom of God, she said she had organized messes, but she knew where everything was at any given time. 'Don't mess with my stuff!' was her slogan. It was like we had come to opposite ends of the spectrum. One day things came to a head and she ran into the bedroom, shutting the door behind her. I knew right then that this was not a good sign.

She kept feeling like my disorganization was trashing a part of her. She felt like I didn't care about her. She took her tantrum into the bedroom, because she had gotten so mad. She was trying not to beat me up, even though she wanted to so bad. 'Conform, or else...' type of thing. 'My way or the highway!'

While she was having this tantrum, lying on the bed in the other room in the Father's presence and crying, she questioned Him. 'Did I hear You right about getting married anyway? This isn't right, You know. I thought he was a believer. There's a lot of things he says, that I don't know where he got this stuff from." Everything was coming to the surface at once and she was having to face it. "I don't want to do this anymore, but I'm not going to quit. Will You please talk to him. Just tell him it matters. He was a bachelor for a while and he had to be clean when he stayed with others. I'm sure he was raised inside, instead of being born in a barn, so would You please talk to him and let him be caring about it. He didn't marry a maid and he didn't marry his mother."

Of course Father always waited until she was through

before He would respond. As she was still crying, He said, "Look over there."

She replied, "I don't want to look over there."

He said, "I want you to look over there."

She replied again, "I don't want to look over there."

He asked, "What do you see?"

She said, "I don't want to look over there."

He kept on, "I want you to look over there."

Finally, Janiece looked over there and exclaimed, "Oooooh!" She didn't like what she saw. It wasn't good. On the other side of the room was a big, black panther. She asked very quietly in a whisper, "What's it doing here?" She knew what was to follow next, deliverance.

He replied, "That's Self-Pity!"

She said, "I heard about that one. I think Jane Aguilar mentioned it once. Okay?"

He continued on, "You know, you're stroking that thing all of the time."

Upon the realization of what's she had been doing, she goes, "Oooooooo! But I don't want to!"

He said, "But you are. You are doing it right now."

She asked, "Okay, so now what?"

He said, "Look over there."

She responded, "Look over there? Do I have to look over there too?"

He repeated, "Look over there."

She looked.

He asked, "What do you see?"

She answered, "Well, it's kind of like a prune, but really big, really big. Okay, so what's that?"

He said, "That's pride. You're too proud to let things go.

You're too proud and you've been holding on to self-pity too. Both of them walk together all the time. They're friends."

Janiece questioned, "So, they're my friends? My friends?"

He said, "Yes."

She asked, "So, I guess you want to deliver me again? Okay, so what do I have to do?"

He said gently, "Confess your sins, let it go and I'll take it away."

She responded by slowly repeating, "Okay, okay, okay, okay!" She was lying there going through 'Okay', but not doing it."

While all of this was going on, the Lord gave me a vision while I was in the other room. It was right at this particular time with her conversation with Him, that I turned the doorknob to the room and opened the door. I don't know if I was brave or stupid.

She was thinking, 'Talk about nerve! Stick your face into the hornet's nest!'

I told her quickly, "I see you in a room with self-pity."

At that moment, she wanted to take my head off. She looked up to the Lord and told Him, "Cheap shot! You send a prophet if I don't deal with it. Okay! Then fine!" Then she looked at me, "You get out of here!"

I closed the door really quick and went back into the other room. Why did I ever do that? Just following orders!

Janiece talked some more to the Lord, "Okay, all right." She gave it up. Now, she hears self-pity when it is around. It is very evident to her, since she had been its friend. She knows it and recognizes it. She hates the thing and what it does to people, but has compassion for the person, its victim. She's been there, so she knows how dangerous it is.

The pride helped keep it there by telling her, 'Oh, I'm not in self-pity, not me.'

She said, "People call it denial, but it is actually pride. 'I'm not letting that go. I don't have any problems, no, not me.' Until they can see, they can't see."

Self-pity is a vicious spirit. Its victims are its prisoners and are deceived into thinking that no one else cares, poor me. If a friend or someone doesn't agree with the spirit speaking through them, it viciously attacks them through words of hatred and anger. When a person tries to see what is going on and tries to get free, the spirit turns on them. It won't allow them to see the truth, until the Lord breaks in. It is a wicked cycle of deception and pain for the victim, as well as those who love and care for them. If you see someone who is in the clutches of self-pity, pray for protection for them and those who are trying to help. Then pray that the Lord will open their eyes to see, and give them the strength and courage to admit they've been wrong and ask for His help and deliverance.

Touching The Fear

There were times, during our early years, she would get angry at me and tell me she was leaving. She had enough of my not caring in the way she needed me to do. Most of the time it had to do with my not cleaning up behind myself, or just leaving things like clothes and papers lay around for a period of time. In the beginning, fear would grip my heart. I would think, 'What did I do? Now, what? Is she going to leave me like my previous two wives did? Here we go again. Lord, I don't think I can handle this? Will You please help?' My heart would start racing as failure started parading its theatrics right before my eyes. He would show me all the same scenes over and over again. I would hear, 'You're just a failure at relationships. Here you go again. You messed it all up.'

However, gradually over time, as I would give these areas over to the Lord, He began to heal my heart in this area. He had to replace the lies with the truth and He was so gentle in how He always brings healing. The scripture says in **Isaiah 42:3, "A bruised reed he will not break, and a smoldering wick he will not snuff out." (NIV)** I would have preferred He just heal me rather than take me back into these dark and fearful places in my heart. He is faithful and He will continue to do everything in His power, to not only set us free, but to see us totally healed and made whole, but He is limited by our choices and how far we are willing to go.

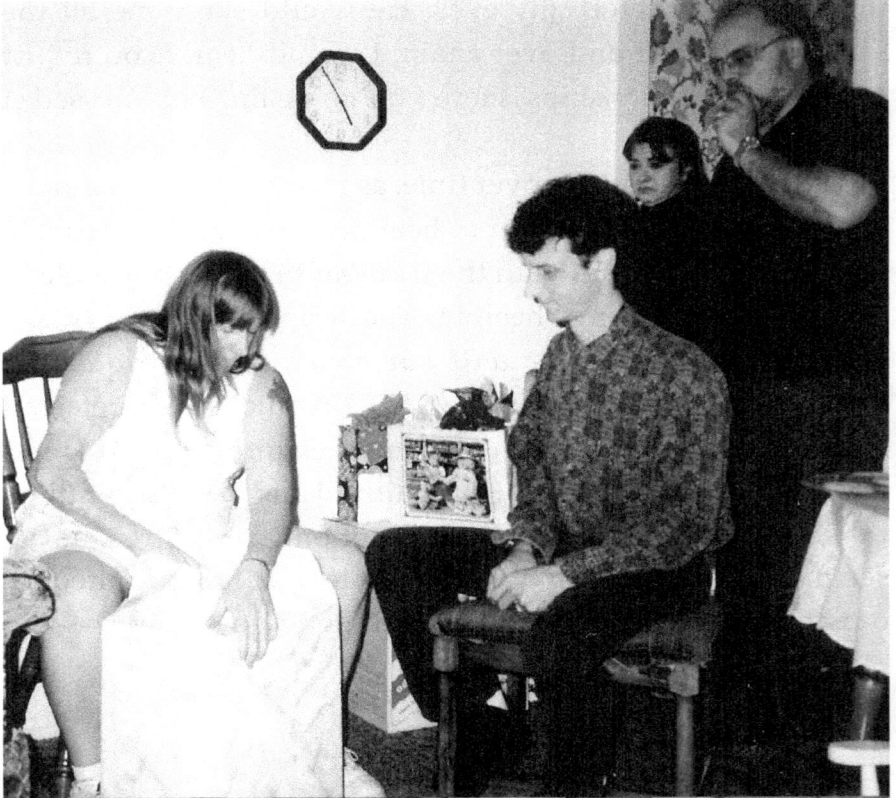

Chapter 14

Another Miracle Of Life

Janiece Pregnant?

The day Janiece decided she needed to get a test to see if she was pregnant, really concerned me because of her past. So far we had been married about fifteen months and we had not needed to face this uncharted territory. Years ago the Lord told me He was going to give me a son, but I wasn't in any real hurry. He just told me one day that He was. I had three daughters and I loved them so much, even though we were all apart. Now, the day had come and I was unsure what events were going to take place.

Well, Janiece decided to call her friend Staci. She felt really close to Staci and safe being around her, because they were similar in their outlook concerning frilly, girly things. They didn't like them. So Staci told Janiece she had an extra pregnancy test and asked if we could come over there, and so we did almost immediately. Janiece got the test and went into the bathroom. She came bounding out of the bathroom with a loud, "Woo hoo!" running and dancing around on the hard wood floor. She went up to Staci and asked her, "Is this what I think it is?"

Staci said, "Yes!"

Janiece asked, "Are you sure?"

Staci said that sometimes they aren't that accurate, but she had another test, so they decided to do another one to make sure. It tested the same.

All my concerns were unfounded. This too, was another miracle and was one of the easiest and most joyful of all. To see this lady, whom I had spent so much time and prayer with, going through so many changes, challenges, and some of them violently, be so full of joy in being pregnant was totally amazing. The Lord was showing His awesome handiwork right in our midst. She came into the Kingdom praying for a 'quick work' and hasn't stopped since. None of this would have been possible if she hadn't missed the appointment with the doctor for a sex change, that was interrupted by an unthinkable accident, and of course, you know the rest of that story.

Some of our journey has seemed like we were scaling sheer cliffs, as we climbed higher on the journey He placed in front of us. It was and is purely by His grace, mercy, love and power. I know that there was no way this journey would have been possible outside of His immeasurable love and miraculous power.

Another Accident

A little over midway through Janiece's pregnancy, we were involved in a car wreck that totaled the car. A lady made a late left turn across the intersection in front of us on a red light and I couldn't stop in time before running into the side doors of her car. Through the rest of the pregnancy Janiece had back and neck pain. Our chiropractor, Courtney Owen, was only able to do certain adjustments and even the massage therapy was limited, due to the pregnancy.

It was after this accident that we were able to purchase a new four-wheel drive Suburban, that we would use to travel cross country after we sold our house.

Please, No More Hospitals

During our early marriage, we became determined to drink pure water and to eat as well as we could on the budget we had. This also included whether or not we would go to doctors. After we found out Janiece was pregnant, we were determined to stay away from doctors and hospitals and go the natural way through a midwife.

A few weeks before the due date for the baby to be born, Janiece was sketching on her sketch pad when her water broke. We called Martha Breeden, our midwife to ask her what we needed to do. She wanted us to come over to her office so she could check Janiece.

Janiece was so scared of going to see a doctor. Even though Martha said she would go with her, it didn't make much of a difference. She didn't want to be around doctors anymore. She didn't want to be in their hands anymore. She wanted to go the natural way.

Martha told her that if it was her water that broke, she wouldn't be able to be the midwife. It was a law and she couldn't go against it.

Janiece was so scared. She was sitting down, rocking back and forth asking Holy Spirit, "Hold me and comfort me. Please give me the courage to go see Martha." She had her arms across her chest, holding herself as if in a hug.

A bit later, we went to Martha's office where she determined that her water had indeed broke. Janiece pleaded with her to no avail. Martha wouldn't back down and she said there was no other way. Janiece told her that she would have to think about it for a while. She had to get her peace back, because she was determined that she wasn't going to go alone. She needed to know that the Lord would be going with her.

Janiece went into another room while I was discussing the details with Martha. She was asking Holy Spirit, "Please comfort me. I need your comfort. Please comfort me. Please comfort me. I just need your comfort. Please comfort me. Go ahead of me and prepare the way. Give me guts please. Give me guts. I am so scared."

A little while later, I took Janiece over to University Hospital. It was a university hospital, because we didn't have the money to have our own private physician and we had planned on going the natural way. Martha had called ahead to set everything up. She had to share information with them, because she was the midwife. Their primary concern was regarding a Staph infection, since the water broke.

Our first major obstacle was getting onto the elevator at the hospital to go up to the correct floor. She was so scared and fear literally overpowered her. She couldn't get on. Finally, after some coaxing, prayer and my reassuring her that I would be there with her, she got on.

After we had gotten up there and they checked her out, they told us that it didn't make sense, but that it had sealed back up. The water was still there. So whatever had happened, it closed back up and that was not normal, nor natural.

They left Janiece alone in the room for a bit and she asked the Lord, "So, it was You again, huh? You set this whole thing up." While she is in there alone, although not really, she was having to look at her heart, her attitude towards the medical community, and she was facing it going, "Okay, I don't know You in this area. I don't know You in this area, but I want to. I don't trust You here, but I want to trust You through people to handle me again." The tears fell from her eyes as she reached out for His love and healing. She forgave every face that popped up in front of her mind, all of the doctors and nurses that had handled her in the past, some gentle and others not. There were a lot of people to forgive and she kept thinking of Stephen when he was being stoned and he said, 'Lord, don't hold this charge against them.' So every time she was forgiving people, she was remembering that. The main problems she had was in the misdiagnosing of her prognosis; putting her on all of those medications, some with dangerous side effects; and all of the pain and suffering in the emotional and mental areas. She had to be around others who were nuts and crazy, even though she was in the same state to a degree, it was very scary for her. She felt totally vulnerable and exposed. They talked down to her like she was a 'nothing.'

Before she had the accident on the press she was a very secure person. She wasn't afraid of people. She wasn't vulnerable. She was a young person who thought everything was going to be fine and nothing was ever going to happen to her. She was forgiving them now, because she had not realized she had copped such an attitude. She had blanketed the whole medical community, for what a few had done, with blame and mistrust. It was a great opportunity to be praying for everyone. She asked the Lord to meet them all where they were, to give them double of what He's given her of His goodness and love. Love them to life. Give them a chance at life. "He had forgiven me of so much, who am I not to forgive people?"

Later on, in her pregnancy, the baby was turned wrong. On one appointment, the doctors tried to turn him while he was in the womb. I watched as they put the cream on her belly, each one on opposite sides of the table would use their hands, press into her stomach and try to move him around inside. Her belly was so contorted as they pushed and pulled on this little life inside. After what seemed a long time, they finally decided it wasn't going to work and stopped, but it was so painful to her. I couldn't imagine the pain she was going through. They had the sonogram going at the time so they could see what was going on. After all I saw through this pregnancy, I saw how resilient babies are and how gracious our Lord is to humankind. He simply puts up with our weaknesses, frailties and most of all our hatred for His ways. In spite of us, He cares so much and keeps the human race alive. Just before the due date, the doctors tried one more time to turn him, but it didn't work this time either.

Wrong Position

As time was getting closer to the due date, he wasn't turning and we had to prepare for a possible Caesarian section, another surgery to this body that had been wracked so many times with pain.

When we finally got to the hospital for his birth, Janiece was still determined to have him natural and without pain medication. She didn't want any of the medication getting into his system. She had watched her diet carefully for nine months and wasn't going to deviate at the end. The contractions kept coming regularly, but the dilation was not increasing. The baby had one leg up, one leg down and was determined to come bottom first, instead of head first. After quite a few hours of intense pain, she finally gave in to having an epidural. They turned her on her side and tried five different times, with that very long needle to find her spinal cord before finally hitting it. They would tell her to be still in the middle of a contraction. I don't think so. She still has the scars today. Finally they found the right place and she was able to rest some.

After over twelve hours of labor, they determined that a C-section was necessary. I followed them into the surgical room, held her hand, talked to her and prayed for her as they cut him out. The Lord came through and kept her through it all. Through all of the trials, He was there. To the doctors amazement, they found an extra layer of muscles in the area they cut. It wasn't normal, but she had done so much body building during her life, we wonder if somehow this could have been the cause. Possibly, it had something to do with her thinking she was a male in a female body for so many years? We really don't know, but it was different. It was so much so that the doctors made a point to tell us.

Who Is This Child?

We had a really hard time getting a name from the Lord for him. To make it even harder, every time Janiece had a sonogram, he would be turned wrong and they couldn't tell whether he was a girl or boy. We had to keep calling him, "the baby" because we didn't know. She was almost ready to pop, when we were in a worship service and the Lord gave her his first name, Daniel. It was a short time later, when we were in prayer and I was reading in Zephaniah and the Lord told me his middle name was Zephaniah. Daniel means, "God is my judge." and Zephaniah means, "Hidden in Jehovah."

When Anthony Chapman had prophesied over Janiece while she was pregnant with Daniel, it really lifted her spirit. They were the same words she had already been praying over him. She was so excited for the confirmation. She kept speaking and prophesying to him daily. She even asked the Lord to give all of us the interpretation of tongues so that we could understand him and he could understand all of us and it was so.

All we had going into the labor room that day was what the Lord had given us, Daniel Zephaniah, a boy's name. We didn't have a girl's name, nor did we know the gender. There were so many elevens on the day he was born. He was born on November 11, 1996, which was double eleven, 11/11/1996. It was in the eleventh hour and in room 11.

I wished we had recorded everything, but in the moment, a person doesn't always think of those things. It is interesting to note that this year, as I finish this book, is 2011. On his birthday this year, the date will be 11/11/11. There is a great significance, but we won't know the whole thing until we get there or until we get the full revelation. He was one who might not have been here, had Janiece had her way with beginning the process of the sex change on the day of the accident.

On the very first day of his birth, she fed him on the same breasts that would have been removed. In fact, she would breast feed him until he weaned himself one week shy of his third birthday. She felt abandoned by him at that time and had to realize the gift she had been given. The Lord intervened. He heard her cry, even in this area and took care of it. He cares so much for all of us, no matter what our outbursts are, He sees our heart and he has a special plan for our lives.

One of my greatest joys was to see the joy on her face and in her heart when they brought Daniel in for the first time. She was a mother and it was written all over her face. She got to be what she was meant to be and she was able to enjoy every moment of it. She had prayed for him everyday he was inside of her. She prophesied to him and sang songs to him. She asked the Lord to help him understand and us to know what he needed, even though he couldn't even talk yet. She poured her life into him and continues to do so today. She wouldn't let just anyone pray for her when she was pregnant. She was very protective. What a gift.

One thing that was so funny over those three years, was that she could raise her shirt up a bit and ask him "You want some num, num?" He would crawl or run over to her. These times were so precious. Had she not had the accident and went ahead with her plans to have the surgery to have her breasts removed, we would not have had these special times.

Also, if someone walked by or was close that had a bad spirit, he would pick up on it and start to get uncomfortable. She would take him and let him nurse and comfort him. It would bring him peace and comfort. He was secure in his mother's arms, a place of safety and peace.

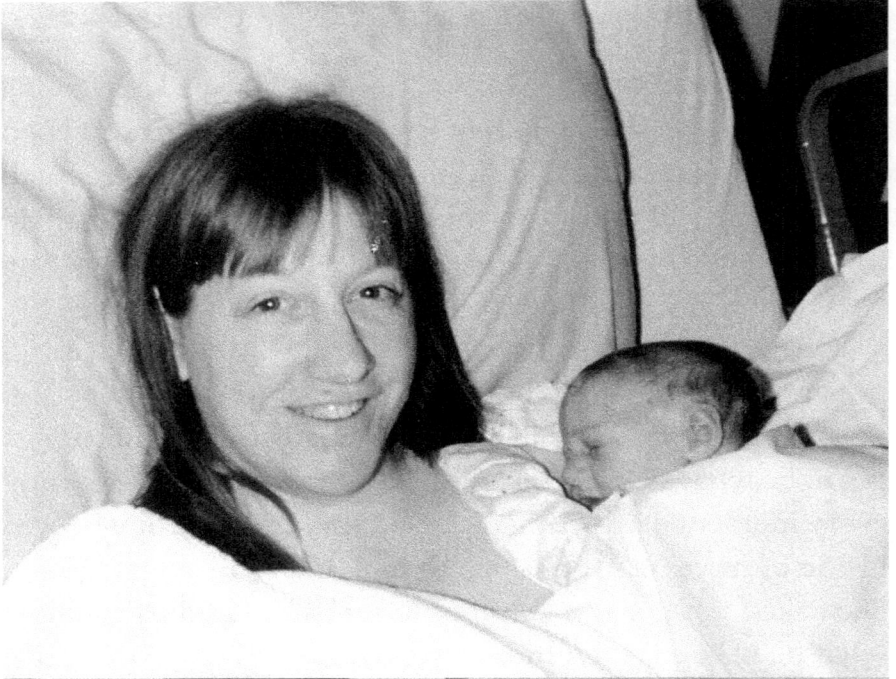

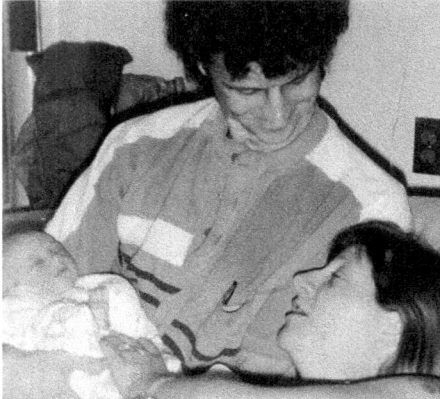

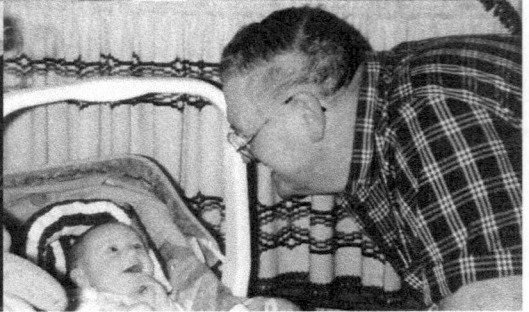

Photos Above: Daniel is in all photos; Top: Janiece; Middle Left: Joseph & Janiece in the hospital; Middle Right: Gin; Bottom Left: Diamond Dixon (Bob's Mother); Bottom Right: Bob

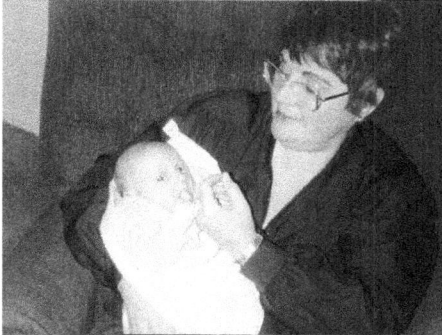

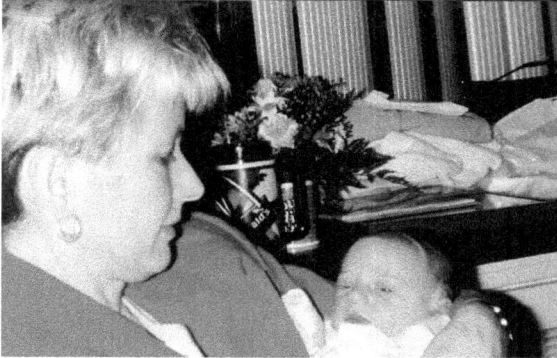

Photos Above: Daniel is in all photos; Top Left: Janiece, Joseph, Krystal, Desiree; Top Right: Deborah Nazemi Lewis; Top Middle Left: Janiece; Top Middle Right: Joseph; Bottom Middle Left: Jane Aguilar; Bottom Middle Right: Christa Edwards, Bottom Left: Christine Davis; Bottom Right: Margaret & Sherrill Tomerlin (Gin's parents)

Photo Above: The burgandy and gold GMC Suburban 4x4 that carried them cross country on many journeys

Chapter 15

Trail Of Tears

Selling The House

We had our house up for sale for about year before it sold. The realtors didn't understand why it wasn't selling, because it was in such an immaculate condition. We kept telling them that it would sell at the right time. From the time we got married until it sold, we worked together to fix it up. We had a new roof put on it as well as a new fence for the back yard. We painted the whole exterior and interior including the ceiling. It had been smoked in over the years, so the ceiling had a yellow tint. We even changed all of the electrical outlets and switches from the ivory to white. We moved the washer and dryer from inside of the kitchen into the garage. We replaced the three section sliding glass door in the back with a double section. We bought some landscape timbers and created a small garden in the back yard. It was good to work together. We were always doing odd jobs together for people who needed help. We would do electrical, plumbing and even mechanical repairs. We loved being together.

When the house did sell, it sold quickly at the beginning of June 1997. Even though we thought we were prepared and had downsized tremendously, we were not ready to be out of the house in three short weeks. We moved our things to storage and bought a small utility trailer to pull behind the Suburban to carry our necessities. Daniel was eight months old and was starting to develop a rash on his face. It was on both of his cheeks. This was only the beginning of some hard and impossible times ahead.

After the sale of our house, we decided to transform our Suburban into somewhat of a camper. Our idea of camping, was sleeping in the Suburban, really roughing it. It wasn't all that great though on those freezing nights. I would have to occasionally start the engine for short periods of time to let it warm up the interior.

Before we left, we found a foam company in San Antonio, and bought a two-inch thick piece of foam. I had constructed a platform bed in the rear cargo area for Janiece and me to sleep on. We made a special place for Daniel to sleep on the second row seat. We learned to eat out of cans and clean up in store restrooms as well as other things that were available to us on the road. Truck stops had the features available, but they weren't always the cleanest.

One of the things dearest to us, was when Daniel would wake up during the night or in the morning hungry. He would stand up at the back of the seat and look over. Our pillows were up against the seat, so I could reach over and grab him and lift him to the back with us. We so enjoyed these special times and still enjoy the memories.

Now, I must illustrate what our transportation looked like to others viewing from a distance. We were driving a 1996 GMC Suburban 4x4. We were pulling a white 5x8 utility trailer with two bicycles mounted on its roof. On the sides of the trailer in large letters, I had painted the words KALEO Ministries and on the back door I had mounted a laminiated copy of my art print, "Destiny Path Of Life." What a sight as I think back to it now.

When we started preparing to sell the house so that we could travel and minister we asked Dennis to bless us and he did. He didn't want us to go and we told him we would be back. As Janiece put it, "We have to be about Father's business."

Across The USA

Mendenhall Missippi, July 1997 - Aunt Emily

After we placed all of our necessities in the trailer along with our sound system, we headed off to Mendenhall, Mississippi to visit a dear friend of Janiece's parents, Emily. We were so excited to be on the road and were ready for adventure.

Memphis, TN - Art Prints

After we left Mendenhall, Mississippi, we traveled up to Memphis, Tennessee. I had a printing company in San Antonio, Texas print an order of black and white prints of my art print and had them ship them to me. When we received the prints, I saw they were incorrectly printed, and so we waited there until they could reprint them and send them to us. We were going to use these on the trip. We had planned to go from Mendenhall to Montrose, Colorado, but this was going to delay our trip. Our money was limited and we ended up not being able to continue our stay at our hotel. As we told the hotel manager we had to leave, because we couldn't afford to stay, she said, "Oh, please don't go!" She reasoned, "You haven't received your shipment yet." She put us up in a large hotel suite that was reserved for their employees and managers. After she got off work each day she would come by the room and we would talk and also minister to her. She received so much healing and ministry from the Lord. She had reached out to us with a gift that was in her power to give, and the Lord responded to her and touched her life in a huge way. We have lost touch with her, but hopefully, some day our paths will cross again. Here was a stranger who immediately became a friend as the Lord led and directed us. This started to become the norm everywhere we went. His favor was with us everywhere we went.

It was during this time, Janiece received a song from the Lord to Daniel. In all that he was going through, the oozing rash on his face, she would sing to him. "Don't give up! Don't give in! Keep on pushing, Daniel!" She would sing that song to him all the time. I don't think the rash on his face bothered him as much as it did us. We saw the things he was unable to do, because of the binding from the harness that I had fashioned to help keep him from using his fingers to scratch his face until it bled, but he just seemed to roll through it all. Seeing him grin over and over again just seemed to touch us so deep with his love and it was very evident that it did the same to those around us, too.

It is interesting how we can sometimes focus on our limitations, rather than enjoy the fullness of the moment and its joys. In his own way, he was showing us what was more important. His life has touched so many already and he is only fourteen. As far as we were concerned, he was a miracle baby and we dedicated him to the Lord, even like Hannah did with Samuel in 1 Samuel 1.

During our trips, we weren't able to take advantage of seeing and experiencing all of the sites we saw, due to our financial situation, but we were able to 'window shop' as Janiece says it. There are places we would like to go back to again some day.

Cimmaron, Colorado - YWAM

During this trip, we visited Youth With A Mission (YWAM), in Cimarron, Colorado, in the amazing Rocky Mountains. This center covers 2,000 acres and is at an elevation of 8,600 feet and it extends up to 11,400 feet. It is such a beautiful place to get away and spend time with the Lord in the midst of His glorious creation. It was good to see how they operated, trained and worked together with each other. It helped to add to our vision of a community that could live together, work together, and be prosperous from a Kingdom perspective.

First Public Ministry

Uncompahgre Lodge, Montrose CO

In September 1997, we went to Montrose, Colorado to visit a pastor friend of mine. We found a bed and breakfast to accomodate us during our stay. When Barbara, the owner heard our story, she wanted us to put on a crusade, as she called it, and to have Janiece share her story. She ended up giving us free accomodations for a period of time. She wrote up the concert details and placed them in an advertisement in the local newspaper.

She and her husband, Rich, had converted the old community school building into the bed and breakfast, so it had a large room in the center of the building with a stage.

The classrooms on the sides were used as the bedrooms. It was perfect for a concert and they would also get some publicity from it. The community was excited when they bought the property and started restoring it.

We had our sound equipment with us and my guitar, so we unloaded the equipment and set it up. This was the first time we ministered together in a public setting. I would share several songs and then Janiece would get something from the Lord and share. Then I would sing some more and this happened again and again. It reminded us of our Pastor friends from Australia who minister this way, Paul & Bunty Collins. It was really cool. We got to get a glimpse of the future in this smaller setting, because we had been asking the Lord to show us how we were going to minister together. My music has a country and folk sound to it and Janiece doesn't really care for that type of music, so we had been wondering how it was all going to work together.

One thing that Janiece noticed the most while we were ministering, was that the churched people seemed to be the most closed off, hardened hearts of the group. The others were very open to this type of ministry and the anointing that was upon us. It was so good to see them get more free. There is such a difference between those who are closed off and those who know they don't have anything and are very needy. When Janiece was ministering, all she could see were hearts.

It was during this trip, we met Mike and Delores Booher and the rest of their family from Yoncalla, Oregon. They were on tour, traveling in their bus, singing gospel and western music. They were so gifted musically and each one played multiple instruments including the violin. We had met their son, Justin, much earlier because he was living in Montrose and was our pastor friend's worship leader. He had told us his family was going on tour and that it would be good, if they had someone to take care of their house while they were gone.

Janiece was used to having money to pay her own way in things and not being a burden to others because of the burden she had been during her illness. During this trek of our journey together, we were having to rely on the Lord and she was feeling like a bum.

On the morning they were leaving town, they came over to Justin's house in Montrose, where we had stayed the night. His father cooked breakfast that morning. Janiece was fasting at the time and doing a cleanse, because she thought the rash on Daniel's face might have something to do with the excess Candida in her body. Right before they were ready to leave, they decided that they wanted us to stay at their house, while they were gone.

They had only met us the night before, but their son had known us for a little while. He was the one who came up with the idea and told them. Janiece questioned Mike, because she wanted to make sure he was okay with it. "Are you sure? Are you sure you want us there at your home? We don't want you to be uncomfortable or have regrets. 'No' is an answer too." They were sure they wanted us to stay at their home. In reality, we were total strangers, but the Lord was putting this together. He gave us instructions as to whom to contact when we got there. They had eighteen acres just south of Eugene, Oregon, an apple orchard and other fruits, and the rainy season was just beginning.

Oregon Trial *(Spelled Correctly)*

Yoncalla Oregon, October - November, 1997

When we left Montrose, we headed north to Interstate 70 that would take us west through Utah, Nevada, California and into Oregon. To every new adventure come the mountains and valleys. The landscape of the trip should have given us an indication of the journey that lay ahead. Although this leg of our journey would feature one of the toughest times in our life together, we would look back on it for years to come with fond memories of how the Lord miraculously met us at every step. For us, many of these times defined how we now choose to face the new challenges we face, as we continue to explore new places in the Lord. Each challenge becomes a new stepping stone that propels us on in our journey.

I don't remember much of the trip and it seems like we drove straight through, although we did go through Lake Tahoe, where we had our honeymoon.

We arrived at the homestead, totally exhausted from the long trip. We had taken turns driving and sleeping along the way. What a beautiful place. There was an area beyond the front yard where the ground had been plowed, evidently for planting something. The Canadian geese that appeared there almost daily, seemed to like what was in the dirt. The two-story house was large and such a blessing to us. There was a flowing creek behind the house with a bridge large enough for vehicles to cross. It was dammed up by a cross section of boards under the bridge that created a nice sized pond during the summer months, when there wasn't much rain. The land behind the house gently sloped up towards a hill. There was a fenced in area at the back that was almost full of red delicious apple trees and they were ready to be picked.

It was the first time we had ever eaten apples fresh off the tree and were spoiled instantly. I didn't realize what I was missing by buying them in a store. There were also Asian pears, Granny Smith apples, and an assortment of grapes and blackberries.

The temperature during our stay was cold for us, being from south central Texas. It was generally in the 40's in the morning, damp and it usually rained every day. It was the beginning of their rainy season. Janiece took on the job of mowing the huge yard with the riding lawn mower. It brought her a lot of peace and solace in the midst of the storm. It seemed that by the time she had finished, she had to start over again. The grass was growing so fast. Occasionally, she would take Daniel with her and let him ride on her lap. He really enjoyed it.

The blackberries were delicious, but they were growing wild over that area of the state. They had weaved their way into the apple trees. As we picked the apples we had to be very careful that we didn't get stuck by or caught on the thorns. Most of the time we would use the loppers to cut the vines out of the trees before we would begin to harvest the apples. The Lord was always showing us spiritual revelations of His Kingdom, through the physical things around us.

Sometimes, in our lives, we have both fruit and thorns. As we share the good things in our life with those around us, if we are not careful, they can get hurt on the thorns we have in our lives, you know, those hurts and wounds where we have set up our own defenses to protect us from getting hurt again. We need to realize that it is difficult to share His love freely with others, unless these things are dealt with. We must receive healing and forgive others and ourselves. Only when we are fully healed will we be really safe to be around. This goes for everyone. What good does it do to minister to someone when they are open and receiving, and then out of nowhere we snap at them or maybe we raise our defense because something gets touched on, and boom, a thorn pricks them and causes another deep wound. These things are going to happen every now and then in relationships, because we are all on a journey, however we can minimize them by becoming open to and allowing the healing to come as Holy Spirit shows us things. When He is uncovering it, His grace is there to bring healing and wholeness.

Another way to see the thorns, is that as we reach for the fruit of the Spirit, (*love, joy, peace, forbearance, kindness, goodness, faithfulness, gentleness and self-control*), the cares of this world try to spoil it for us. Because we worry and are stressed about things that we should let Him carry, we can miss out on the goodness that He has for us. The Lord has His continuous banquet table spread out before us. According to *Galatians 5:22,23*, it is always full of *"love, joy, peace, forbearance, kindness, goodness, faithfulness, gentleness and self-control." (NIV)* The question is, do we sit down at His table and take what He has prepared for us, or do we try to get it in our own flesh? The Lord also has a store room of gifts that He wants to give His people. He showed it to me in a vision. The problem is that most people don't know how to access it or even know that it is there and available to them. He told me to tell others that He wants each of us to distribute these gifts to those who don't know how to get them. When we are around others, if we see a gift He wants to give them, then we should tell them and if they are willing, take it from Him and give it to them. So simple and yet so profound!

After a few weeks of being at their place, they asked me if I would be willing to pull out the boards that were damming up the water. With the rainy season beginning, the creek would have too much water flowing through and the dam wouldn't be able to handle it without the creek flooding out of the banks. It was an eerie feeling going under a bridge where the boards were taller than I and there was water flowing over the top. It was a great way to face some fear though. I would take the crow bar and push the boards up one at a time, very slowly and the water would gush through the small gap under the board. The boards were about 4 x 8 inches as I recall and were in a steel channel on each side. After the water had come down to the level of the top of the next board, I could remove the board I had pryed up and begin the process with the next board. It was probably in the 40's and 50's while I was doing this. I am glad they had rubber boots in the house to keep my feet and legs dry. The water was really cold.

Translated

These six weeks of our married life were very, very difficult, but we were in a special place. It was like a small paradise to us. It was during this time that Daniel's face broke out all over, even onto his forehead. It was constantly oozing and scabbing and we didn't know what to do. If we got two hours with uninterrupted sleep at night, it was a miracle. I had sewn together this little harness out of material that we would velcro around his waist with a piece that was attached behind his back and went through his legs and attaced to the front. On each side I had a piece long enough to secure his hands by his sides for short periods of time, so that he couldn't scatch his face to where it would bleed. We had to watch him constantly. We tried all sorts of natural remedies and treatments to try to keep the area dry and non-itchy. People everywhere always had ideas for us to try. We tried some of them. Mainly, we were told to just keep it clean and dry. We found that Desitin Ointment worked the best.

One day, Janiece asked me to find a Naturopath who also had an M.D. I searched the phonebook and found one in Eugene, Oregon and we went to see him. It was at this point we found out that the rash had developed into Impetigo. The doctor told us what we needed to get, but we didn't have the money to get those things and to also pay him for the cost of the visit too. He was so touched by our situation that he told us not to worry about the office visit charges, but to use that money to get Daniel what he needed. Our hearts were deeply touched by his compassion and generosity. We went over to the Wild Oats grocery store and a pharmacy, where we found everything and then left town to go back to the Booher's home. It was normally a 45 minute trip. I was in the middle seat of the Suburban with Daniel to make sure he wouldn't start rubbing his face again on the sides of the car seat and Janiece was driving. We were so tired and exhausted. I looked up at one point and saw our exit coming up next. I told Janiece quickly to not miss our exit.

She was surprised, "It can't be already! It's only been about 20 minutes."

She had cried out to the Lord as we were leaving Eugene for Him to get us back quickly and safely, that we were so tired. He heard her cry and tranlated us through time and space. What an absolute miracle. He showed us how much he cared and how close He was walking with us through this journey, this tremedous trial that was constantly pricking our hearts with pain.

Lots Of Fruit

It seemed like there was no end to all of the apples. We picked apple after apple, until we had so many stacked in the house. We wanted to bring some apples back with us, but we also wanted to come back to Texas through California. The problem was that California wouldn't let us bring fruit through the state, so we had to alter our course. We went up through Idaho, down through Nevada and into Arizona to meet up with the Booher's again, where they were performing in Tucson. It was a great reunion.

One note about the rash that lasted about six months, it didn't matter where we traveled or what restaurant or hotel we visited, Daniel was always smiling through it all. There was such an anointing on him that seemed to just attract people, especially the waitresses. As they would come up to him and talk to him, he would look at them and grin. They were so touched by the love that seemed to come from his whole being. There was always an openness for us to share the Lord's goodness with others. There were times we would run out of money, but the Lord always provided. We were given lodging, and extensions of hotel stays for free.

Sometime later, after our trips, I asked the Lord about this. I was concerned that we had just gone off and done these things on our own. I was asking Him where the fruit was, because we didn't seem to be blessed financially in it. He reminded me about Paul, the apostle in *1 Corinthians*

4:3,5 "I care very little if I am judged by you or by any human court; indeed, I do not even judge myself ... Therefore judge nothing before the appointed time; wait until the Lord comes. He will bring to light..." (NIV) This brought me comfort. I asked Him why he sent us to just these few people and why we traveled so many miles criss-crossing the USA. He simply answered me, "No one else would reach out to them." He trusted us enough to go and He made the way possible. It wasn't for me to judge in the natural, what I couldn't see that was accomplished in the spirit. It was a great lesson for me and it brought peace to my soul and my walk with Him. It is a simple walk of obedience.

When working with a large jigsaw puzzle, sometimes we can work on many different areas of the puzzle at the same time. Just because we can't see the whole picture doesn't mean progress isn't being accomplished. The Lord sees the whole picture, while we see the small fragmented area we are currently working on. Sometimes, we will go to different areas and do little bits here and there. If we judge it prematurely, we can get discouraged and quit too soon and the whole project becomes a failure. It might have been just before all the segments were going to be joined together and completed. What a waste it would be to miss it all after getting so close.

On one of our trips, we were in Salt Lake City, Utah. We were low of fuel and money, and needed to get back to San Antonio. We drove up to a gas pump and I got out to put some fuel in the Suburban. There was a man on the opposite side of the pump who was fueling his car. We started talking and he asked me what we were doing in Utah. I guess he saw the Texas license plates. I told him and he handed me a twenty dollar bill. He said he wanted to sow into our lives. From there, we found a pawn shop and sold our sound system. Then we drove back to San Antonio.

East Coast

North Carolina, Virginia, DC, West Palm Beach Florida, February 1998

During our early two years of marriage at our house in San Antonio, Texas, I had invented a special type of water sprinkler for watering landscapes using professional sprinkler heads for maximum effectiveness. It used a special set of sprinkler heads from a company in West Palm Beach, Florida. In February 1998 after we had sold the house, we went on a trip to visit some friends in North Carolina, Andrew and Kitty Ford. We stayed at their place for a few days and enjoyed the snow too.

We visited Rick Joyner's church in Charlotte, North Carolina. Without even knowing us at all, one of their ministry teams prophecied to us about our current situation and saw exactly what we were doing at the time, even living in our Suburban while we were traveling. It brought confirmation to us that we were on the right track with the Lord.

From there we visited Jan Rogers, a dear friend of ours who had helped us as a midwife and nutritionist during Janiece's pregnancy. She had moved to Virginia and it had been a long time since we had seen her. It was such a good time of getting back together, sharing what the Lord was doing and learning more about nutrition and health.

We made a brief appearance in Washington DC and drove by the nation's capital. We would have liked to stay and visit more places, but we had to continue on the journey. We drove up to Pittsburgh and then down through West Virginia on our way to West Palm Beach, Florida. As we traveled the interstate and proceeded to get closer to Florida, we noticed a lot of bikers heading south. Also, vehicles towing trailers with motorcycles started going by us on the freeway with more frequency. We wondered what was going on. We arrived in Daytona Beach late in the afternoon and decided we would try to find a place to camp for the night and then we would continue on our journey the next morning.

Well, we found out what all of the motorcycles were all about. There was a huge biker's rally going on in Daytona Beach. There were bikers everywhere, literally thousands. As we drove around we came upon an outdoor concert featuring "Bad Company." We found a place to park and walked down to the concert with Daniel. They also had a carnival. We felt really special to have been in this place at this time. We were able to enjoy being a part of something without even planning for it. It was dark by this time and we didn't stay long because we were tired from the trip. After we left, we drove around for a while until we found a place to camp for the night. It was right next to a railroad track, wouldn't you know. Waking up in the middle of the night to the sound of approaching trains was not fun at all and happened quite a lot on our trips.

We arrived at the sprinkler manufacturing company the next day. We drove through the front gate and all the way around the edge of the parking lot before we could find two parking places we could park in because of the length of the truck and trailer. As we entered the parking lot, we saw two men standing in front of the doors to the main office. They looked up and watched us as we drove around in their parking lot. I got out of the Suburban and walked up towards the office. Before I got there, one of the men looked up and asked me if he could help me. Keep in mind that I had not contacted this company before now. I told him I would like to speak to the owner about an invention that I had that would use their product. He introduced himself as Chip, he was the president of the company and his vice president was standing next to him. He told me to go in and talk to his secretary and he would be in shortly to talk to me.

Chip was very intriqued with the invention and did his part to help me with it. It was going to cost me about $100,000 to pay for the tool they would need for the plastic injection molding process and I would have to come up with this amount. I left somewhat discouraged, because I couldn't see any way that I could come up with that much money. To this day, no one has ever produced this type of product, so maybe it will still come about. I think the main thing the Lord showed us that day, was that nothing was impossible for him. He could put us in the right place at the right time to get us in to see the people we needed to see. How many times is it possible to talk directly to the president of a company or any other important people without going through a long drawn out process of communication? I simply walked right in. That was favor and it keeps happening in other areas of our lives too.

Chapter 16

Growing In Grace

Middle Of Nowhere

Janiece's parents had given us some land in Colorado City, Colorado. On one of our trips out west, we decided to try and locate it. It was a lot on a large piece of land that was being developed back in the late 60's. We didn't know exactly where it was, so we started driving around. There were actually 16,000 lots that had been plotted for the development. As we drove around on the gravel base roads, seemingly out in the middle of nowhere, because very few people had actually built houses and the land was basically still raw, the fuel pump went out on the Suburban. Back then we had a bag cell phone, analog. I had to climb up on top of the Suburban, hold my arm up with the phone to get reception so that I could call a tow truck. We also had a small trailer on the back, so I knew the tow was not going to be cheap. Then we found out that the nearest dealership was in Pueblo, some 35 miles to the north. The fuel pump was in the tank and we had just filled up with fuel, so I

Photos at Left: Top: Daniel, Yogi Bear and visitors at Yogi Bear Jellystone RV Park in Bandera Texas, March 2000; Middle Left & Right: 1954 GMC Bus; Bottom Left: 1971 International Travelall; Bottom Right: Yogi Bear & Daniel hugging

knew this was a job I wouldn't be able to do. A dear friend of ours, Larry Larsen helped us tremendously in our time of need.

We received a lot of favor with the dealership. We ended up having to stay in town over the weekend, because it was too late for them to work on it by the time the tow truck got us to town. We managed to get favor with a hotel across the street for a good price. That Monday, one of the guys at the dealership, started talking to me about what we were doing, so I shared the story with him. He reached inside his pocket, pulled out his wallet and gave me twenty dollars. He said he wanted to sow into our ministry. After they replaced the fuel pump, we were on our way back home. We were unable to locate the property at this time, but the Sangre de Cristo mountains around it were awesome. (Sangre de Cristo means "Blood of Christ")

Yogi Bear

In 1998, we decided to buy a 1954 GMC bus, that had been partially converted into a tour bus by a gospel family. The plan was to convert it into a nice motor home, so that we could tour in it, take our home with us wherever we go, but the Lord had other plans. Sometimes it seems like you go backwards before you go forwards, but it is really about the relationships and skills developed along the way. We were entering another one of the hardest times in our marriage, but in a sense, it was a picture of what the Lord was doing inside of us.

We started the conversion at Janiece's parent's home, ripping out everything, especially the carpet that had been glued to the walls and ceilings. There was brown glue showing on the ceiling for a long time after that. We replaced the floor and sealed it. During this time, the air compressor went out on the engine and we had to take it back to the place we bought it, in Pipe Creek, for them to repair it. So, we aired up the air tank that the brakes used to stop the bus and took off. We hoped it would be enough air for all the stops along the way, with the final one at the shop. We made it with just enough air in the tank to park. We also found out that the generator was not working and so they had to replace it too. Jack, the owner of the shop, let us park in the back of his parking lot and hook up to his electrical connection, so that we could live in the bus while we waited. Eventually, he ended up offering me a job. We repaired the bus and later moved it to Yogi Bear Jellystone RV Park in nearby Bandera, Texas. Jack told me he would give us an old International Travelall, if I could get it running. Now I had two restoration projects, a vehicle to get around in as well as our home. Restoration work is really hard work, especially when you are living in it while trying to restore it. We really didn't have a choice, as we didn't have the money to do it any other way. As I worked for Texas Custom Coach, I was trained by a master electrician, Steve Mauldin, and learned to do cabinet work and laminating also. I already had basic skills in all of these, but evidently the Lord wanted to increase the skill level. I worked at the shop during the day, and then on our bus in the evenings and weekends.

Janiece would be alone with Daniel during the day, in a place that at most, was ugly and unfinished. We used the showers at the park and their recreation center. The Medina River flowed through the RV park down below.

We were privileged to meet a lot of the people as they came and went. Some we helped tremendously and prayed for those who would receive from us. Daniel was like the park mascot. Everyone loved him, and every Saturday morning, Yogi bear would appear at the camp store and there would be a special celebration and parade around the small circle.

It was during this time also, Janiece got so angry one day, that she punched the unfinished cabinet with her fist. Unlike the drywall in the house, the solid wood didn't give, but the pinky bone in her hand did as it broke through the skin in a compound fracture. It also broke her heart that Daniel witnessed it. Miraculously, the Lord healed it quickly, but it was the last time she punched anything in anger.

Shortly after this, we parted with the bus and moved into San Antonio. As my skills improved, so did our income and we were able to move into an apartment and buy a different vehicle. We did take the bus on one journey to Dallas to see my daughters. Looking back on it, it must have looked really funny to others, but the Lord was doing a work inside of us too. No matter what came at us, we had to rely on Him. He was the One Who put us together, and He would have to be the One to keep us together. Many were the times, we would each look up to heaven and tell Him, "Father, You said! You started this! Help!" He always did.

In 2002, I left Coachworks, (Texas Custom Coach had been bought and the name changed), to do phone book deliveries with Janiece. She had started to do a delivery in San Antonio part time to make some extra money and we realized we could make enough money for me to quit. We ended up traveling again, this time paying our way through these jobs. We did deliveries in Bryan/College Station; Irving; Fort Worth; Austin; Fort Wayne, Indiana; Santa Fe, New Mexico; Denver and Colorado Springs, Colorado.

Albuquerque, NM

In 2003, we drove to and stayed in Albuquerque, New Mexico and commuted to Santa Fe to do the delivery, because it was too expensive for us to get a hotel in Santa Fe. We were privileged to see, from our hotel room on the second floor, the hot air balloons take off every day. It was a lot of fun. Most of the balloons were very colorful and it was quite a sight to see. It is amazing to me, how a bag of hot air could transport people through the air. Of course, travel is according to the wind, so you have to make sure how long and how far it will travel in a particular direction or you might end up somewhere other than where you wanted to go.

One day we drove around in Albuquerque just to see what was there. We drove by a Chevrolet dealer called Bob Turner Chevrolet. Bob Turner was Janiece's dad's name, so we went in to talk to them. We ended up getting her dad two license frames with the Bob Turner logo on it for his truck. He really enjoyed the gift. Oh, and he drives Chevrolet pickups so it was a perfect fit.

Colorado Springs, CO

From Albuquerque, we drove up to Denver to do a book delivery. We stayed in Colorado Springs and drove daily to Denver to do the delivery. One day, as we were headed back from Denver, a Suburban passed us on the interstate. On the back window it had written, "Mother's House Publishing" and all of the contact information. Janiece was driving at the time, so I asked her to speed up so I could get the phone number.

As soon as we were able, we called and talked to the owner, Jackie Haag, who was also a great inspiration in getting us to write this book. When she heard Janiece's story, she was so determined that it had to be written correctly, so that her story of God's goodness could touch a multitude of people and bring them hope. Thank you Jackie for the years of encouragement and help, and also for the completion of this project which is still to come. She confirmed what Gin had been telling me for years to do. Thank you, Gin.

Why Me Lord?

Janiece had questioned the Lord, "Why did you want me? Why did you pick me?"

He told her, "Because I will have mercy on whom I will have mercy, and I will have compassion of whom I will have compassion."

She said sheepishly, "Yes Sir!" She didn't know that was in the Bible yet. When she found the passage in Jeremiah, she thought, 'So I must have heard You.'

That was how my walk began too when I began to write songs. Holy Spirit would give me the words to the songs and later He would show me the scriptures to back it up. What a way to live and walk with Him. That is communication and it is available to everyone who wants it. *1 John 2:27,*

"As for you, the anointing you received from him remains in you, and you do not need anyone to teach you. But as his anointing teaches you about all things and as that anointing is real, not counterfeit — just as it has taught you, remain in him." (NIV)

We pondered that this is how it was for the early apostles as they wrote the letters of the New Testament. The Lord has never stopped speaking to His people, rather, His people have stopped listening due to the hardness of their hearts, religious beliefs and opinions that are contrary to scripture.

It was now the year 2003, and we had finally made it to Colorado Springs again and this time we were determined that we were going to stay there. We ended up spending the summer there, but the Lord had other plans. Some time in September, I had walked out onto the porch of our hotel room and was looking at Pike's peak. Every morning we walked out, sat on the steps there to be with each other, pray and talk. This morning was different. This time I heard His voice, "You are going back to San Antonio."

Now, I didn't want to hear this. I didn't want to go back to San Antonio, again. A few weeks later, when we were again in Denver, Janiece got a call from her dad. Before she answered it, I had this deep sense of death, like there were going to be two deaths that would occur. He told her we needed to come back because her grandmother was not doing well. He didn't think she was going to make it much longer. After we got back, there were two deaths within seven weeks, her dad's mother and her mother's father. The word was so clear and direct.

Land Of The Cheese & Snow

Wausau, Wisconsin

In January 2004, the phone book company needed someone to supervise a delivery in Wausau, Wisconsin in February. We agreed to do the work, so they sent us, expenses paid to Fort Worth to train for a month. In February, we took off for Wausau. We stopped in Mineapolis and Daniel was able to see the huge Lego store in the "Mall of the Americas." We had never seen so much snow as we saw on this trip. Whoever thought that scheduling a phone book delivery during the middle of the winter was a good thing, I think needed to be brought to reality. We had people calling in that their snowblower had been damaged, because some delivery person had thrown their book into the snow instead of placing it next to their door like we instructed them to do. I don't think I need mention trying to navigate some of the back roads in all of the snow and ice in our van without snow tires or chains. It was another experience and through it all, we had a lot of fun times. Wherever we went, the Lord used us to reach out to others and bring encouragement and hope.

We stayed at the "Best Western" there. They had an indoor pool and their people were great. It was just a wonderful experience.

After this job, we went back to Dallas to drop off all the equipment and then on to San Antonio. Krystal was graduating from High School in June in Irving and we decided we would do another delivery in Dallas while we were there. Well, there would be a lot more to this trip than we would ever expect.

Set Apart

Dallas, Texas - June 2004

We arrived in Dallas shortly before my daughter, Krystal, graduated from high school in June of 2004. We weren't able to do a lot with my daughters over the years, because of distance and our financial situation, so the few things we were able to do with them, were very precious to us.

We had a phone book delivery job lined up and did that for a while. After that was completed, we talked about moving our stuff up to Dallas so we could be near them for a while. Janiece said, "Sure, why not?" We found a place to rent by the month and went back to San Antonio to pack.

On the day we were packing the trailer and heading to Dallas to live, I was attacked by two red wasps. They stung me on my back, right behind my heart. The temperature was around 100° outside and I was overheated. I didn't think much about it, because I had been stung by many different insects and wasps over the years. About fifteen minutes later though, I began getting dizzy. Finally, I went inside to get Janiece to pray with me. Then I started blacking out and that scared everyone except me, because I was unaware of what was going on. Gin had an Epipen and asked me if I wanted a shot. I said sure, but she had to do it. I had blacked out a multitude of times and vomited three times, before I started coming out of it. Something did not want us to get to Dallas, but we went anyway.

Shortly after we moved, I took a courier job that didn't pan out. We had a full size van and it didn't do well enough on gas mileage to make any profit, so I had to find something else. It was during this time we felt like the Lord wanted me to go back to school. I wanted to do something that would help us in the ministry, so I decided on Web Design & Development. We checked out Westwood College and The Art Institute of Dallas. I felt like Westwood was a better choice because of price, even though I really liked the Art Institute better. Janiece felt like the Art Institute was the one and so we went for it. The Art Institute was almost double the price of the other, but the Lord made a way for us through scholarships and grants. In fact, with the grants and scholarships, they ended up being the same amount. Nine quarters later, I graduated with an Associate Degree in Multimedia & Web Design with a 3.8 GPA. In high school, I had missed graduating with honors by less than a grade point, mostly because I was working so much at the time. This time, I made it. I felt like the Lord was so gracious and that He allowed me to have something that had been stolen from me at a younger age. It really meant a lot.

Bare Necessities

We didn't have any furniture when we first arrived in Dallas and Deborah Lewis told Janiece about freecycle. We were sleeping on a two inch foam mattress and Daniel on a pallet on the floors. Through freecycle and some other groups, we were able to get some furniture for free. Janiece continued her surveys and home schooling Daniel. A short while later, shots were fired in the apartment above ours. I had gone to the grocery store and Janiece and Daniel were there. She was scared and called me on my cell. We moved from there as soon as we could into a sister apartment complex in the Village.

I worked about 32 hours per week at T. D. Jakes during this time to help us financially for a while, but then I hurt my back and this didn't work out. I couldn't do the lifting any more and they didn't have anything else at the time. It was during this time on Workman's Comp, we got so far behind on our bills that we had to file for Chapter 13 bankruptcy. After I was released for light duty work, I was hired by OfficeMax, in the Impress copy and print department. It ended up being a good thing, because it enhanced the educational course I was taking at the Art Institute. During most of this time, we were also home schooling Daniel and things were getting tough. Janiece and Daniel were having a rough time together with the home schooling. There were things he just wasn't going to do and it was very hard on her. I was in school full time and working around 30 hours per week. That and the tremendous amount of homework was really tough.

I had only been at OfficeMax for a short time, when Carol Blackwood, the Marketing Director for Our Redeemer Lutheran School came up to me for a print job for their school. We got to talking and after a meeting and some tests, Daniel was enrolled into their private school with a scholarship. That was awesome timing and a great bunch of people they were. It was so good for us. Because of my course of study, I was able to also bless them with some projects I did for their school.

Less than two months before I graduated on October 4, 2006, Janiece's mom took a turn for the worst. She was dying and we didn't have the money to send Janiece to San Antonio for an extended stay, because of my school, work, and Daniel was back in school. I wouldn't be able to handle everything by myself.

She had decided she would wait until the last moment, before she would fly out, so she was praying and listening intently to know when that time was. Although Deborah had told her it was close, it wasn't time. It came suddenly one afternoon and we had her on a flight that evening. Early the next morning, her mother, Virginia Sue Turner, went to be with the Lord. Janiece did get to see her and talk to her before she left. The passing of her mother brought her tremendous grief and sorrow for years to come. She would dream of her mother and woke herself up constantly, crying in her sleep. She would lay awake at night and just cry, or even during the day, when she would think about her, the tears would flow again. Her mother had become her best friend after Janiece had been miraculously healed.

After I graduated, I did a few freelance jobs before I got on with a commercial real estate company in Dallas. It was good money, and finally, we were paying things off and had some extra for ourselves. We could even buy a few things and had new clothes and shoes to wear. We could even fly to San Antonio to visit friends and family instead of having to drive the long hours. Things were starting to go really well.

Restoration

Janiece likes to spend time with the Lord in the mornings before she comes out of the bedroom. Not long after we were married, she came out and told me that the Lord had told her to read Job and remember the end. Here was where the argument began between her and the Lord. She said, "I don't want to read Job again. I know what happens in there. Can we just skip to the end already?" He restated to her the same thing. She agreed, "Yes, Sir!"

One day in March, Janiece received a word from the Lord on restoration. In receiving the word on restoration, she had pretty much lost all hope by now. She questioned Him, "Is this You, Father?" She had so much pain in her back and joints for so long. Her nails were brittle, her hair was thinning out and she was gaining so much weight. She even participated in different medical research programs. It was during this time she found out that she was anemic too. She studied different books over at Borders and found that she had every symptom of a non-working Thyroid. She was so mad at the Lord during this time. She wanted it fixed, but He wanted to strip off all the old before He adorned her. Check out the book of Esther in the Bible for more on this. Janiece didn't want to be around us much, because she didn't want to hurt us. It messed with her demeanor. She was always in pain to some degree or another. Her thoughts were, "You fixed everything else, fix this too!" Sometimes, she wished the Lord had a necktie on and that she could grab it and pull Him closer so that they could talk face-to-face. You have to be stripped in order to see what He wants you to see and how gracious He is and He is the One Who adorns us. Even though all of this was going on, she took the word, 'restoration,' and began speaking it on us and to everyone as she was praying for them. She learned that 'hope' is a gift too and how she had accused Him of so much unrighteousness during that time. That is what broke her heart. He already knew what was in her heart, so when she saw it and confessed, He started the healing and restoration process.

Dennis once told her that she was the Lord's trophy. She didn't have a clue what that meant and she didn't want to be just a trophy. People have trophies and they just sit around on the shelf collecting dust. She wanted to be more than a trophy. She wanted to be doing something because she is a doing person, not a sitting around, doing nothing, collecting dust, getting old thing on the shelf. Now, to her, a trophy means to display the glory of God. She gets it. Go out and tell about it. Show off His glory. A trophy shows off. If anyone is broken, it is a good thing, because at least you can be fixed.

Then one day in March of 2009, Janiece walked up to me and told me, "You are not going to want to hear what the Lord just told me!"

I said, "Probably not. What is it?"

Photos Above: Top Left: Coach Gary Frieling & Daniel at Our Redeemer Lutheran School in Dallas, Texas; Top Right: One of the fountains in one of the lakes in The Village in Dallas where they lived; Bottom Left: Janiece, Daniel & Joseph at the other lake; Bottom Right: Joseph at his graduation from the Art Institute of Dallas in October 2006

Chapter 17

Mountain Of Hope

Back To San Antonio

Janiece said, "He said that we need to move back to San Antonio."

I said, "You're right. I don't want to hear that. I'll pray about it." I didn't want to move back to San Antonio. It had been a hard place to live for me. There was a lot of pain and failure there and I didn't want to return, except to visit. I really knew that she had heard, but I didn't want it to be real. It wasn't long and the Lord confirmed it to me, when I surrendered and let Him speak. Then I told Him, "If You want us to move by the first week in June when our lease is up, then You are going to have to provide." We didn't have the money for a move like this, but He did. We ended up with more than enough from the extra work He created ahead of time to make everything work seamlessly, so we could leave. So amazing!

We moved into a temporary two bedroom luxury apartment in the Colonnade, until we could find a place to

Photos at Left: Top: Pike's Peak taken from the Garden Of The Gods in Colorado Springs, Colorado; Bottom: One of the tunnels on Gold Camp Road just outside of Colorado Springs

live. Three months later, we found a beautiful, four bedroom house that had like a turret in front, where the staircase was located. Janiece called it her castle and it was. It was just what we needed and we stayed for one year.

Close to the end of this year, the finances really started getting tight and we knew it was time for another move. The Lord was telling us that it was time to get this book finished and the house was costing us so much that I was having to work too much to pay the bills. We needed to downsize.

We wanted to get away to Colorado Springs to finish writing, but didn't have the funds at the time, so we started looking around for a temporary place to stay. Janiece found an RV park with cottages in a neighboring town and we were almost ready to move in there, when a friend, Jeannie Pircher, suggested we look in the Sea World area. We found a cottage in a luxury RV park called Blazing Star Luxury RV Park. They even had a small basketball court where we could all play basketball together as a family. It was wonderful. I wrote the first 242 pages of this book there, but we ran out of time and money and had to move out. The book was going to have to wait a bit longer.

Close to the end of our time there, Janiece had a dream about her dad having a really tough time and that we needed to be near him. Through a series of events, we decided we would move in with him to help. He has a prosthetic foot and can't do all the things he needs to do to keep up with the house by himself, plus all the depression he was going through after he lost the love of his life, almost five years previously.

We moved on March 7, 2011 and started helping with the outside work. He has an acre and a half of land, of which a half acre is wooded. We helped him plant a garden again and started doing a lot of landscaping and tree trimming and removal. The Lord's presence came upon the land, the song birds have come back and there is fruitfulness upon the fruit and nut trees and the garden. It is so beautiful. Our relationship with each other has blossomed like never before and we know the Lord is not only with us, but His blessing is upon us.

Unity Among The Brethren

During our time back here in San Antonio, we also rejoined our church group, now called Oasis International Christian Center with Dennis Goldsworthy-Davis. Janiece had heard a word from the Lord about 'restoration' before we left Dallas, and now it was happening in all areas of our life. We were welcomed back with open arms and so much healing was spread about. We had gained maturity through the paths we had walked. Those who were there before, who had caused many problems, were no longer around.

We were back only a few months when we were asked to start a group at Oasis, doing the thing we were doing everyday, just reaching out to others with His love. My design business was one I could do from any internet connection and our favorite place of business was Panera Bread Restaurants. They opened a new one near us in July 2009 in Huebner Oaks and we were there every day for the first two weeks. We became regulars and well known with the staff. It has been almost two years now, the staff has changed, but the new ones seem to adopt us too. One of them told us one day he was glad to see us, because the day had been so chaotic. He was a new employee and had not been there long. Wow! This is what it is all about. His presence and His love emanating out from us and touching those around us without us saying a word. They notice the difference. We have prayed for this for years, that He would get the glory.

Direction

On Janiece's 50th birthday, Dennis spoke out publicly to her, "Jubilee." He also let everyone know that I was writing her book, this book. Since then, the pressure has been on by the Lord for me to finish it. We have prayed about it all and are following counsel to finish writing the book before we share the story abroad. That way, we have the book to offer alongside the testimony and ministry. ***Revelation 12:11, "They triumphed over him, (the devil), by the blood of the Lamb and the word of their testimony." (NIV)***

Here is the testimony. It is true to the best of our recollection. Our relationship with the Lord is real and can happen to anyone who wants it. God is no respecter of people. He plays no favorites, but He can get close to those who want Him to be close. The more that we throw off the things that hinder us, the closer we are able to walk with Him. Repentance is how Janiece got closer. It cancels the devil's hold on our lives in certain areas, and gives us freedom through the blood of Jesus, to walk free and deeper in His purpose for our lives.

Photos at Right: Top Left: Janiece with Jackie Haag, their publisher inside of Mother's House Publishing in Colorado Springs, Colorado; Top Right: Daniel & Janiece at the Cave of the Winds; Bottom: Daniel, Janiece & Joseph in front of Soda Pops in Boerne, Texas which is owned by their friends, Maurice & Staci Andrews

Photos Above: Top; Janiece & Joseph at the visitor's center to the Garden Of The Gods in Colorado Springs, Garden Of The Gods and Pike's Peak in the background; Bottom: Janiece, Joseph & Daniel at the Cave of the Winds

Chapter 18

Gather My Sons & Daughters

Kingdom Directives

Our directive from the Lord is simple. "Go tell My people I love them." Our answer is to simply go where He leads, whether it is to individuals or groups. People need to know the truth and walk away from the religious lies that have no power to save them.

Our goal is to help establish Kingdom communities around the world where people can live and work together in safety. Where broken and wounded people can be brought in and receive the healing they so desperately need. The proceeds from this book will help us begin to accomplish this goal. We purpose to help raise up Kingdom businesses that operate according to His purpose and principles along with local governments that operate according to His plan. Our small publishing and design business is the beginning of this. It is what we used to design and publish this book as well as design and develop our web sites.

On May 21, 2011, we flew from San Antonio to Colorado Springs to put the finishing touches on this book, complete it and send it to the press. We could sense His awesome peace and His presence as we waited for our first plane in

San Antonio, to waiting and boarding our second plane in DFW. The flights were so smooth, even though they were the small M80 jets. I had rented a full size car for us to drive during our stay, but when I went up to the Budget counter at the airport, they handed me the keys to a Jeep Liberty, four wheel drive. This spoke volumes to us. First of all, the Jeep Rubicon is Janiece's favorite vehicle in a Detonator Yellow color. Even though this was charcoal gray and not the right model, it was four wheel drive that signified that this would be a new adventure for us. By its name, Liberty, it signified a new freedom in the Lord. On the flight, He had told Janiece again these words, "I'll meet you there." Where? There! Once again, we were in a special place, out of the natural surroundings into a place where we needed His guidance through the unfamiliar territory He had already charted for us.

We left San Antonio at an altitude of approximately 902 feet above sea level. We arrived in Colorado Springs at an altitude of 6,035 feet, with Pike's Peak measuring 14,110 feet. By the time we left, the last weekend, it was like He lifted us up to the top of Mt. Everest. We attended a conferece, at Wellsprings Church, where we received revelation from Him through Robert Henderson and Natasha Vermaak, that again, challenged and changed our lives. We weren't going back the same as when we came. Kingdom life and living is a new adventure everyday. What does He have planned for today? We have a new focus, a new road to travel, and now, let the Journey Begin.

AUTHOR'S COMMENTS

Writing This Biography

Although the journey of writing this book has been long and at times even stressful, it has been such a blessing to go back and remember all the things that we journeyed through. Sometimes, we tend to forget the little things in the midst of the storms and trials that come our way. It is these very storms that produce the glue, that can strengthen us when we face similar situations in the future. We can look back and say, "Lord, You met us there when we needed You, so therefore, You will meet us here today!" These hard and difficult places can become altars and monuments that strengthen us in our walk.

Arranged marriages do exist today and those arranged by Him, are foremost the best. What He joins together, has a supernatural ability to stay together, because He is the third part that can hold it together. If you know that you know that He put it together in the first place, then your faith is more secure. If doubt enters in, then the devil has a foothold and a crack can form in the foundation. I know, I've been there twice before and I can attest to the difference. It is good to wait upon the Lord to confirm His Word and His will for the purposes and destiny for your life. He will not fail you, nevertheless, He will not go beyond the freedom He gave each of us to make choices, even if it is in the wrong direction. By His mercy, we don't get what we truly deserve and by His grace, He enables us to do that which we can't in our own strength.

I can't think of a better life to live, than to walk daily

in His presence. There is so much peace and rest, even in the midst of temporary storms. I've been through a lot of trials and traumas, and He never once, left me. In fact, there were many times that He carried me when I could not walk. So grateful! So Awed! So honored that He cares so much for us.

Photo Above: Helen Hunt falls near Gold Camp Road, outside of Colorado Springs - Our lives can be as refreshing as a waterfall to someone else, if we let the refreshment of His love and joy flow through us.

330

APPENDIX - A

Electrical Career

Janiece's Electrical School & Career

June 1978 - June 1982 Bexar Electric Co.

Apprentice Record - Hours - June 15, 1978 - October 25,
1982 - 7,884 hours
Bexar Electric Company
MT Electric
Allied Electric & Air Conditioning Co.
Bexar Electric Company

Photo in magazine article - July/August 79

Certificate of Completion of Apprenticeship - Electrician
- May 24, 1982.

IEC - Apprenticeship Training Program Certificate - 144
hours - September 10, 1982

IEC - Independent Electrical Contractors Inc. Certificate
Of Achievement - Journeyman Electrician - September
10, 1982.

...es to whether he or she could finish the period of indenture, one Ft. Worth graduate expressed everyone's feeling with the comment. "Stick with it. It's all worthwhile."

Contractors in the seventeen AIECA chapters administering apprenticeship programs soundly agree. They are pleased to have apprenticeship-trained electricians available to augment the work force. As one said, "I read a report that said 60 percent of this year's 201.5 billion of new construction would be done by open shop. We cannot do sixty percent of the work with 40 percent of the labor."

"AIECA apprentices are dependable, adaptable, develop good work habits and are consistent in day to day production. These are the employees we will build the future of our companies around. They will be the people we will promote to estimator, supervisor and superintendent," said Steve Humphrey, AIECA Apprenticeship and Education Chairperson.

Overwhelmed Houston graduate Dan McCullough.

San Antonio first year apprentice Janiece Turner.

Despite the costs of apprenticeship, more chapters are developing programs. The growth of apprenticeship is mandated. Existing apprenticeship—electrician programs are meeting only 31 percent of each year's demand. Chapters are developing programs because they want employees who have received the systematic training which will enable them to adjust to new industrial processes and materials. And, as more contractors elect to run open shop businesses, they recognize the need to develop programs to replenish the labor pool. AIECA contractors recognize that if America is to remain economically strong during its third century, they must promote the apprenticeship structure.

Many people are surprised to find that journeypersons are auditing the AIECA apprenticeship classes. Their motivation stems from the fact that apprentices often have skills which took the veteran years to learn. Those auditing apprenticeship training freely admit that they don't want rookie electricians to "out perform" their professional efforts.

Jack Turner and Henry Bravenec at Houston ceremony

They, and others, are additionally requesting classes to upgrade their skills. Apprenticeship programs have served as this catalyst for developing continuing education programs in all industry areas.

No workforce training program has been as effective and rewarding as the apprenticeship system. Nothing else has offered the wide range of skills and mastery of a trade as the combination of job related study and on the job training under the eyes of uncompromising master craftspersons and demanding employers.

The seventeen AIECA chapters administering apprenticeship programs are:

Alaska	Nashville
Atlanta	North Texas
Chattahoochee	Oklahoma City
Dallas	San Antonio
El Paso	Tri-Cities
Fort Worth	Tulsa
Tarrant County	Rio Grande
Houston	Valley
Lubbock	Wichita
Midland-Odessa	

Over 65 percent of the contractors in these chapters have apprentices.

Image Above: Janiece was featured as 'San Antonio First Year Apprentice' on page 19 of the AIECA publication in the July/August 1979 edition as an Electrician Apprentice.

APPENDIX - B

Printing Press Images

The following illustrations were used in court to illustrate the press and show the rollers where Janiece got her thumb caught while cleaning the press. The rollers then pulled her in all the way up to her shoulder.

Photo Above: Bob's finger is actually pointing to the place between the two rollers where Janiece's thumb was caught pulling her in to her armpit and degloving the flesh and crushing her bones along the way

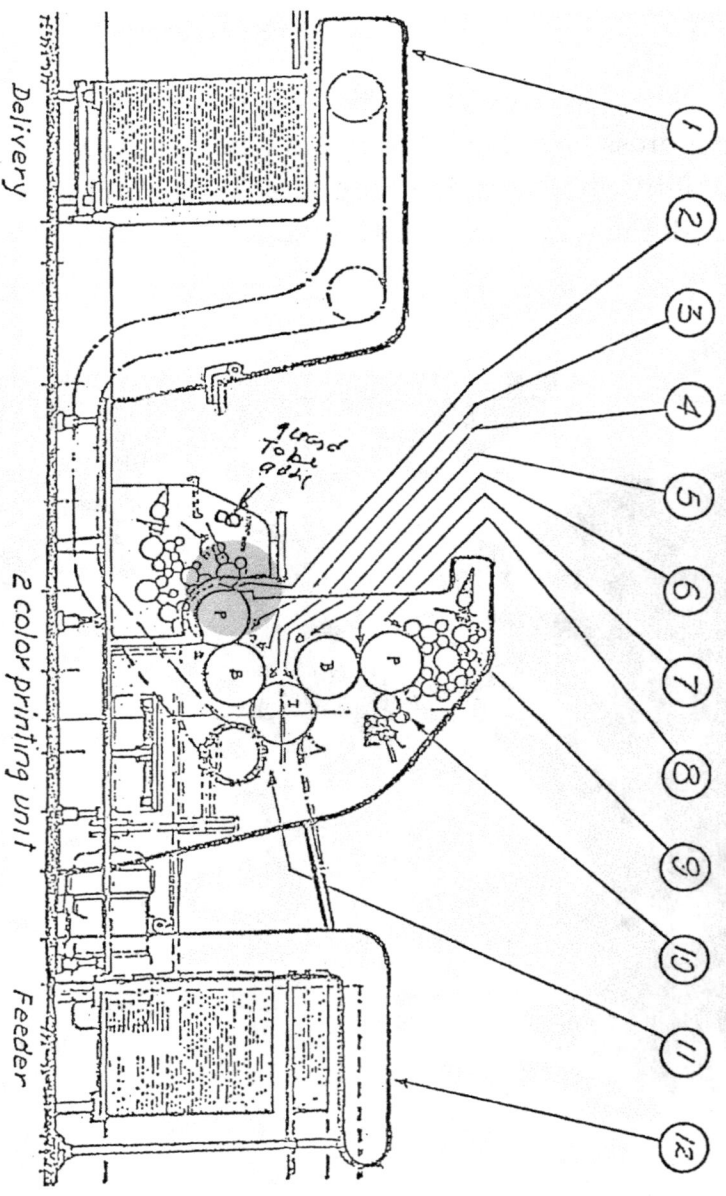

Typical Feed Side Elev. - Sheet Fed Offset Press

Delivery

2 color printing unit

Feeder

① ② ③ ④ ⑤ ⑥ ⑦ ⑧ ⑨ ⑩ ⑪ ⑫

Illustration Above: #2 line above points to the point on the press between the highlighted rollers where Janiece got her thumb caught and was pulled in up to her armpit. Notice the position she would have been in as she was bending over and being pulled into the machine.

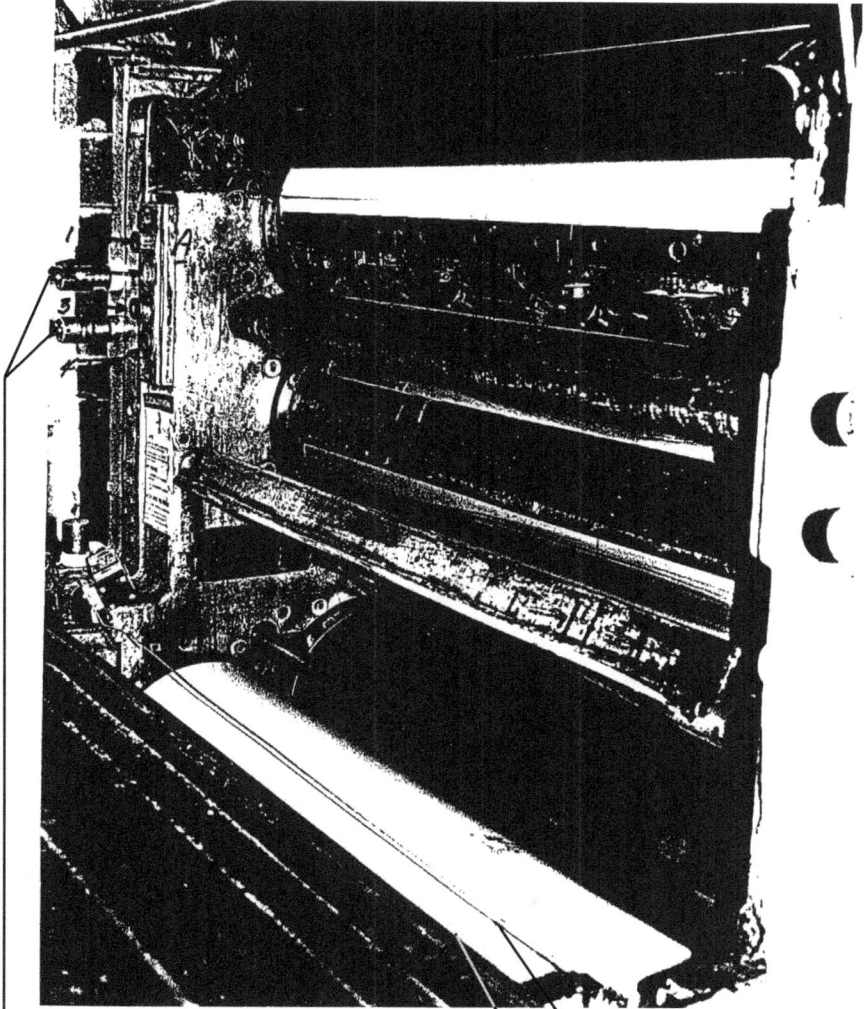

The recessed shut off buttons
have been replaced with easy
to push buttons.

Shut off wire to shut
down the press when
touched

In between the rollers
where her thumb got
caught

Photo Above: The same press that pulled Janiece into the rollers is now
fitted with the safety features it should have had in the first place.

APPENDIX - C

Guardianships Granted

Letter of Guardianship - May 7, 1985

Letters of Guardianship

In the matter of:
JANIECE ELAINE TURNER,
A PERSON OF UNSOUND
MIND

NO. 85-PC-1227

In Probate Court
Bexar County, Texas
In Matters Probate

The State of Texas
County of Bexar

I, Robert D. Green, Clerk of the PROBATE Court of Bexar County, Texas, do hereby certify that on the 7th day of _____ May _____ A.D., 19 85 _____ VIRGINIA SUE TURNER _____ duly qualified as such as the law requires (having been appointed by said court) as guardian of the _____

☒ Person and Estate
☐ Person only
☐ Estate only

of _____ JANIECE ELAINE TURNER, A PERSON OF UNSOUND MIND _____ and that said appointment is in full force and effect.

Witness my hand and seal of the PROBATE Court of Bexar County, at San Antonio, Texas, this the 7th day of _____ May _____ A.D., 19 85 .

ROBERT D. GREEN, Clerk
Probate Court, Bexar County, Texas
By: _____
CYNTHIA CHANDLER

Letter of Guardianship - January 20, 1987

Letters of Guardianship

In the matter of:
JANIECE ELAINE TURNER
A PERSON OF UNSOUND
MIND

NO. 85-PC-1227

In Probate Court
Bexar County, Texas
In Matters Probate

The State of Texas
County of Bexar

I, Robert D. Green, Clerk of the Probate Court of Bexar County, Texas, do hereby certify that on the 20th day of _____ January _____ A.D., 19 87 _____ BOBBY D. TURNER and / VIRGINIA SUE TURNER _____ duly qualified as such as the law requires (having been appointed by said court) as guardian of the ☒ Person and Estate ☐ Person only ☐ Estate only

of _____ JANIECE ELAINE TURNER, A PERSON OF UNSOUND MIND _____ and that said appointment is in full force and effect.

Witness my hand and seal of the Probate Court of Bexar County, at San Antonio, Texas, this the 20th day of _____ January _____ A.D., 19 87 .

ROBERT D. GREEN, Clerk
Probate Court, Bexar County, Texas
By: _____
CYNTHIA CHANDLER

APPENDIX - C

Guardianship Absolved

CAUSE NUMBER 85-PC-1227

IN RE GUARDIANSHIP OF	§	IN PROBATE COURT
JANIECE E. TURNER	§	NO. 1
AN INCOMPETENT PERSON	§	BEXAR COUNTY, TEXAS

ORDER ADJUDGING WARD TO BE OF SOUND MIND

On this day the Application for Adjudication of Legal Competence of Ward was heard and considered by this Court, and the Court finds as follows:

1. Notice and citation have been issued or duly waived in accordance with the provisions of the Texas Probate Code. Guardian and Ward both appeared in person and by attorney before this Court.

2. The Court has jurisdiction of the subject matter and of the parties, and Court has venue in this matter.

3. Janiece E. Turner, Ward, has been restored to her right mind, and the facts in support of such restoration are not doubtful.

IT THEREFORE ORDERED, ADJUDGED, AND DECREED as follows:

1. Janiece E. Turner, Ward, is hereby adjudged to be a person of sound mind.

2. Bobby D. and Virginia Sue Turner, Guardians, shall prepare and file a verified final account. When the final account has been approved, Guardians shall be discharged from this guardianship and their bond.

Page 2 - (Excerpt)

SIGNED this ___25th___ day of ___August___, 1992.

_____
JUDGE PRESIDING

Final Guardianship Absolved - August 25, 1992

APPENDIX - C

Dr. Raymond Potterf Letter

Raymond D. Potterf, M.D., Ph.D.

DIPLOMATE, AMERICAN BOARD OF PSYCHIATRY AND NEUROLOGY

7410 JOHN SMITH DRIVE, SUITE 206
SAN ANTONIO, TEXAS 78229
TELEPHONE: (512) 692-1988

July 21, 1992

Mr. Mark Stanton Smith
Law Offices of John Heard
3737 Broadway, Suite 310
San Antonio, TX 78209-6547

RE: Janiece E. Turner
Competency Determination

Dear Mr. Smith:

In my medical opinion, Janiece E. Turner, has regained control of her mental faculties. She is now able to handle her own personal financial affairs with good judgment, is able to transact her own personal affairs, and is competent to enter into legal contracts and agreements.

She will no longer require guardianship of her person and estate as she is currently competent to conduct her own personal affairs.

Her present diagnosis is:

Axis I   - Schizoaffective Disorder

Axis II - Borderline Personality Disorder

Axis III - Seizure Disorder

She is not on any prescribed medications at this time, and her prognosis is good for continued functioning and mental competency.

I, therefore, recommend that Janiece Turner be returned to full competency as she no longer requires intervention in handling her personal and business affairs.

Sincerely,

Raymond D. Potterf, M.D., Ph.D.
Board Certified Psychiatrist

RDP/pab

cc: Mr. & Mrs. Bobby Turner
    Janiece Turner

ABOUT THE AUTHOR

Joseph James

"Sentenced To Death, Destined For Life," is the third book that Joseph has penned. His first, "Destiny Path Of Life: The Journey Begins," is an allegory of the two different paths in life. His second, "Islands In The Sea," is a prophetic, romantic novel of what happens when the King steps into His Church, His Bride. It is being released shortly after the release of this book.

Joseph is also a musician and songwriter, playing the guitar, piano, and drums. He has written over 200 Contemporary Christian songs, and shares them in small groups and in small public settings separately and in conjunction with him and his wife as they minister together about her testimony and theirs together.

He has also created a "Path Of Life" art print which is scheduled to be released in large print soon. He has written several poems as well as created photo collages to help illustrate biblical revelations. More information is available on his web site at: DestinyPathOfLife.com.

He loves the Rocky Mountains of Colorado and enjoys seeing the Majesty of the Lord in the awesomeness of His creation. All of the heavens declare the glory of the Lord. Man is without excuse, because even if he were never told by a human voice, creation tells the story. All of creation groans for the sons of God to be made

manifest. We must find our place, walk in it and reverse the curse placed on it at the beginning of time as His Kingdom is ushered in, in its fullness.

Joseph writes in his blog on his websites bringing hope and encouragement to his readers around the world. His Destiny Path Of Life blog is translated into 48 different languages by the Google translator plug-in and has been read by people in over 54 different countries including the Middle East. He believes one life and one voice can make a difference for good in this world, how much more a multitude for our generation. Each of us has a story to tell, and just like this book, people read the pages of our lives everyday. They see our expressions, our attitudes, our character and our love or the lack thereof. We must make our life count, every moment of every day.

Photomontage: Destiny Awaits - Your destiny awaits you. Every day is new and the old is gone. (One of the art prints Joseph designed. They will be available in print soon. Please check our websites for the latest updates.)

RESOURCES

Joseph & Janiece Hartmann
        SentencedToDeathDestinedForLife.com
        DestinyPathOfLife.com
        BeneficialZone.com
        VaryMedia.com

Dennis Goldsworthy-Davis
        GreatGraceInternational.org

Oasis International Christian Center
        OCC-SA.org

Robert Henderson
        RobertHenderson.org

WellSprings Church
        WellSpringsChurchCS.org

Deborah Nazemi-Lewis
        DeborahNazemi.com

Jackie Haag
        MothersHousePublishing.com

OUR MISSION

"Tell My People I Love Them!"

We are committed to carry out the mandate issued to Janiece by our Lord, by going where He leads and as He provides. We are sharing the good news of the Gospel of the Kingdom, helping others to find their God-given destiny. In heaven is a scroll written about each of us. It is our privilege to find out what is written about us and then to walk it out. Father has created a special walk for each of us and gifted us to run the race victoriously. Our purpose is to help each person find their path and encourage them to finish their wonderful, adventurous race. By doing this individually and corporately, the whole Body of Christ grows up into the unity of the faith and makes herself ready for His return. Come Lord Jesus, take Your place on this earth.

If you would like us to come to your area to minister to your organization or speak to your group, please contact us through one of our websites: DestinyPathOfLife.com or SentencedToDeathDestinedForLife.com. Our e-commerce website is BeneficialZone.com. We have a shopping cart for products as well as to receive donations there to help support our outreach.

We are also planning to build communities in strategic places to help those who need time to regroup, heal, be strengthened and refocus before they can begin to walk again. Will you help us? Let's hear what the King is saying and then do our part to help Him build His Kingdom, one stone upon another, one life joined to another. He alone deserves our praise.

Joseph, Janiece, and Daniel Hartmann